THE SPIES OF WINTER

SINCLAIR MCKAY is the bestselling author of *The Secret Life of Bletchley Park*, *The Lost World of Bletchley Park*, *The Secret Life of Fighter Command* and *The Secret Listeners* for Aurum. He lives in London.

THE SPIES
OF WINTER

The GCHQ Codebreakers
Who Fought the Cold War

By Sinclair McKay

Aurum
Press

Brimming with creative inspiration, how-to projects and useful information to enrich your everyday life, Quarto Knows is a favourite destination for those pursuing their interests and passions. Visit our site and dig deeper with our books into your area of interest: Quarto Creates, Quarto Cooks, Quarto Homes, Quarto Lives, Quarto Drives, Quarto Explores, Quarto Gifts, or Quarto Kids.

First published in 2016 by Aurum Press,
an imprint of The Quarto Group
The Old Brewery
6 Blundell Street
London N7 9BH
United Kingdom

www.QuartoKnows.com

This paperback edition first published in 2017 by Aurum Press.

A catalogue record for this book is available from the British Library.

ISBN 978 1 78131 298 8
eBook ISBN 978 1 78131 618 4

10 9 8 7 6 5 4 3 2 1

2021 2020 2019 2018 2017

Typeset in Minion Pro by SX Composing DTP, Rayleigh, Essex

Printed and bound by CPI Group (UK) Ltd, Croydon, CR0 4YY

Contents

Prologue

The Masters of the Game

The piercing cries of seagulls, combined with the deep roar of cold waves crashing on black pebbles, did not help the concentration of the highly strung Soviets. These men, the Soviet Union's supplest minds, were already agitated enough after an unsatisfactory trip around the tourist spots of London, followed by this journey to the freezing south coast, where the contest was being held. The English did not play the game in the same way: instead of deep focus, there was rush and commotion. They started too early in the morning, and added to this was an unusually heavy haze of tobacco and the unbearable hum of pointless chatter from onlookers. The Soviets – and the grim undercover NKVD security men who were supervising them closely – were growing increasingly tense.

This was a tournament that was quietly weighted with global consequence, lethally serious yet at the same time – thanks to the English hosts – charged with some ironic wit. The setting for this clash between violently opposed ideologies could not have been more pleasingly incongruous; it was an out-of-season theatre near the promenade at the seaside town of Hastings, in Sussex. It was January 1954, and the weather by the seafront was ferociously wet and cold. Doughty women out walking their dogs in the freezing spume dodged into the tea-rooms attached to the theatre in order to avoid the knife-keen winds. The Russians regarded their constant entrances and exits as further intolerable distractions. These ladies could have no conceivable idea of the significance of the contest being played here; they could never have guessed that among those crammed into this room of brightly painted pillars and velvet curtains were agents of a foreign power. Before the dog-walking ladies, at a range of tables, and operating in a dense mist of cigarette smoke, were many men in suits, some young, but most middle-aged. They were hunched over chessboards.

These were the world's chess Grandmasters, gathered from all over for an annual competition – the Hastings International Chess Congress – which was (and is) held every winter in this otherwise unassuming seaside town. Among the players, for the first time since the Cold War had begun, were participants from the USSR: Alexander Tolush, David Bronstein and Vladimir Alatortsev. They had arrived in Britain at a time when relations between the British and the Russians had reached a point of permanent mutual neurosis, distaste, suspicion and contempt. And the game of chess was regarded as being very much more than a symbol of national intellectual prowess. Unknown to the wider world, there was a battle taking place here in this hall that in some way was as significant as any movements of submarines, tank regiments or intercepted coded messages.

Soviet pride – and concomitant insecurity – was at its most intense. Even with Joseph Stalin – leader of the Soviet Union from 1924 to 1953 – recently dead, senior figures in the Kremlin were tormented by the idea that the Western powers looked down on them. If the Soviets knew what a particular branch of British intelligence had waiting for them here in Hastings, they might have thought again about allowing their Russian Grandmasters to make the journey. As it was, the main English representative at this tournament was not immediately familiar to the Grandmasters. In such a closed and hermetic world, they must have wondered quite where this handsome, amused-looking man had materialised from. And as intellectually confident and dazzling as Bronstein and Tolush were, these towering giants of the game must have wondered how it was that this English player came by such effortlessly confident body-language – even an easy smile – as he settled down before the chessboard.

Hugh Alexander was the perfect emblem of a new department of British intelligence that was fast establishing its indispensability. He – and several of his friends dotted around those smoky Hastings halls in that dark winter – were brilliant codebreakers. For several years, Alexander's own work had been devoted to penetrating Soviet encrypted messages gathered from deep in Eastern Europe, their codes devised by men such as those he was now playing chess against. Alexander and his colleagues were rich in experience and, indeed, success. Hidden deep in the darkest shadows of British establishment secrecy, there was only a handful of people in and around Whitehall who knew the full extent of their extraordinary accomplishments. The NKVD agents in the hall could not have imagined, as they watched Alexander locking wits with their team, that this was the man who, in 1942, had helped steer Britain through the worst of the Battle of the Atlantic by penetrating Hitler's most unthinkably complex codes.

The codebreaking triumphs carried out at Bletchley Park, a large house and estate to the north of Buckinghamshire, was one of the more astonishing stories of the Second World War. The unravelling of the Nazi Enigma codes had enabled the cryptographers, and Prime Minister Winston Churchill, to see right into the heart of the enemy's plans. When the war ended in 1945, the senior codebreakers understood very well the frightening fragility of this new peace. They had developed an extraordinary new espionage muscle. Unlike human intelligence, which often relied on unstable, untrustworthy double agents and psychologically damaged individuals, codebreaking and intercepted messages had a kind of crystalline, unblemished purity. The cryptographers knew that they had to sharpen their skills and their scope further in order not only to defend the nation, but also to ensure the stability of other regions. This was a world-spanning game. In that January of 1954, Hugh Alexander – now one of the mainstays of the regenerated codebreaking department known as Government Communications Headquarters (GCHQ) – took several days away from his secret duties in order to accept a symbolic challenge from an unwitting Kremlin.

Curious though it may seem, this chess tournament – covered by the world's press – offered a chance of victory that Britain's spies badly needed. The last few years had been very difficult. British intelligence had suffered the humiliating exposure and defection of the MI6 double

agents Guy Burgess and Donald Maclean in 1951. The revelation
of treachery at the very heart of the secret state was compounded by
concomitant repercussions among Britain's allies. A notable irony in the
torrid saga of these traitors – Kim Philby and Anthony Blunt were to
be exposed later, and the alleged 'Fifth Man' John Cairncross only in
1979 – was that their activities had been uncovered first by American
codebreakers and then by their British GCHQ colleagues. This was one
success – both bitter and horrifying – that had even initially been kept
from the British prime minister and the American president, so volcanic
were its implications.

But the wider point was this: the generation that had emerged from
Bletchley Park was very swift to find its operational feet in those first few
traumatic years of the Cold War. The international climate froze over fast,
and generals on either side anticipated the world at any moment being
convulsed with conflict once more. The codebreakers, after having gone
for a few years under the title of 'London Signals Intelligence Centre', were
by the 1950s a completely free-standing department. The initials 'GCHQ'
were never referred to in public, its existence unspoken in newspapers and
even in Parliament. Quietly, and invisibly, the codebreakers established
themselves as an all-seeing, all-hearing force, concealed at the very centre
of British life.

The world was faced with the entirely new prospect of global devastation. First, America detonated two atomic bombs over Hiroshima and
Nagasaki in 1945. Then, the subsequent treachery of atomic scientist Klaus
Fuchs, who passed the scientific secrets of nuclear weaponry over to the
Russians, enabled Stalin to build his own atomic bomb by 1949. There was
now for the first time the possibility of a war which could poison and kill
generations to come. From the start, the codebreakers trained themselves
to be alert, not merely to messages from on high, but also to the seemingly blander encoded communications from Soviet fleets in the Arctic,
or between Russian military figures in Kazakhstan. Any day might bring
the indication that an atomic offensive was being planned.

The codebreakers were also learning to stretch beyond simple
cryptography into the new dimensions opened up by fast-developing

technology: listening devices that could be used hundreds of yards away from the target; aeroplanes armed with super-focused cameras; submarines that could prowl the darkness of the deep, intercepting communications and also other signs of nuclear activity. Cunning wireless interceptors, engineers and scientists built secret tunnels under city streets. From these claustrophobic warrens beneath Vienna, and later Berlin, they could tap unseen and undetected into telephone cables that were hot with calls to and from Moscow. No method of eavesdropping would be deemed too outlandish; all that mattered was the capture of as many conversations and commands as possible. Bletchley Park had been the incubator for the codebreaker's brilliance. In this freezing new world, they were now ready to listen to the world's every heartbeat.

What was happening in Hastings in January 1954 was far from frivolous: it was the symbolic affirmation of the codebreakers' new powers. By taking on Soviet Grandmasters, senior GCHQ operative Hugh Alexander was letting the Kremlin know that even though Britain's imperial era was ending, the country still possessed the intellectual arsenal to thwart the creep of Communism. The first years of the Cold War had been jagged, harrowing, uncertain: an entire continent was suffused with blood, the millions of displaced survivors trying pitifully to find some tokens of familiarity and home amid poverty, malnutrition, local violence and some of the cruellest winters seen over the last 100 years. The word 'peace' was almost laughably empty: Europe was exhausted and the wounds were gaping wide. It would not have taken much for the violence to begin all over again. It had already resurfaced in the Soviet brutalisation of German women, and in the fate of Jews who tried to return to their old villages. From the point of view of the Western Allies, Russian ambitions and desires were unreadable. Stalin had been swift to lay claim to vast tracts of Eastern Europe. Western policymakers fretted as to just how far his territorial plans extended.

In Britain, most of the men and women who had fought and worked for the war effort were returning to their old roles, in offices, factories or indeed back at home. At Bletchley Park, by August 1945, the number of people involved in the production of thousands of daily decryptions – a workforce that at its peak numbered around 10,000 – started thinning out with some speed. This was quite natural; but those who ran this (still gravely secret) operation were concerned. The world was scarcely more stable now than it had been at the heart of the conflict; the Bletchley Park directorate, who were soon to move premises, still had need of the very finest minds to unlock the codes of rival nations and powers.

A codebreaker is a quite different creature to other intelligence opera-tives. The discipline of cryptology, which experienced its true renaissance in the Second World War, was at that time becoming very strongly aligned with the pure theory of mathematics, and indeed philosophy. Before then, code-cracking had been the realm of classicists and linguists. The elec-tronic age would completely change this approach. Pure mathematicians dive deep into oceans of abstraction, where numbers may or may not be symbols of a quantifiable reality, where algebraic and geometric theories that can have no conceivable application in the outside world may be explored for decades. Yet in the late 1930s, when the generation of math-ematicians spearheaded by the likes of Alan Turing were drawn into the fight to break Enigma, suddenly all those ethereal abstractions found a concrete application: here, with these German encryption machines that could generate 159 million million million combinations of letters, was an area where the sheer force of pure mathematics could be gleefully unleashed in the effort to bring meaning to unfathomable chaos.

And so from the very start, the codebreaker was both a proud personality and also – owing to that ability to stare into incalculable intellectual depths – rather difficult to anchor down. It was often said of Alan Turing that he was hopeless at eye contact, and tended to sidle awkwardly into rooms. He was not the only codebreaker to be viewed as eccentric. But he has, of late, become an emblem or an archetype for the entire discipline. The point was that, unlike the rather public-school/clubland and socially assured ethos of MI6 – Britain's foreign-intelligence service – this new generation of cryptographers was less predictable in its working methods and could frequently be the cause of exasperation in Whitehall, where senior civil servants recoiled from accounts of apparent anarchy. The war had proved that this apparent disorder had worked magnificently – when yoked to a properly structured organisation. Halfway through the conflict, when Commander Edward Travis had taken the helm, the work of Bletchley Park was transformed from resembling a cottage industry – the work carried out in wooden huts – to a sleek industrial production line, with specially built blocks housing fantastic new technology. In these, the codebreakers produced thousands upon thousands of decrypts each day.

More important than that was the fantastic reliability of the intelligence that Bletchley Park produced. There were no rogue double agents who would say anything to ensure that they got their money; here simply were decrypted transcripts of the enemy talking. And talking freely, since they were so confident that their codes could never be broken. What Bletchley Park gathered in was usually the truth. In the world after the war, the possibilities of listening in had multiplied unthinkably. The codebreakers were very much the future.

They had vaulting, intuitive minds, working with fast-evolving technology, but in many ways the ethos was unchanged. When Hugh Alexander walked into that old theatre in Hastings in January 1954 to face the most formidable opponents any chess player could hope to meet, there was a blitheness, almost a studied carelessness, about his approach. Throughout the Cold War, the stakes for the codebreakers grew ever greater as the superpowers evolved new weaponry, extended their control over fresh territories, and sharpened their influence over geo-strategic hotspots right the way across the world. But Alexander and his colleagues – together with their American counterparts – understood that to remain effective, their minds had to have a diamond clarity. There were some who relieved that extraordinary mental pressure by immersing themselves in antique-coin collecting; one who used madly energetic Highland dancing as a release. For Hugh Alexander, recreation was a chessboard, and the adrenalin rush of facing outstandingly brilliant rivals.

The early evolution of GCHQ was far from an unalloyed success story. In those fractured, nervous years after the war, there were stumbles and mistakes. Yet from a department of seemingly ungovernable geniuses emerged an organisation that continues to work to preserve national security from within the (necessary) shadows. These days, GCHQ is showing a more open face to the world; newspaper journalists have, for the first time, been invited to see a few (though obviously not all) of its workings at its impressive headquarters in Cheltenham, Gloucestershire. The GCHQ that works endlessly to ensure the security of the nation is the direct legacy of Bletchley Park. The men and women who broke into Hitler's codes were to build an institution that would go very much further. But the story of the genesis of GCHQ is also about a world in violent convulsion. In those first terrible years of the Cold War, security agencies in Britain and America alike were thoroughly infiltrated and undermined, the rules of this brand-new game were still being fathomed by two brand-new world-dominating superpowers, and all the continents of the earth were suffering the traumatic aftershocks of war. The codebreakers were among the very few to be able to divine a route through this new and hazardous labyrinth of mirrors. The men and women who built a new codebreaking institution in the late 1940s and early 1950s very soon became sharply aware that the nation would – quite without any member of the public knowing it – come to rely not only on their ceaseless vigilance but also on their free-wheeling ingenuity.

Chapter One

If War Should Come Again

The music echoing out of the house on that warm spring evening, across the large green lawn and the lake, was not unusual. This Victorian mansion and the wooden huts dotted on the grass around it had echoed with everything from opera to Highland dance tunes in recent years. The young people who had been putting in round-the-clock shifts at this country property had an unusual susceptibility to melodic compositions of all kinds. They were keenly aware of the intricate structures of music. Very often, it was an invaluable pressure valve, helping to relieve the sometimes suffocating pressure that they were all under. But now, on that May evening, the soft strains of the gramophone from within the house, combined with the ripples of conversation and laughter outside, spoke of quite a different atmosphere.

It was 1945, and the war in Europe was over; but here, on this unremarkable English country estate, among the huddles of young people drinking glasses of beer and gin on the grass, looking out at the perpetually furious geese on the lake, there was also an understanding that their work could not simply end.

An entirely new world was being shaped, even in the space of those few hours and days when the Germans finally capitulated. There were teams of brilliant men and women, pioneers all, who understood very well how vital their efforts had become. From a slightly hit-and-miss operation back in

1939 to a sleek, super-efficient decryption production line which by 1945 unlocked thousands upon thousands of secret enemy communications daily, the work of Bletchley Park had played an enormous role in victory. Winston Churchill had been particularly grateful for his daily boxes of intelligence provided by these glittering intellects.

A few months before the end of the war, a triumvirate of young codebreakers had been asked to give their thoughts on facing up to new kinds of conflict. These men – senior cryptologist Gordon Welchman, Edward Crankshaw, and a 26-year-old Harry Hinsley – immediately saw where the threats of the future would come from; and they were astringent in prescribing what Bletchley Park as an institution would have to become in order to face them.

'This organisation should cover all types of intelligence about foreign countries, including scientific, commercial and economic matters as well as diplomatic activity; for in the handling of both foreign and domestic affairs, it is important for the Government to have the best possible knowledge of developments and intentions in other countries,' declared their top-secret jointly written memo.

'The Services, also, in order to be fully prepared, must have all possible knowledge about the developments of methods of war that are being carried out by potential enemies.

'Further, the organisation must be so planned that, if war should come again, the Services will have the best possible operational intelligence from the start. The applications of intelligence to civil problems may well prove to be of greater value than they could ever have been before, because it appears that the handling of foreign affairs is going to be exceedingly difficult after this war. The value of a good intelligence organisation to the Services may well be critical, because the steady development of methods of war will tend to make the first blow of an aggressor more and more devastating, giving less time for an unprepared country to develop its war potential.'[1]

The most senior figures at Bletchley were among the very few, before August 1945, who knew how such a 'first blow' might be landed: they were part of a tiny elite who had knowledge of the development of atomic weaponry at Los Alamos, New Mexico. They were aware that the United States had developed the capacity to drop atom bombs. They also knew that it would not be long before other, less friendly, powers, would develop their own equivalents. Looking back now, we tend to see the end of the war as being a neat line: one day there was fighting, the next peace. That is not at all how it seemed to many people then. If anything, there was a pervasive fear that worse was to come.

For those senior figures who worked in the Bletchley Park Directorate, overseeing the continual stream of top-secret and invaluable coded signals intelligence flowing in from every region on the earth, there was a terrifying awareness of the fragility of peace. The Park's director, Commander Edward Travis, was thoroughly human, though, and Bletchley Park – which at that point had many thousands of people working in and around the estate and at out-stations too – found its own way of marking 8 May 1945. The Park's administrative officer Captain Bradshaw sent out a memo to all codebreakers setting out arrangements to celebrate the great day. It was to start with appropriate solemnity; the music and laughter came later.

'On VE Day at 0915 hours, there will be a brief Thanksgiving service, on the lawns, in front of the main building,' the memo read. This referred to the area directly in front of the distinctive Victorian house. It was to be 'conducted by the Rev JL Milne, Rector of St Mary's Church, Old Bletchley'. The Reverend would have been acutely aware throughout the war of these multitudes of young men and women, many not in uniform, passing in and out of the big estate, and living and socialising in the town and surrounding villages. But the Reverend Milne, even on VE Day, would not have had the slightest idea what they were actually working on. The secret remained tightly kept, even among respected Bletchley locals.

'In accordance with Government policy,' Captain Bradshaw's memo continued, 'all staff except the minimum necessary for operational work . . . will be granted a paid holiday on VE Day and the day following . . . in anticipation of congestion on the public transport services (road and rail), staff are advised in their own interests not to attempt long-distance journeys.'[2]

The note of caution filtered down to all sections and departments. Women's Royal Navy recruit Betty Flavell recalled: 'The chief officer gave us all a pep talk. I think she thought we were all going to lose our honour, because of everyone feeling free and throwing caution to the wind. Celebrating, drinking.'³

According to codebreaker Major Neil Webster, there had indeed been quite a gaudy night. 'Bletchley Park put on a terrific VE party,' he wrote in his memoir, 'a fancy dress ball with oceans to drink, a top band, our own cabaret, special décor, soft lights and all the trimmings.'⁴ The 'top band' was most likely formed of Bletchley personnel; figures such as Eric de Carteret, who was to stay on, had a genius for music. Added to this was a wide range of acting and writing talent (among the codebreakers was Angus Wilson, the soon-to-be-feted novelist); the Bletchley Park players were so accomplished that they had taken their productions around the county, and raised a great deal of money for military charities. The fancy dress for their VE Day party would have been an extension of their limitlessly inventive costume departments; and the night, for many, would have been an acknowledgment, possibly a melancholy one, that this extraordinary and intense life that they had known was almost over.

The authorities need not have worried about excess: after so many years of ferocious self-discipline, it was hardly likely that a full-scale bacchanalia would break out. In any case, victory in Europe was overshadowed by the knowledge that conflict in the Far East was still raging on. There is a photograph of a large group of Bletchley codebreakers, men and women, a few in uniform, all smiling and raising glasses. There were some who had ignored the dire warnings about the crowded railways, and hoofed it to London on the express in order to be able to catch the night of celebration there.

Everyone gave thought, though, to their colleagues across the world: the dedicated codebreakers stationed in Ceylon; in India; in the scorching sun of Heliopolis, Egypt; in the turbulent political atmosphere of Mandate Palestine. In Colombo, Ceylon (now Sri Lanka), young women such as Jean Valentine, then 19, were still working deep into eerie tropical nights, burrowing into Japanese encrypted intercepts. In India, young men such as the Oxford undergraduate Alan Stripp – like so many, his university education interrupted before it got going – were still deciphering Japanese communications in sweltering huts, while coping with extraordinary heat and with ceiling fans so slow that birds would sit on them and be rotated gently.

Back at Bletchley, obviously there were warm words too. Some of these words came from a man that very few of the codebreakers, Women's Royal Navy (Wrens) or Auxiliary Territorial Service women would ever have seen, or even been aware of. On VE Day itself, a letter from Sir Stewart Menzies was circulated. It was signed from the 'Director General'. Sir Stewart was the head of MI6 at that time, which oversaw the work of Bletchley Park. MI6 was never publicly acknowledged or referred to. The vast majority of those working in all departments at Bletchley would have had no indication that they came under the aegis of the Secret Service. The place was so efficiently compartmentalised that most had no idea even what happened in other huts and blocks.

'On this ever memorable day,' Sir Stewart wrote, 'I desire that all those who are doing duty in this Organisation [sic] should be made aware of my unbounded admiration at the way in which they have carried out their allotted tasks. Such have been the difficulties, such has been the endeavour, and such have been the constant triumphs that one senses that words of gratitude from one individual are perhaps out of place. The personal knowledge of the contribution made towards winning the war is surely the real measure of the thanks which so rightly belong to one and all in a great and inspired organisation which I have the privilege to direct. This is your finest hour.'[6]

The achievements had indeed been extraordinary: from the 1939 Enigma code-cracking inspiration provided by three pioneering Polish mathematicians to Alan Turing and Gordon Welchman's development of the revolutionary 'bombe' machines which partially automated the decyphering of German codes; from the first cracking of the daily Luftwaffe codes to eventual triumph against the almost unthinkable complexities of the German naval Enigma; from the development of an extraordinary proto-computer that opened the door of the future to the decoding of encrypted messages from the desk of Hitler himself. The work of Bletchley Park had – as many distinguished figures were later to aver – shortened the war by two years, if not by three.

By the summer of 1945, some of the leading intellects who had shaped these codebreaking triumphs had been pulled elsewhere. In the case of Alastair Denniston, the original wartime director of the institute and the man who had assembled this quirky array of minds, his time at Bletchley had ended unhappily in 1942, when he was bumped sideways into a role in diplomatic cryptographic intelligence, heading up a much smaller department back in London.

The man whose name is now synonymous with Bletchley's success – the mathematician Alan Turing – had himself been rather more gently removed. First, he was transferred from his position as the head of Hut 8, where he and his team had been fighting desperately to crack the apparently insoluble naval Enigmas. Rather than have him anywhere near administration, which was clearly a misuse of his almost preternatural intellect, Turing was first set to working on more advanced code and technological problems (helping Professor Max Newman and the engineer Dr Tommy Flowers to bring the Colossus, the world's first proto-computer, into being). Then, in 1942, he was sent across to the States, to join the top-secret research work at the Bell Laboratories. Turing's gift, as one colleague put it, was that he was capable of thinking thoughts that others would not even have thought it was possible to have. Towards the end of the war, after Turing had returned to England, he was diverted to another highly secret research establishment: Hanslope Park, just a few miles north of Bletchley, in North Buckinghamshire.

But back at Bletchley itself, the senior figures who worked on the first floor of the main house represented a certain sort of continuity. These codebreaking veterans were now to be the architects of the computer-age future, staying firmly in place to ensure that the organisation was ready for the new world. Their experience was beyond value. Brigadier John Tiltman, born in 1894, had joined the Government Code and Cypher School (as the operation was then known) in 1920, in the wake of the First World War. He was sent out to India for a few years, where his job involved more codebreaking duties. As the sophistication of encryption grew, so too did his ideas for unravelling it. This was still largely the pre-Enigma machine era; the Germans bought up this electric encryption technology for use in the navy in 1926, and extended it to the rest of the military thereafter. Others were still relying on less sophisticated – though still fearsomely complex – means of scrambling communications.

And this is where Tiltman's astonishing skill came into play. Rather than rely on machinery and technology, he had an almost intuitive approach to cracking codes, a blend of mathematical, linguistic and philosophical brilliance. Returning to London and working at the Government Code and Cypher School throughout the 1920s and the 1930s, his chief focus became the agents and diplomats of the Stalin-era Soviet Union. He uncovered a quite remarkable volume of intelligence, particularly involving links between Soviet agents and organisations in Britain. Tiltman's approach to codebreaking was, in part, immersive: he would plunge into unfamiliar languages and dialects, absorbing them completely, and in so doing pick up an instinctive feeling for the thoughts of others and the patterns of their communications. Tiltman had the most extraordinary facility for language, and later, at Bletchley, he swiftly mastered Japanese, and was responsible for running the intensive schools in the nearby town of Bedford that threw young undergraduate recruits into the esoteric mysteries of Japan's encryption system.

In the early days of Bletchley Park, Tiltman had specialised in military codes, and in 1941 broke specific German army and railway Enigma cyphers that revealed the imminent Nazi threat to Russia. But despite his senior military rank, Brigadier Tiltman was the opposite of a uniformed martinet; indeed, he was often amused to see younger Bletchley recruits, fresh from university, working in uniform instead of perfectly acceptable civilian clothes. 'Why are you wearing those damned silly boots?' he asked of one uniformed codebreaker. His office in the directorate – in the house that had once belonged to the Leon family – was in what had been the family nursery. It was still decorated with Peter Rabbit wallpaper.

Working alongside him in the Bletchley Park directorate was another formidable codebreaking veteran: Nigel de Grey. Born in 1886, de Grey was an Old Etonian with quite a nuanced background. As a boy, he had shown a real gift for languages, but decided against going to university. He had aimed for the diplomatic service instead, but despite his linguistic skills, failed the exam. As a result of this, he moved into the rather more raffish, bohemian world of publishing, joining the firm Heinemann prior to the outbreak of the First World War. At the start of that conflict, Nigel De Grey served as an observer with the Balloon Corps (an unenviably vulnerable position, even by the standards of that most harrowing of conflicts), but by 1915 was drafted into naval intelligence.

This was the start of an extraordinary career; indeed, the colourful de Grey might now be said to have been at the very epicentre of some of the century's most pivotal moments. He began working alongside other codebreakers in the Whitehall forerunner of Bletchley Park, a department called Room 40. It was here that he met Alastair Denniston and Alfred Dillwyn ('Dilly') Knox, with whom he was to work so closely over the next several decades. And it was here, in 1917, that he decrypted, among countless other documents, one very particular German diplomatic message. From the German foreign minister Arthur Zimmermann, it was a telegram that had been sent across to Mexico, via the Atlantic underwater cable, to the German Ambassador there. It concerned the stepping up of submarine warfare in the Atlantic. In the telegram, Zimmermann told the ambassador that he was to approach the Mexican government with an offer of an alliance against the Americans. The reward for Mexico would be the acquisition of the southern states of Texas and Arizona.

Though the provenance of the intelligence was suitably disguised (it would not do for the Germans to see that their codes had been broken – still less would it do for the Americans and everyone else to see that the British had tapped the transatlantic cable), the news was released. As well as the resulting uproar, de Grey's decrypt had the effect of bringing America into the First World War, which in turn helped ensure Germany's defeat.

Yet even after this dizzying triumph, de Grey did not stay on with the Government Code and Cypher School at the end of the war; instead, he went to Piccadilly to head an art concern called The Medici Society. Its purpose, in part, was to provide prints of Old Masters to various smart figures. One such, in the inter-war years, was Winston Churchill; the Churchill archives contain correspondence between the two men discussing various art works. Home was a house in the Buckinghamshire village of Iver, close to where Pinewood Studios now stands. De Grey had married in 1910, and he and his wife had three children. This also meant that despite a privileged background, he very much needed to work. De Grey was an aesthetic soul; occasionally he was given to wearing a cloak. Because of his smart family connections, he would often spend his weekends at vast country estates, shooting. He was a keen painter himself, and was also an enthusiast amateur actor, appearing with a group calling itself the 'Windsor Strollers'.

Just before the outbreak of the Second World War, The Medici Society ran into financial turbulence, and de Grey's position looked precarious. After a gap of nearly 20 years, he was welcomed back into the embrace of the Government Code and Cypher School (though on a rather modest salary). Dilly Knox had been making terrific headway with different versions of the Enigma encryption machine; soon de Grey was on top of this, as well as other encryption methods. In 1941, he was one of the first people to comprehend the scale of what the Germans had planned for the Jews; breaking codes coming out of Eastern Europe, he saw and understood the meaning of orders for villages to be razed, and communications involving the logistics of mass transportation on the railways.

If Brigadier Tiltman represented the best of the military mind – ideal for analysing the territorial intentions of the Soviet empire – Nigel de Grey exemplified the value of the artistically refined codebreaker, versed not in mathematics, but in language and culture. His languid fluency would prove to be a great advantage in the late 1940s and early 1950s when dealing with the more stubborn corners of Whitehall. And the man who was their commander – Edward Travis – brought his own formidable codebreaking expertise to what, by the middle of the war, had become a dizzyingly efficient intelligence factory, unravelling thousands upon thousands of messages, from all theatres of war, every single day.

Commander Edward Travis was a bulky figure, born in 1888 in the marshy south-east-London suburb of Plumstead. He joined the navy at the age of 18 and sailed on HMS *Iron Duke*. His aptitude for code work was spotted early on when he decrypted some of Admiral Jellicoe's messages to prove that the system being used was weak. By 1916, he was working full-time on naval cyphers, devising as well as decoding; and he did a great deal of work alongside the French and Italians. When the war ended, he elected to stay on full-time with the fast-developing Government Code and Cypher School. Alastair Denniston became the director and by 1925, Travis was his deputy – a state of affairs that would last until 1942. It was said of Travis – five foot seven (1.7 metres), inclining to the portly – that his gruff, brusque manner gained him few friendships, though he commanded loyalty. In fact, though, many who were to work at Bletchley and GCHQ regarded him with enormous affection.

He also caught the admiring attention of senior figures within intelligence and Whitehall. Whereas Alastair Denniston, in assembling and constructing the codebreaking teams at Bletchley Park, encouraged anarchic-seeming lateral thinking and wild abstraction, Travis was the man who kept it all very firmly rooted, and who ensured that even the airiest mathematical theorising led to concrete, well-organised results.

At a time when codebreaking representatives of all the services – the army, the RAF, the Royal Navy – were competing furiously for valuable time on Alan Turing and Gordon Welchman's bombe machines (which could check through thousands upon thousands of potential code combinations at speeds that no human could match), it was Travis who put an end to the shrill bickering, and found a way to turn Bletchley Park from a cottage industry into a vast, slick, efficient factory. It was also thanks to Travis that in the latter years of the war, machinery and personnel materialised in ever greater numbers.

And it was in recognition of this organisational genius that Alastair Denniston was told to move aside. In a mark of Travis's own loyalty, he refused for a couple of years to take the title of 'Director', sticking firmly to 'Deputy'. Only in March 1944 did he relent. By VE Day, and the night of those fancy dress celebrations at Bletchley Park, Travis was not some distant authority figure but a man who kept closely involved with all the departments and personnel; there is some suggestion, in fact, that the lavish VE Day party was funded entirely by Travis from his own pocket.

Travis, Tiltman and de Grey were to be the cornerstones of continuity as a new, more shadowy war loomed in 1945. They would have known, throughout 1944 and 1945, that they would have to find ways to ensure that cryptography stayed ahead of vast technological leaps. But another senior Bletchley figure, who might very reasonably have been expected to stay on, had been thinking for some time of quite different enterprises. Gordon Welchman, a bullish young academic plucked from Sidney Sussex College in Cambridge, was in many ways Bletchley's great logistical genius: as well as devising brilliant innovations, such as an addition to the bombe machines that greatly increased their calculating speed and efficacy, he was an expert in ensuring that all lines of communication between huts and machines flowed like mercury.

Welchman was an innovator who had been able to demonstrate to his superiors (and indeed on one occasion to a visiting Winston Churchill) how brilliant new technology could be melded with organisation to produce a lightning-fast stream of intelligence. It was his view – and that of Travis too – that the possibilities of this new world, hovering just at the edge of the inception of the computer, were the real future of intelligence. The cloak-and-dagger antics of MI6 were, by contrast, starting to look slightly antiquated, a fit subject for entertainment in Hitchcock films, but out of step with a fast-changing landscape.

Given all this responsibility, one might almost have expected Gordon Welchman to be officially compelled to stay – a man who simply knew too much to be allowed to go anywhere else. Yet at the end of the war, he could see setbacks to a career in cryptography. Welchman was married with three children and his ambitions, though not quite in focus, were rather larger than a place in such an organisation as the Government Code and Cypher school would allow.

Welchman, like Turing, had been sent over to America for a time in 1943, and the experience for him was an extremely happy one, from the VIP dinners on board *Queen Mary* on the voyage over, to the open, friendly (and by implication, breezily classless) community of cryptanalysts in Washington DC and New York. And perhaps it was this that was to set the course of Welchman's days. He had caught the sniff of opportunity, the idea that he might be able to vault much further than what was, in essence, a modest wage packet with the civil service. So in 1945, as the Bletchley operation started to wind down, Welchman was anxious to get out. Equally, he looked back at Cambridge, at his old academic role, and realised that a return to that life would be terribly stifling and claustrophobic after all the days and months of nerve-fizzing adrenalin that he had been through. Where could a restless young man go to make some money?

At first – with a few words in the right ears from elegant fellow-codebreaker Hugh Alexander – Welchman headed into the slightly unlikely sphere of corporate life. Before the war, Hugh Alexander had worked in a senior position for the John Lewis Partnership which then, as now, ran department stores. With his recommendation, Welchman would move into the same position, commuting to central London every morning from the village of Cookham in Berkshire. Yet very quickly it would become apparent that the contrast between this and the life that he had led bordered on the bathetic. As we will see, even the codebreakers who left actually never really did so; Welchman and many others eventually reconnected with this much more satisfying secret world. How could the secret world ever let them go?

For the women, there were other, stronger, social pressures. Young female codebreakers such as Mavis Batey and Sheila Lawn, there right up until the end, had met their future husbands at Bletchley; and while Keith Batey and Oliver Lawn, young postgraduates, set their sights on the civil service, their wives would be expected to make homes. A young mother was emphatically not welcome in the workplace; she had children to look after and a house to keep. The cruelty of this was that Bletchley itself had opened up a hitherto unimaginable range of possibilities for women; at the age of 20, Mavis Batey had cracked the Italian Enigma code that resulted in British triumph at the Battle of Cape Matapan. Sheila Lawn found the most influential use for her significant linguistic skills. But in that summer of May 1945, there was one young woman who knew that she would be staying on. Joan Clarke – the only female codebreaker in Hut 8 – was a formidable mathematician. And even though she had started out at Bletchley performing largely clerical duties, her talents had quickly been recognised.

For a time, Joan Clarke had been engaged to Alan Turing. They had been on holiday together. She was very much in love; and on some level, he was too. But Turing was honest with her: he explained how he had 'homosexual inclinations'. Such things were not as well understood in that era, and she felt that it didn't matter. However, after a few months, Turing called the engagement off. It is a testament to them both that they remained very close friends until his tragic death in 1954.

But Joan Clarke, 23 years old when she had been recruited by Gordon Welchman for Bletchley in 1940, had proved one of the mainstays of Hut 8 following Turing's replacement by Hugh Alexander, and then the subsequent merger with a party of American codebreakers. She had proved herself to be sinuously dextrous with Bayesian Probability Theory – a mathematical set of cartwheels that resulted in the fantastically complex codebreaking method known as Banburismus, and which greatly increased the speed of the work on the bombes. More than this: she had been notably calm in the vortex of tension of the Battle of the Atlantic, when the new four rotor Naval Enigmas would not yield, Britain's shipping was being sent to the bottom of the ice-cold ocean in terrifying volumes, and the nation's lifelines were being inexorably severed. The political pressure on Hut 8 throughout those months of 1942 would have been enough to drive anyone to nervous collapse. Joan Clarke and her Hut 8 colleagues knew that the only thing to do was to push on.

And now, in 1945, she was working alongside American naval cypher experts – her own field of expertise was the Shark and Dolphin keys, used by German submarines. After VE Day, naturally, her office would be very much quieter. But even by then, even with all the secrecy surrounding the work that she and her colleagues had done, the satisfaction must have been immense. On VE night, as Travis's fancy dress party spilled out of the house into the crisp May evening air, Joan Clarke surely experienced a helium buoyancy, the sense that the aching responsibility had lifted. But like so many of her fellow codebreakers, she would have found that the work itself had bred a sort of compulsion: intense intellectual duels that had instant, concrete impact on events around the world. At this point, she was unmarried, and had no dependents. Unlike so many other women, there was nothing to stop her continuing to lead this extraordinary life. For this, her superiors would prove to be intensely grateful.

The unfathomable stress of breaking into the enemy's every communication was one thing; being right at the heart of the secret war effort was another. The pressures that came with this unspoken knowledge were invisible. There was also a delicate element of diplomacy involved, for the British were – unprecedentedly – sharing both full intelligence and decrypting techniques with their allies, the Americans. While the military side of the Special Relationship was rather more fraught and ill-tempered than anything 'special', the codebreakers worked in unusual harmony. Unlike among the Allied military, there was a huge amount of mutual intellectual respect on both sides. A contingent of American codebreakers had come over to Bletchley, just as Alan Turing had been sent over to the States. And Travis was the man who kept this partnership on smooth rails, negotiating with some skill the few aspects of codebreaking work that both sides were keeping back from one another.

But the truth was that not much diplomacy was needed: the American personnel at Bletchley, some of whom worked for a unit called 'Sixta', had been utterly beguiled by what they had found there. Captain William Bundy was one young American cryptologist – an extremely nimble one, solving a Hut 6 coding difficulty in record time – who fell head over heels in love, not merely with the place but with the ethos, that curious blend of military and civilian. Bletchley had an apparent lack of iron hierarchy – but there was a concomitant ferocious self-discipline and self-reliance. Even though he later rose to be a defence adviser to President John F Kennedy in the White House of the early 1960s, Bundy always looked back at Bletchley as a career high-point.

The Americans were by and large the first to leave Bletchley Park after VE Day; beforehand, General Spaatz of the US Army paid a visit to the site to make a general speech to all – British and American alike – thanking them for the amazing work that they had done, and for the invaluable contribution that they had made to the victory.

This close relationship worked the other way around as well: for example, by 1943, the work of Hut 8 in burrowing into German naval codes was in part taken over by the American naval codebreaking department. The head of Hut 8, Hugh Alexander – born in 1909 and pulled into Bletchley in 1940 – focused, in turn, on the Japanese Coral cypher. There was none of the bitter competitiveness or jealousies to be found elsewhere in the military. Instead, the knotty intellectual challenges of ever-evolving encryptions seemed to provide their own satisfaction. As Travis's VE Day party got underway, Hugh Alexander was on the other side of the world, installed for a couple of months at the codebreaking establishment in Colombo, Ceylon.

During the summer of 1945, there was much about the Far East codebreaking effort that was a little routine, but still very necessary. After his brilliant work applying some of Alan Turing's most labyrinthine mathematical theories, Hugh Alexander might have thought that this tropical office with its bamboo roof and its nightly incursions from giant winged insects was the conclusion of his cryptological career. Indeed, for a very short while, it was. But the end of the war did not diminish Alexander's appetite for the constant stimulation of coding challenges. His future lay in those cyphers.

The atomic bombing of Hiroshima and Nagasaki in August 1945 brought the world to a shocked stop. At Bletchley, among the personnel who were now left, it brought a sense, not of relief that the war was over, but of nauseous unease about the sort of world that might emerge from the ruins. The summer of 1945 had seen a certain amount of winding down – the young aristocratic ladies decanted back to London, the undergraduates prepared to resume interrupted academic careers. Indeed, the sparser staffing arrangements had already caused some tension: even more rigid shift patterns made it difficult for codebreakers to arrange things such as dental appointments.

There were outbreaks of unalloyed happiness, sometimes from Wrens who had come to detest the bombe machines, which required a great deal of tending (they frequently came shuddering to unintended halts, and wires had to be teased with tweezers, often in the small hours of the morning). Now the monsters were to be dissected. 'I remember having to dismantle the bombes bit by bit, wire by wire, screw by screw,' recalled one

Wren. 'We sat at tables with screwdrivers, taking out all the wire contact brushes. It had been a sin to drop a drum [the machines had rows of rotating drums] but now we were allowed to roll one down the floor of the hut. Whoopee!'

The social life was winding up too; as well as the theatrical troupe, the classical music societies and the film appreciation societies, which met in the main house, came to an end. Now one very particular task remained for the occupants of all the myriad huts and blocks: getting rid of every particle of classified intelligence. That which had not been spirited upwards into the Directorate, and thence to Whitehall, had to be destroyed. Slips of paper with five-letter groupings – indeed, every last little bit of paperwork – were to be carefully gathered up and burned in bonfires. Most of the machinery on site was to be destroyed too: the secrecy was still vital in a shifting, uncertain world. As we will see later, some vital instruments, such as the world's first proto-computers, were to survive, but the silence surrounding that survival was so complete that their heartbroken creator had no idea.

The cleansing of the Bletchley Park estate was not perfect, as a very recent discovery has made quite plain. In 2015, workers performing restoration work at the old Hut 6 for the Bletchley Park museum were startled when a wodge of scrumpled paperwork fell from the ceiling. Upon closer examination, it turned out to be a great mass of decrypts. How and why had they been pushed into the hut's ceiling cavity? The answer was hilariously simple: during those wartime winters, the huts were cruelly cold. The wind and freezing draughts crept in from all angles. The discarded decrypts had been used as a primitive form of insulation.

Commander Travis and his colleagues had known for some time that, once the war was over, the work of Bletchley Park would be moving back to London, or at least its suburbs. While the numbers of personnel were to be reduced to a fraction of their wartime height, the operation still needed a substantial (and secret) base from which to operate. The ideal candidate had already been in use since 1943 as an outstation, largely for the vast bombe code-checking machines tended to by armies of Wrens. The new site was fiercely utilitarian and in the winter months rather depressing.

Unlike Bletchley, there was not the sociable focus of an architecturally striking grand house. The site was at Eastcote in Middlesex, near the north-western end of the Piccadilly line, and some 15 miles (24 kilometres) from central London.

A return to the Government Code and Cypher School's pre-war HQ at St James's Park, round the corner from Westminster, was no longer practicable. In the course of the previous six years, signals intelligence – that is, intelligence captured over the airwaves, or through intercepts, as opposed to the intelligence gathered on the ground by agents – had evolved to the most striking degree. Thanks to Turing, Welchman, Newman, Flowers and many others, bulky new technology was indispensable for unlocking encryptions. Added to that, a base was needed which also had room for a properly sized radio operation. Bletchley itself was not to be wholly abandoned by the Government Code and Cypher School; the codebreakers didn't make the move until 1946 and even then some traces were left behind in the form of a training establishment. It was still used, right up until the 1980s. But the more compact post-war operation needed to be closer to London, as opposed to in the middle of the countryside.

There was another pressing question to be addressed by Commander Travis, and it was one that had been indirectly posed by Sir Stewart Menzies, head of MI6, and his proprietorial letter of congratulation to all Bletchley staff. With the end of the conflict, who was now to be in charge of codes and signals intelligence? Was Travis's team destined to become an offshoot of MI6 (and answerable purely to Sir Stewart)?

There was a strong case to be made that Bletchley's core team should form its own department, not as a branch of MI6, but as a fully fledged organisation in its own right, answering only to the Foreign Office and to the prime minister. Obviously, the codebreakers and the secret service could hardly be completely divorced; the nature of clandestine intelligence gathering meant that overlap would be inevitable. But Commander Travis could see the shape of the future, and the scale of the work that his new team was going to have to do.

It is always officially said that during the war, once Britain and the Soviet Union had become allies against the Germans, the British stopped intercepting and decoding Russian messages. Indeed, Bletchley Park obliged further, giving Stalin the (carefully edited) fruits of their German decrypts, so that the Russian army could find the weaknesses and vulnerabilities of the Wehrmacht. But the British codebreakers had – before the war broke out – been most assiduous in their blanket monitoring of Russian encrypted communications. It seems not merely decent but also rather reckless of them to have simply stopped, especially in the later stages of the war, when Stalin's ambitions for Eastern Europe became ever clearer.

Also unprecedented had been the warm intelligence partnership between British and American codebreakers; even more unusually, it was to continue. Never before had two nations forged such a tight alliance over the sharing of top-secret material. And in this respect, once again, the British were a little ahead of their Allies. For thanks to the Y-Service – the British wireless interceptors who grabbed all messages from the airwaves and with pinpoint accuracy relayed them back to Bletchley Park – the codebreakers had operatives in every region on the earth. From Mombasa to Murmansk, Cyprus to Hong Kong, these listening posts were beyond value. America's codebreakers (many of whom were based in Arlington Hall, a former girls' school a little to the west of Washington DC) were greedy for the sheer volume of raw intelligence that these worldwide outposts were continuing to scoop up.

The Americans wanted to point out it was a two-way process: that their British friends would be allowed in on their own codebreaking results. In July 1945, Commander Travis wrote to his opposite number, Captain Wenger of the OP-20-G US codebreaking arm, to acknowledge this happy continuity. 'Many thanks for your offer to continue direct cross-Atlantic communications,' he said. 'Fully appreciate difficulties created by economy drive, as I am experiencing them myself. Suggest that negotiations now proceeding with you may lead us both to conclude that good Atlantic channels are essential for close collaboration on future problems that may arise. Shall therefore keep subject under review . . .'[6]

Britain had its own concerns too, from the impending independence of the subcontinent of India from British rule to the feverish tensions in Palestine and the increasing pressure to honour the 1917 Balfour Declaration, which promised British support for the creation of a homeland there for the Jewish people. The need for signals intelligence did not diminish.

In those last few weeks of Bletchley Park, a local newspaper reporter wrote sadly that the Park's theatrical troupe was disbanding, and that its talents would be dispersed far and wide. Neither he nor any of their audiences had any idea what it was that these gifted amateur actors had been doing as their day job. It is natural now to imagine with hindsight that this was symbolic of the change that was coming to the codebreakers – that frenetic yet eccentric world being replaced by something far chillier, much more professional, and far less amenable to whimsy or the sort of Bohemian behaviour that Bletchley recruits had displayed. And yet this is not so: while the site of Eastcote itself was drab, the ethos of Bletchley Park was to be transplanted; there were still battalions of bright young women and owlish young men. And they were to be joined – as symbolically befits the new age of Clement Attlee's Labour government which came to power in 1945 – by a swarm of fresh new recruits from all sorts of social backgrounds, united by intellectual dexterity, the ease of youth and indeed a love of music – though this time, the musical form was jazz.

And it would not be long before the talents and capabilities of these younger codebreakers were to be tested: in some key regions of the earth, peace was little more than an illusion.

Chapter Two

Storm Warnings

For those working amid the sand and the flies in the piercing heat, or indeed for those thousands of miles away again intercepting messages in wet warm emerald forests, mesmerised at night by the flickering glow of fireflies, it must have seemed for a time in 1945 that the British Empire would carry on much as before. The war was won and, superficially, the old order had not itself been called into question. Empire was a matter of administration and bureaucracy, or so it must have seemed to many. What could be more natural than Britain's holding on to its bases in Egypt and Palestine, in Ceylon and India, and in Cyprus and Hong Kong?

Winston Churchill was gone, unsentimentally voted out before the war had even ended. His Labour deputy, Clement Attlee, was now prime minister. Ernest Bevin was his pugnacious foreign secretary. Britain was financially shattered: it had been driven practically to bankruptcy by the pressures of war production from 1940. Yet the economy alone was not Attlee's main spur when he considered Britain's position in this ruined, traumatised world. He was already thinking in terms of Britain voluntarily surrendering its imperial influence to a new technocratic council of nations (what would shortly become the United Nations).

But for the moment, the British codebreakers were at the absolute centre of influence. They were faster than many to understand that the Soviet Union under Stalin would be seeking to expand its own interests ruthlessly, not just through Eastern Europe, but into Asia as well. The codebreakers saw too that the Soviets would have a keen interest in the Balkan states, all the way down to Greece and the Mediterranean; and that the rich oil fields of Saudi Arabia and Iraq would be a new crucible of tension. The Combined Code and Cypher School in Heliopolis, just outside Cairo, Egypt, had proved more than invaluable throughout the Desert War against the German forces led by General Erwin Rommel, sometimes knowing more about his supply lines than he did. Now, although the focus of its work had shifted, it remained vital.

Because most aspects of the Second World War are now so intensely familiar to us, it is slightly startling to look instead at those immediate post-war weeks and months; to imagine how the peoples of Europe and Russia, of China and Japan could function amid such utter devastation. It is sometimes assumed or imagined, for example, that the liberation of the Nazi concentration camps was an occasion of tearful joy; in fact, on the part of both the liberators and the prisoners, it was anything but. There was horror on the part of the liberators, a sort of paralysed trauma from the prisoners. Those Jews who survived – who had seen their entire families murdered in the most appalling circumstances – what were they to do now? For some, the immediate and macabre-seeming answer was simply to stay put in the camps: the world outside was not to be trusted to any degree. At least now, within the fences of these obscene compounds, there was a bizarre measure of security among familiar faces. Beyond the gates were the people who had consigned them to this hell in the first place. There were some Jews who started to think of making the return to their old towns and villages deep in Eastern Europe; as we will see later, these journeys were not to end well. Forget any semblance of delicate justice: what were these people to do, where and how were they to live?

And although some might be tempted to see a satisfying symmetry, the same was quickly being asked of 20 million displaced German citizens: as Nazi rule ended in Czechoslovakia and in many parts of Eastern Europe, so the local populations in those countries immediately turned to look at the German speakers who had been sent to live among them. Those Germans, too, were soon to understand the pitilessness of persecution.

This, then, in 1945, was the Europe that the codebreakers were listening to. Germany itself was bloody, broken and mute. Once busy city streets had been crushed into grey dust; entire urban skylines had been obliterated. Women quite beyond number had been raped by invading Soviet soldiers, and these countless individual traumas were to resonate. Food was in desperately short supply; rations in Germany were down at one point to a few slices of bread, a herring and some jam to last a week. In many senses, the continent of Europe had been thrown back to the Dark Ages, fractured by war and threatened with famine.

Berlin, the German capital, was carved up into four sectors, run by the victorious Allies: the British, Americans, French and, of course, Russians. There was a solid practical reason for Bletchley Park's wartime triumphs to remain completely secret, and that was that some of the codebreaking technology that they had pierced during the war was still very much in use. The Bletchley secret had also been assiduously kept from the Russians; although intelligence from decrypts had been carefully filtered through to Stalin, its exact provenance had always been disguised. This secrecy was later to pay off: for instance, some years later, as East Germany (or the 'German Democratic Republic') went behind the shadow of the Berlin Wall, officials sometimes still used Enigma machines.

The months before the end of the war had brought other developments that foreshadowed the secret cypher conflicts to come. Of particular significance in late 1944 was the discovery, in Finland, of a partially burned Soviet code-book, the vital key into a wide range of Russian communications. The Finnish cryptographers had made some use of it, feeling their way into the Russian codes, but they passed it on in turn to the Americans. The US cryptographers at Arlington Hall were quick to get to work. The Americans had as much of a knack for recruiting from unexpected quarters as the British. A key cryptographer assigned to this vitally important task was a woman called Gene Grabeel, 'a Virginia schoolteacher,' who, according to NSA history, 'began the effort to read the Soviet diplomatic messages'.[1]

What she started snowballed into one of the most shattering revelations of treachery, for amid the thousands of Soviet messages that Grabeel and a very small (and hyper-secret) team of American and British codebreakers were to set to work on were communications that would uncover double agents working at the very heart of the Washington and Whitehall atomic establishments. As a result, that partially burned code-book found in Finland – together with more Russian encryption material discovered in May 1945 in Saxony and Schleswig, Germany – was to become a vital part of a mosaic of intelligence finds.

The Government Code and Cypher School successfully fought for its independence. It has been suggested that the wartime achievements of Edward Travis and his team had been rather appropriated by Sir Stewart Menzies and MI6; that Menzies wanted to see his own department garlanded with lavish praise; that if it had not been for Bletchley, MI6 would have emerged with very little credit from the conflict. But now the codebreakers were a service in their own right, under the auspices of the Foreign Office – because, despite the ruins and the human devastation and the financial chaos, it was also perfectly clear in this new world that the fast-evolving technologies of signals intelligence would be on a par with what was called 'humint' (or human intelligence), involving secret agents on the ground.

There was another incentive for a greater concentration on code-work: it was a great deal more economical than the expensive business of running spies and double agents. Also, unlike the skittish agents (just exactly how skittish, the security services were to discover to their terrible cost in subsequent years), codebreaking work was reliable: there was no treachery.

The cabinet and Whitehall knew that Britain's imperial status would be changing; that India would soon be making the transition to independence. But as an empire within an empire, Commander Edward Travis's global network of listening stations was, at this point in history, pretty much unparalleled, and indeed more powerful than any other on earth. No other nation, not even America, had an equivalent scope.

Naturally, America was keenly aware of this fact. The codebreakers at Arlington Hall had maintained extremely good relations with their British counterparts. Even though the Americans had been focused on their struggles against Japan, they had been quick to see what the British were seeing; that if there was to be further war in the years ahead – when, perhaps, economies had recovered sufficiently – then it would most likely be against Stalin's Soviet Union.

As well as enjoying a sense of fellowship with director Edward Travis, Captain Wenger of the US Navy codebreakers had formed a firm friendship with Bletchley's Frank Birch, a longstanding senior veteran who blended his brilliant codebreaking career (stretching back to the First World War) with an equally lively (and incongruous) curriculum of professional acting on stage, screen and early television.

'Dear Birch,' wrote Captain Wenger on 7 September 1945, 'I trust you will forgive me for not having written sooner but we have been in a mad whirl here ever since peace broke out. As with you, we are in the midst of demobilisation and post-war planning and are struggling to find solutions to complex problems while many of the basic policies are still undecided or unknown to us.' (In other words, it was all very well the codebreaking partners having ears all over the world, but they also required those in charge to indicate what their priorities should be.) 'My object in writing at this time is simply to express my great appreciation of the great relations we have enjoyed throughout the war. Your unfailing spirit of co-operation and helpfulness was in no small way responsible for the fine teamwork that prevailed throughout our operations.

'It seems to me,' Wenger continued, 'that the joint efforts of the two organisations can always be looked upon as a model of combined action. I trust,' he added, 'that this will find you in the best of health ... Please convey my best wishes to Mrs Birch and to all of my good friends at Bletchley Park.'[2]

Wenger had supposed that Frank Birch was now going to take a break from this intense life. He was wrong. For the post-war codebreakers in 1945, there was to be a foretaste of the continuous nerve-stretching crises to come. It centred on a small and rather obscure region of western Asia: Azerbaijan, then part of the north of Iran.

The chief protagonists in this tussle were the British and the Russians. This was the first time since their wartime alliance that the two powers had found themselves in active dispute. The skirmish was to serve almost as an orchestral prelude – a tight, local outbreak of hostility that encapsulated the fears, neuroses and misunderstandings of the conflict to come.

The importance of this region was little to do with its extraordinary history. It had more to do with the gulping appetites of the motor age, and the mineral wealth of the land. In the latter years of the war, the Allies had kept a very tight grip on Iran, which had originally declared its neutrality in the conflict; the area had been absolutely key, first for transporting supplies to the Russians after Hitler had invaded the Soviet Union, and also for its flow of oil. For their part in this wartime control of the country, the Soviets occupied the north-west of Iran.

Naturally the Soviets showed no signs of wanting to move out again after the war, and when Azerbaijan declared its independence from Iran – with the backing of Stalin – Britain and America felt their interests to be imperilled. The British interest was particularly acute: it more or less owned the oil that was pumping out of Iran's wells and it had every intention of holding on to this advantage. So at this point, the British needed to delve deep into the minds of Iran's rulers: where did they secretly stand? Would they use this crisis as a trigger for rising up and ejecting the deeply resented British colonial presence?

And so it was in late 1945 that the Bletchley Park codebreaker Alan Stripp, a bright young man who had been cracking Japanese cyphers in Colombo, found himself being sent on a new mission to listen in to Iran and to break its codes. In order to do this, he was to be posted to the extensive 'Wireless Experimental Depot' in Abbottabad, in India's North-West Frontier province, around 100 miles (160 kilometres) from Afghanistan (Abbottabad was to claim greater geopolitical fame in 2011 when it was revealed to be the refuge of the al-Qaeda leader Osama Bin Laden, assassinated by an American squadron). Signals from Iran and Russia poured into this station.

Though the journey across the continent, largely by rackety railway in sweltering weather, was arduous, Stripp relished the new challenge, which combined codebreaking with a more old-fashioned kind of approach. Cryptology, for all its terrific satisfactions, was a desk job. The posting to this remote station – with all of its historical resonances dating from the 19th-century 'Great Game' (ie the military manoeuvring) in the region between Britain and Russia – spoke more of high adventure. 'My job . . . was to study Farsi, the main language of Iran and Afghanistan, and much closer to the languages of north-west Europe than many found in between,' Stripp wrote. 'It is a beautiful and flexible language with a strikingly simple structure and a fine literature.'[3] According to Stripp, this top-secret cryptological listening station in the wild and beautiful foothills of the frontier had been established before the war – indeed, it might have even been there since the First World War. The unit that Stripp found was small, and was presided over by a Colonel Harcourt who had read Persian at Oxford.

Stripp insisted that even though the station had been reading Afghan and Iranian encoded messages for years, they had 'certainly' stopped working on the Soviet messages that they would surely also have been overhearing. Now that the war was over, this was changing fast. 'Abbottabad was concerned with finding out what it could about Iran's real intentions,' wrote Stripp. 'The traffic we studied, therefore, was not military but diplomatic, with a single code system covering every aspect of diplomatic and consular activity from summaries by overseas press attachés of local newspaper reports on Iran, at the brighter end, to routine requests for permission to issue a visa at the more tedious extreme.

'This may sound pedestrian,' he added, 'but after the Japanese grind, it was a welcome distraction; moreover, the atmosphere of the small unit was very appealing.'[4] These were the deep twilight days of Empire in the region; Stripp was in a world of manservants and 'native bearers' that was soon to disappear. But the dispute with Russia – the Soviets continuing to arm the rebels in the north of Iran in their struggle with Tehran – was a dress rehearsal for the tense stand-offs to come. Out there among the rich foothills of India, Alan Stripp was at the heart of the first Cold War skirmish.

But in early 1946, the truth was also that Russia was still weak and wounded; it needed time to convalesce. Even though Iran was starting to bubble with resentment not only about Soviet interventions, but also about British and American military occupation, the Kremlin felt that it had to stand down. As they did so, Stalin's men attempted to wrest an oil concession from the Iranian authorities. But as soon as the Soviet forces had pulled back, the Iranian government tore this agreement up. Moscow was not quite able at this stage to retaliate. This relative weakness only served to exacerbate the neurotic paranoia and aggression within the Kremlin: the proof they needed of Britain and American perfidy.

And it was Alan Stripp and his colleagues who were in place, instantly intercepting, decrypting and analysing Russian movements. This was a test case for the new incarnation of the codebreakers: their ability to garner invaluable intelligence from every corner of the earth, no matter how remote. (Incidentally, these events of 1945 and 1946 also had repercussions that can be felt to this day – many parts of the modern Iranian establishment still nurse poisonous resentment of the British interference in their affairs, to say nothing of the sequestering of their oil, which continued with even greater establishment cynicism throughout the 1950s.)

Stripp was blithe, however. In his station set amid a stunning landscape of mountains and wildflowers, there was much in the job to be relished. He was so at ease with the Farsi language that he regarded the actual codebreaking as a crossword-style relaxation. And he could see history unfolding before his eyes in Abbottabad and northwards: how local politics in the region was to take on global consequences. 'The fly in the Afghan ointment was the Faqir of Ipi,' Stripp later wrote. 'A celebrated old rogue who, with his forebears, had long played a tune which many tribesmen in the whole Hindu Kush area were happy to dance to. He was again becoming restive and the Pathans were getting excited. A lot of this was simply letting off steam: the rugged local tradition expressed joy at fairs, festivals and weddings, or grief at funerals, by firing rifles into the air. Sometimes things got out of hand, and kidnapping, arson, murder and attacks on local forts (on both sides of the border) led to the risk that any clumsy action by the civil or military administration could produce a dangerous flare-up.' The town of Abbottabad was no less restive. 'With the end of the war, the "Quit India" campaign was gaining strength and there were many points on which Muslims, Hindus and Sikhs could not agree.' Given the subsequent partitioning of India and Pakistan in 1947 – with the resulting carnage and vast death toll – there was an element of macabre understatement in this.

Yet Stripp also wanted to pay tribute to the ferociously hard-working 'Indian wireless operators' attached to the station who were utterly committed to their interception duties 'at a time when their loyalty to the British might well have been in question, for any appeal to their patriotism would have been diluted by the ending of the war.'⁵ They were also rather brilliant cricket players.

In 1946, it was time for the Wireless Experimental Depot team to pack up – and each of the men was offered the chance to apply for a full-time job with the codebreaking HQ. Some did and were accepted; but Stripp felt that this would be his chance to return to academia.

His story, though, throws light on a wide web of British interception and codebreaking that had been carefully constructed over a period of decades; indeed, as soon as the very first telephone cables were being laid under oceans in the earlier years of the century, and across continents, the British had been pioneers in making arrangements to have those cables tapped and monitored. By the mid-1920s, the Government Code and Cypher School had made a secret deal with the communications company Cable and Wireless which was laying down the connections: even back then, few were the cables that ran across borders which were not being actively monitored.

Meanwhile, a far-sighted Commander Edward Travis, preparing for his organisation's move to Eastcote, had decided to take stock not only of British intercept stations, but also of the set-ups in the Commonwealth and the Dominions, interception bases ranging from New Zealand to Canada. He set off on an epic journey around the world.

Travis's grand tour started at the station in Heliopolis, based in the old Flora and Fauna museum with its elaborate glass and steel architecture; then he progressed to Mombasa, where the codebreakers were ensconced in a rather ornate old school house overlooking the Indian Ocean. Travis then travelled across that ocean to inspect the rather more extensive cypher base at HMS *Anderson* in Colombo, Ceylon. And from there it was onwards to the Antipodes. Australia had a formidable interception and decryption setup and there was a lot of cross-traffic and co-operation between stations in Melbourne, Canberra and HMS *Anderson*. Commander Travis wanted to be sure that in the post-war landscape, the British operation retained its essential superiority; that there would be no worrying outbreaks of independence in the passing upwards of intelligence. On top of this, there had been concerns about the occasional instance of leaking in Canberra. It was vital that no-one knew of code systems that had been broken. According to security expert Professor Richard Aldrich, the Australians were actually quite happy to swallow the British arrangement, for it equally gave them access to all the latest developments in British signals intelligence.

The grand tour did not end there. Travis and his party then journeyed on to Hawaii, which again was the hub of a complex listening operation, this one obviously run by the Americans; and thence onwards to Washington DC. Canada was key to this codebreaking alliance too. It was recognised in Ottawa that Canada's own codebreaking efforts could give the country some independent heft in the alliance of intelligence communities. But as with Australia, so with Canada: Britain was for some time to remain very much the senior partner. As a worldwide operation, the scale was quite breathtaking. And because of Empire and Commonwealth and Dominions, the British briefly had what the Americans did not have: the ability to listen to any nation in any corner of the earth.

The manpower and machinery to cope with the interceptions being received from all over the planet did not all converge at Bletchley Park: it would have been a physical impossibility and the teleprinters would most likely have melted. Instead, there were numerous out-stations, filled with the young men and women of the 'Y' services (the 'Y' was short for 'wireless'). These operatives, high-speed Morse experts all, would receive both encrypted and decrypted messages sent on from Y Service colleagues around the world. The domestic out-stations were spread across the Home Counties of England, which took in all the raw intelligence and then fed it on to Bletchley; and in the new post-war world, they continued to do so. The staff, though, had gone through a bit of reconfiguration, and the intelligence now went to the new headquarters at Eastcote.

Naval signals were intercepted in Hampshire at HMS *Flowerdown* – a pleasingly bucolic name for what was in fact a rather utilitarian establishment just outside Winchester, noted among Wrens not only for the pressure and demands of the work, but also for a certain amount of knicker-theft. *Flowerdown* was also unusually progressive: throughout the war, this had been one of the few places where uniformed sailors and Wrens had worked side by side. Consequently, it had also been a simmering hotbed of romance.

In the aftermath of war, HMS *Flowerdown* was also where many young male Morse interceptors – who had been based everywhere from the remotest, bluest isles of the Indian Ocean to the wild shores of East Africa – now came back to address new challenges. These were young men with sharp, agile brains and reflexes, enabling them to take down accurately 30 coded words per minute. One such operator, barely 19 when he got back to Hampshire from the Cocos Isles, remembered how striking it was that the sole focus of their efforts was now Russian messages; as ever, the young Y Service operatives were never told why. Equally, they were still very strictly working under the Official Secrets Act: no-one was to know that they were listening in to all the Soviet communications that they could.

Other branches of the services had their own arrangements. The Royal Air Force, for instance, also employed secret listeners. Their intercepted encrypted signals were routed through to Chicksands Priory, in Bedfordshire, a rather more aesthetically pleasing prospect than HMS *Flowerdown*, with its pre-fab Nissen huts; parts of Chicksands Priory dated back to the 15th century. This antiquity was counterbalanced by an arrestingly futuristic spectacle nearby of a Stonehenge of radio masts – vast concentric circles laid out in an array across the land. Chicksands was later to stand as the perfect symbol of the close relationship between the British and the Americans, as an American team of interceptors in essence took the site over in 1950. But the great – and sometimes comical – point of continuity, from the point of view of the Bedfordshire locals, was the secrecy. Throughout the war, everyone knew better than to ask questions; after the war, inquisitiveness increased. Any local people asking whether it was true that Chicksands was some kind of spying headquarters were told matter-of-factly that it was not: it was simply an ordinary RAF establishment. But everyone could see with their own eyes that rather beautiful array of aerials.

Chicksands had played an honourable part in the codebreakers' secret war with Germany; originally based at RAF Cheadle, in Cheshire, there were men and women there who were faster than their counterparts at Bletchley Park. Before the advent of the computer age, in fact, these young people came to be known as 'the human computors' (sic). Among their number was a bright young man called Arthur Bonsall who some decades later – in the 1980s – would rise to become the Director of GCHQ. As well as getting early crowbars into Luftwaffe Enigma codes and pilots' messages, the team at Chicksands were, in 1941, at the centre of the operation to sink the German battleship *Bismarck*. It was their intercepts of Luftwaffe communications – some of which involved an anxious Luftwaffe officer who had a relative serving on board the *Bismarck* – that, once decoded, gave clues as to the elusive co-ordinates of the much-feared vessel. Once this intelligence had been passed through Bletchley Park, the British were able to act: first, by sending RAF planes flying over the *Bismarck* as if by chance, to give the impression that the ship had been spotted from the air; nothing could be allowed to hint that in fact the *Bismarck*'s messages had been read and decyphered.

There was the occasional outbreak of friction between Bletchley and the out-station 'human computors'. Because of security, the codebreakers at Bletchley hated it when codes were broken unbidden, and off site; and this was the case with young Arthur Bonsall's team (as indeed it was elsewhere with another department, the Radio Security Service, and one of its brilliant young operatives, Hugh Trevor-Roper).

The Chicksands operation, together with those spectacular mast arrays (and occasional concerts from American band leader Glenn Miller, attended by hundreds of adoring WAAFs [members of the Women's Auxiliary Air Force], further proof of fruitful Anglo-American accord), made the interception work even slicker and faster. The main building at RAF Chicksands had once been a priory belonging to the Gilbertine order, and it was said to be suitably haunted. The chief spectre was that of a nun. The story went that she had become pregnant and had been walled up alive for her sins; her lover was beheaded.

By August 1945, Germany's defeat had been followed by that of Japan. VJ night saw a number of Chicksands personnel off duty at last; in that warm summer darkness, WAAFs gathered around the nearby YWCA for a huge bonfire and celebratory drinks. But as with the other corners of the codebreaking enterprise, the work went on. And in the new post-war chill, RAF Chicksands had been designated as 'European Signals Centre'. For the next five years, the personnel left on base would be focusing on the signals coming out of Central Europe.

Wars do not just suddenly stop, like a heavy rainstorm followed by sunshine. Treaties may be signed, but the violent aftershocks are felt by everyone for an extraordinary amount of time afterwards. How were the Allies to deal with the German people? How were they to be, as the phrase came to be used, 'de-Nazified'? How was the country to be run? Who would feed the population and try to ensure that they did not begin the whole murderous cycle all over again?

Agonising questions branched out from that: the survivors of the concentration camps – what was to become of them? Added to this was the terrifying and all-embracing oppression that came with Soviet rule, which itself always teetered on the edge of state-approved anti-Semitism (and indeed, by the 1950s, openly tipped over into it). The continent was swarming with displaced persons (or DPs). There were, for example, a great many Polish men who had fought with the Allies, but who had no intention of returning to their own country, now under the domination of their implacable Russian enemies and their Polish Communist collaborators. Many of those who did return would be subjected in the months to come to grotesque trials for having fought alongside capitalists and imperialists, regardless of whether they were Allies or not. The Poles knew that to return would be to face either face instant violent death or the protracted living-death of the Gulag. But where could they go?

And over all these individual and mass traumas flew the spectres of disease and starvation. The shadow that had fallen over 20th-century Europe disfigured many thousands times more lives than any previous conflict. For the Western Allies, the overwhelming question was: how could a semblance of civilisation be restored so swiftly after the savagery of the war? And what sort of government would Germany have? Could it in fact be trusted to govern itself? And the nation was clearly bankrupt, so how could it be expected to pay out reparations to compensate those it had so implacably conquered and destroyed?

Decrypted messages – signals intelligence – were to be absolutely at the centre of these efforts to try and keep the continent stable. The British may no longer have been monitoring armies, but they had to stay sharp and alert and pinpoint-accurate, to ensure that the continent did not slide into an even deeper abyss. They needed first warning of trouble or violence from a hundred different quarters; and most secretly, they needed to understand precisely the thinking of the governments of so many different nations, and in particular, those in the east. They needed – through monitoring and deciphering the airwaves – to judge and anticipate the actions of others; this applied to everyone, from the Jews in Palestine to the separatists in India.

Most particularly, it applied to Stalin's Soviet Russia. Commander Travis's codebreakers were light years away from the British public in their views of Stalin's regime. The cryptographers had a long-standing, deep-rooted distrust and loathing of the Bolsheviks; the general public had, throughout the war, developed a much more favourable view. Throughout the war, 'Uncle Joe Stalin' had become hugely popular, especially in more working-class areas. Maisky, the Russian ambassador to Britain, recalled how warmly he was received in visits to the East End of London. He also reported on how images of Stalin, when flashed up in cinema newsreels, always drew cheers. With no public knowledge of the true nature of Stalin's rule (famines and the deaths of millions were shrugged off as dark rumour), Soviet Russia and Communism looked to many like the image of the future. Codebreaking veterans, long-standing foes of the Soviet regime, must have listened to such sentiments in grim silence.

Of course, it was not only the codebreakers who had a more realistic view of Stalin. But even though it was believed in Whitehall that Russia would clearly be the enemy in a future conflict, not everyone believed that the Soviets would be in any immediate position to fight a conventional war. There was physical and economic exhaustion. The losses and the traumas inflicted by the Nazis would require a lengthy period of recovery. But there was another fear, of a more insidious form of invasion. The anxiety was that the Soviets would not actually have to pick up a weapon; that all they had to do was to infiltrate Soviet sympathisers into the political classes and the trades unions of France, Italy and other countries such as Czechoslovakia. They would work to convert the countries from within to the religion of Communism. In the moral disorientation of the war's aftermath, there would be a great many who would succumb. There was evidence that huge numbers already had.

Given the rumbling, violent weeks and months after the war, it is easy to imagine both the dread of Communism spreading and also, for many on the ground, its overwhelmingly seductive desirability. For a younger generation of Europeans, the world and all its promise had been torn down around them, and the fascists had done more than anyone to destroy it. This, it seemed to many, was the end result of capitalism. It was a system that had made a continent collapse in on itself. Therefore, surely the only chance for a proper new start, a society where men stood a chance of being equal, lay with the purity of the Soviet system?

So the listeners at Chicksands and other locations were not merely focusing on the Russians, but also on the sort of political noise coming out of regions such as provincial France; codebreakers were alert to any traffic, any communication, passing between Paris and Moscow.

The army also had its own band of dedicated wireless listeners. The signals intelligence that they picked up was sent on for analysis not too far away from Chicksands: it went to Beaumanor in Leicestershire (the main house of which again outdid Bletchley Park in terms of its pleasing aspects). All three of these establishments – Bletchley, Chicksands, Beaumanor – had lively, youthful atmospheres; the operatives at Beaumanor took this a stage further with their own quarterly magazine, devoted to gossip, jokes and satire, which continued well after the war, up until 1950. After August 1945, the numbers of people based in and around this fine 19th-century house naturally thinned, but there were some young men – there as civilian operators – who now found themselves facing National Service. That is, they were to do the same job – the high-intensity interception of Morse code messages from every continent – but they were to do so in uniform, and with sergeant majors bawling at them.

Close by the elegant Beaumanor Hall was the equally pleasing 19th-century property Garats Hay, which not only hosted wireless interception work, but was also a training camp for a great many young people; despite the secrecy of the work, there are photographs from the 1940s and 1950s of young smiling men, either in huts or in the grounds. And equally, there are many fond recollections of the pub in the local village of Woodhouse Eaves. These youngsters – drawn from all sorts of backgrounds, but quite often linked by a fanatical and almost obsessional love for radio – underwent extraordinarily intensive Morse training. One poet, simply calling himself 'Wireless Operator', contributed this verse to an in-house magazine:

'Livid pulses striking free/In beatings of the rhythmic Morse

Up to the stratosphere, over the sea/Away from the tall and virile source . . .

Hands outstretched, a million masts receive/Electrical sensations, ethereal words,

Faster than the gods perceive,/ Smoother than the birds.'[6]

Which makes the work sound rather tranquil; the truth was different, especially during the war years. Gwendoline Gibbs was an ATS girl with the Y Service who had been posted to Garats Hay in 1944 and who stayed on a little after the war's end, as the interception targets were reconfigured. She recalled the crushing pressure she and all her colleagues had been under. It was not simply a matter of transcribing signals; they were also battling against interference and jamming, knowing that the messages they were taking down could mean the difference between life and death. On top of this, the hours were murderous: long shifts, followed by uneasy sleep. There were a few nervous breakdowns. Operators were moved to different posts, different shift patterns – but when on leave, they still alarmed their families, looking as they did like the living dead. Of course, the work during – as well as after – the war was very strictly under the Official Secrets Act; no-one in the Y Service could tell a soul what it was that they were doing.

That said, Gwendoline Gibbs also recalled that the young atmosphere of Garats Hay – the Regency house surrounded by utilitarian Nissen huts – could often make people combust with hilarity. At the end of the war, the focus of her work swiftly shifted to the monitoring of Russian signals. The intensity was undimmed; but youthful energy sought other outlets too. As with HMS *Flowerdown*, and the intermingling of young women and men, there were outbreaks of romance everywhere. Yet these were also more innocent times. 'As one girl said, at a later reunion,' recalled Gwendoline, 'if someone had said "rape", I would have thought that they meant cattle food.'[7]

Amazingly, at a time when the nation was still struggling on the tiniest rations of butter, meat and sugar, the food at Garats Hay was extremely good. 'The cooks were first class,' wrote Gwendoline. 'We had plenty of salads, with chopped raw cabbage, dried apricots and apples as well as fresh fruit. One of the cooks made superb pastry – we all looked forward to her apple pies.' The women of Garats Hay also became adept at adapting the less flattering aspects of their uniforms. Especially hated was the army regulation underwear. 'Most of us had cut off the long legs of the khaki knickers, the "passion killers",' remembered Gwendoline Gibbs, 'and sewn the bottoms so that they resembled French knickers – so much sexier!'[8]

There was also more of that Anglo-American co-operation. Gwendoline recalled that until the end of 1945, there was a trio of 'American intelligence chaps' who proved very popular. There was 'Forbes Sibley, Fred Allred and "Mac", a charming trio,' she said, 'one of whom, Mac I think, was reputed to have a little black book containing all the names of the girls he'd been out with.'

In 1946, in common with so many other grand properties at the time, Beaumanor Hall was put up for sale: the passing of the owner, W Curzon

Herrick, had left the family and estate with unsupportable death duties to pay. They could no longer afford the place. Landed gentry were hardly the priority for Clement Attlee's post-war government. The *Loughborough Monitor* reported: 'Mansion bought by the War Office. It is remembered that the Mansion was taken over by a Radar Station (sic) during the war and considerable money was laid down on equipment and permanent fixtures. It is still used as a radar centre and the War Office have already stated that the building will be maintained in its present state so as to preserve the beauty of its setting.'

The end of the war was also bringing prodigious leaps in technology: at Bletchley, codebreakers had been working with pioneering electronic decryption techniques and at Garats Hay, there would be similar preparation for a new era of what would be termed 'elint' – that is, electronic intelligence. Which, once again, would prove catnip to new young recruits fascinated by this world of secret communications.

In this new environment, Commander Travis had faced another important consideration: large numbers of academics – the professors and scholars who had been so essential and innovative in their codebreaking work – were now returning to Oxford, Cambridge and the other universities from which they had been drawn. Obviously, since they had all signed the Official Secrets Act, there was no fear of any indiscretions. Equally, though, it was important that they should understand that their secret expertise could well be called upon in the future. Strong and congenial links were to be maintained. Indeed, such links served the double purpose of giving the codebreakers a form of occasional informal consultation, and the academics the supreme flattery of knowing that their superior intellects were still confidentially required.

Among the younger academics who had worked in those Bletchley huts, mathematicians Shaun Wylie and Irving 'Jack' Good were examples of men who either were kept closely in the loop on matters cryptological or indeed were hauled back into it full-time (as was the case with Good).

So it was that Commander Travis, when in discussion with the Treasury about the sort of personnel this brand new branch of intelligence would need, was swift to pay the academics proper tribute. 'The war proved beyond doubt that the more difficult aspects of our work call for staff of the highest calibre,' he wrote in a memo. 'The successes by the Professors and Dons among our temporary staff, especially perhaps the high grade mathematicians, put that beyond doubt.'[9] These were the sorts of minds that he wanted to carry on attracting. Curiously, there was to prove a strong line of continuity in terms of personality types, running from the nascent Government Code and Cypher School, through Bletchley Park and now into this computerised future: in other words, the new generation of codebreakers were to prove every bit as focused yet whimsical and quietly eccentric.

Chapter Three

'The Merest Indication of Corpses'

It had never been Brideshead; there were few who could have sighed with piercing nostalgia over halcyon hours spent beneath its gables. Yet the eccentric architecture of Bletchley had come in some curious way to reflect the ungovernably quirky codebreakers. The move was inevitable though: the directorate understandably wanted to return to London. The country location had only ever really been a Blitz precaution. Gradually, over a period of some months into early 1946, the red-brick mansion was abandoned by the codebreaking directorate and the remaining cryptologists, and they moved into their new base on the green, hilly fringes of London.

The district of Eastcote, situated at the north-western end of the Metropolitan and Piccadilly Underground lines, was an incongruous location, though. From the start, there was something almost comical about the contrast between the sharp lightning-fast intelligence work shaping the contours of a new Cold War geopolitics and the wide leafy somnolent suburban avenues in which this work was being carried out.

Eastcote was well-to-do and still had imitations of village life: the white wooden signposts, carved fingers pointing west to Uxbridge and Ruislip, east to Harrow and Stanmore; the village green and the war memorial; the dainty high street, with its little shops and dressmakers. The railway had first come to Eastcote in 1905, and reached proper frequency by the 1920s and 1930s, at the point when London was beginning its last great expansion outwards. And with the transport direct to the city came charming whitewashed villas with green-tiled roofs, windows and fanlights with red and indigo stained-glass designs. Their architects took ideas from the Arts and Crafts movement.

There were the grander properties still dotted around: Eastcote House and Highgrove Hall were two notable estates, which had provided much of the local employment at a time when the area was still largely agricultural. Then in early 1940, when the War Office acquired some of the local land, there came a new institution, housed in a series of monotonous grey single-storey concrete blocks. The initial purpose of this new establishment was to have been a military hospital. Swiftly, though, other uses were found. The name of this new establishment was HMS *Pembroke V* – or, as it was to become later, RAF Eastcote. You would never have known it was there if you had not gone looking for it. Obscured on one side by a thick wood, and from another by a charming 1930s housing estate – at the end of which it lay – HMS *Pembroke V* was not far from the main street of Eastcote. By 1942, it was in operation as an important out-station of Bletchley Park. The bombe machines – the hulking, wardrobe-sized creations of Alan Turing, Gordon Welchman and engineer Harold Keen – were fantastically successful at sorting through thousands of possible code combinations. As a result, in the early days when there were few of the machines, there had been a great deal of friction about which departments could use them the most, with naval and military sections arguing fiercely that they had to have priority.

When more bombe machines were built, there was then the question of where to put them. Bletchley could not be expected to house all of them and nor, in the case of a bombing raid, would the authorities anyway have wanted so much invaluable technology all gathered together in the same place. This fairly rudimentary base about 30 miles (50 kilometres) south of Bletchley seemed ideal.

However, right from the start, Eastcote never seemed hugely popular with the young women – the Wrens – who were posted there. There was a long badly-lit path that ran between the grey concrete blocks of the base, and in the middle of the night, when shifts were changing, or as young women ventured out for a brief break from tending to these temperamental machines, there was often a sense of unease. Male personnel worked at the base too and there had been stories of attacks upon young women made on that long, dim, unwelcoming path. It was only a little after the war that this new codebreaking HQ began to acquire a slightly more congenial atmosphere, livened up with everything from jazz concerts to cricket and tennis societies.

The Eastcote operation, if one had gone looking for it, presented a formidable prospect from the outside – forbidding fences and rolls of barbed razor wire. Security was intense, even within the base – those whose work centred around Block A would have no idea at all of what was going on in Block B. To get in, one needed an identification card with a photograph on it. One of the administrative staff who made the transfer from Bletchley to Eastcote in the new era was secretary Mimi Gallilee. An evacuee from Blitz-torn London, Mimi had first worked at Bletchley as a messenger girl, leaving school at the age of 14 to do so. She was mentored by Bletchley's senior personal assistant Doris Reed and in time came to work with her in the office of Nigel de Grey, who was now deputy director of the new post-war codebreaking operation.

When the war ended, Mimi agreed to the transfer, having not given much thought by that stage to other career opportunities. However, after the large house and lake and grounds of Bletchley, these new suburban surrounds were, she felt, markedly drearier.

'At Eastcote, we went into the quarters where the bombe machines were,' says Mrs Gallilee. 'And I think there was only one bombe left. I didn't know anything about the bombes.' (This had been because of the extraordinarily tight compartmentalisation at Bletchley – even some of those working in the Directorate would have had no idea precisely how those Enigma codes were being broken.) 'Those of us who had nothing to do with it wouldn't have known,' she says. 'So we just moved in to where the Wrens had worked. I of course stayed within the Directorate.'

Mrs Gallilee felt quite strongly, even as a very young woman, that she did not want to live on the fringes of London: she wanted to be close to the colour and life of the centre of town. This however, caused some practical difficulties. 'I was living in Bayswater and I had to pay the full fares all the way to Eastcote,' she says. 'On such a low salary.' The London of 1946 was still in a twilight of bomb damage: in parts it had been utterly destroyed after the Blitz and the onslaught of V-1 and V-2 missiles. Even once-elegant districts like Bayswater were straitened and peeling, formerly grand houses now subdivided into murky flats with cold shared bathrooms. The brutal truth was that after the romanticism of Bletchley – certainly to a girl in her teens, mesmerised by the aristocratic young women and the brainy young men roaming what seemed to her like a university campus – this new world of secret work was, for Mimi Gallilee, simply exhausting and drab. 'They tried to do something for me in terms of an increase in pay,' Mrs Gallilee says, 'but you just didn't have that kind of system.' In the civil service pay structure, Mimi's youth counted against her – she would have to wait a couple of years until she was 21 before she could be considered for a suitable wage boost.

'And there were no such things as merit awards in those days,' she adds. 'Besides, the government wouldn't have had the money to pay us anyway. I hadn't got enough money to live and stay in London. And I don't think I stayed at Eastcote for more than six months. I said I'd take the first job that I could get as long as it paid more money. And the first job I went after was as a copy typist for Burroughs Wellcome, the research chemist outfit. They took me on. I earned a pound a week more, straight away. That was a hell of a lot of money.'

There was a twist though. 'After maybe just a couple of days,' says Mrs Gallilee, 'I thought: "I can't stand this." I felt as though I had been dropped from one world into another. It was nothing like anything. Perhaps I thought everywhere would be like Bletchley Park.'

Indeed, that sense of rupture was felt quite keenly by many who had worked at Bletchley and who had streamed out of the place to take up positions of academic or administrative importance. There was one other factor too: the authorities gave Mimi Gallilee and all others departing an intensive debriefing reminder that the work that they had done – and indeed, perhaps any work that they might do on similar lines in the future

– was very strictly classified. They were not to breathe one syllable – even to one another. And so it was later in life that Mimi, on the point of joining the BBC, found herself being interviewed by someone whose face she had recognised from Bletchley. On her application, she had written simply that her war had been occupied with work for the Foreign Office. Her interviewer, although recognising her, made no comments at all.

One of the charming and perennial fascinations of even the most incredibly secret and pivotal organisations in Britain is the careful bowler-hatted bureaucracy that surrounded their urgent work. The move to Eastcote, for instance, meant a certain financial readjustment. 'I am directed by Mr Secretary Bevin,' ran a 1946 letter to Barclays Bank from the Foreign Office, 'to request that the Foreign Office account maintained with your Bletchley branch may be closed at the close of business on the 30th March 1946 and that the balance may be transferred to Barclays Bank at Eastcote to be placed to the credit of the Foreign Office account "Government Communications Headquarters".'[1] At this stage, various departments referred to the codebreakers under varying titles. Although this was an early use of the term 'GCHQ' (the use of which would come to be discouraged in official correspondence for security reasons), Eastcote was also known as the London Signals Intelligence Centre.

There were also careful memos – strictly within Civil Service rules – to do with selecting recruits. Interviews were to be carried out. 'Generally speaking, selection will be made on the basis of the forms of application for Post-War employment which have been completed and which contain recommendations by the Heads of Section,' ran an order from the Directorate from late 1945. 'It should be clearly understood by individuals that selection under the above scheme is no guarantee of an offer of permanent employment. Such an offer can only be made when approval for numbers, grades, etc of the signals intelligence centre have been given by the Treasury. Recommended civilian candidates will continue to be employed as temporary civil servants pending the establishment of the Signals Intelligence centre on a peace-time basis.'[2]

There were obviously to be special cases, including those returning from the field. Added to this would be a continual alertness to the brightest intellects of the coming generation, though this new establishment at Eastcote was – for the moment – only a fraction of the size of Bletchley. The codebreakers numbered in the hundreds, rather than thousands. In the coming years, as Commander Travis constructed this regenerated institution, that position would be reversed.

As well as this, there was a new element of centralisation – one of the factors that strengthened the codebreakers' case to be a wholly new service, independent and answering to the Foreign Office. All the different cryptology branches that had emerged from the main Bletchley operation were now to be pulled back in and overseen by the Eastcote directorate. 'The transfer of certain sections (to Eastcote) will commence in November,' ran another internal memo. 'This includes sections now at Bletchley Park, Berkeley Street, Aldford House and Queens Gate. Oxford may not move for some months after the other sections . . .' The numbers were being settled, too. 'The proposed peace-time establishment of the Sigint Centre totals 1,017, exclusive of personnel attached from the Service Ministries and "domestic" staff. The present war-time establishment is being reduced to approximately that figure by 31 Dec 45, the total being made up of the following groups: a) cryptographic (including tabulating and machine sections) 475; b) Intelligence 83; c) Traffic Analysis 180; d) Technical (incl Communications etc) 93; e) cypher security 150; f) administration 36.'[3]

No matter how exceptionally so many women had performed at Bletchley Park, civil service rules – which had ensured that they never received any kind of parity in terms of pay – were still very much in force. Added to this, if they got married, they were required to leave the service altogether. This was considered quite usual. A married woman's duty – no matter how towering the intellect of that married woman – was to make a home for the working husband. The Eastcote codebreakers, conscious of how much brilliant work had been done by women like Mavis Batey, tried to find some kind of fix for this, rather than slam the door on so much vital talent. 'Although, under present regulations, married women cannot be considered for "establishment" in the civil service,' ran one Director's memo, 'they may be employed as temporary civil servants.'[4] Nonetheless, it was still insanity: as a means of illustration, if Joan Clarke and Alan

Turing had gone ahead with a wedding, and had, despite Turing's true orientation, remained married, then Clarke – one of Hut 8's most dazzling codebreakers – would only have been permitted to continue her brilliant codebreaking work as a temp.

And despite the fact that the new establishment was facing up to the prospect of a grim and profoundly uncertain world, there were soon to be yelps of indignation over other outbreaks of perceived short-changing. 'Rates of Pay,' began one incendiary communication. 'It is pointed out, particularly for the guidance of junior staff, that as Eastcote is a "provincial" area, the rates of pay will be on the same scale as those of Bletchley Park.'[5] But as a few people were to point out – Mimi Gallilee included – working in and living near Eastcote very much involved London prices. There were rows to do with relocation and re-accommodation; even in 1946, London was not cheap. Indeed, the scale of the bombing over the last few years had put a strain on the housing market. 'A billeting office is being established,' declared a November 1945 Eastcote memo. The idea was partly to circumvent the kind of disputes that tended to result in triplicated letters of complaint. Originally – as Mimi Gallilee recalled – there had been a rather stark option of staying in a hostel near Notting Hill Gate. Then that was discontinued; there was an idea that another hostel, nearer Eastcote, might be established. But as the memo stated, this was not intended as a 'permanent base of residence'.

Others turning up for duty at Eastcote were similarly dismayed at what they found. According to Professor Richard Aldrich, in 'June 1946, William Bodsworth, a British codebreaker, returned from a period in America to the cold and rain of an English summer to take over GCHQ's Soviet section. He found his first sight of Eastcote 'frankly shattering'. Expecting a 'nice old country house', instead he found it to be 'more cheerless than any of the temporary buildings I have seen in this racket either here or abroad'.[6]

William Bodsworth had a good excuse for his gloom: the year previously he and a small number of other codebreakers had been posted to Washington DC as a liaison team; quite apart from the thrill of being right at the centre of pan-global intelligence operations, there was also the great abundance of fresh food, coffee, even the fruit juices that were quite unknown in Britain. Even tomato juice from a tin was then regarded by the British as impossibly sophisticated. To huge numbers of young people in Britain throughout the war, America symbolised the future; this younger generation danced to swing and yearned for the perceived classless style and cool of their transatlantic cousins. Imagine, then, William Bodsworth sailing back to sad, rain-swept, bitterly cold England, and taking up his new work behind the barbed wire of what looked like a Soviet-style correction camp.

Yet curiously, as 1946 progressed, this most secret site – or at least a disused part at its northern extreme edge, separate from the codebreakers, an area which had once housed some army personnel – proved mightily attractive to others. The gaping holes left all over London where once there had been homes had created a terrible shortfall which, despite the government's best efforts with pre-fabricated bungalows, had not been solved. There were thousands of families desperate for somewhere decent to live. And so – aided in part by former soldiers who knew the sites well – there began a London squatters' movement which focused on what had been bustling military and air bases. The vast acreage at Eastcote became one such target. Prospective squatters and their families noted the group of now disused military buildings, a little distance away from the barbed-wire enclosed blocks of the cryptographers. Indeed, just weeks before the squatters moved in, there had been a question raised in the House of Commons to the housing minister about what might be done with some of the spare huts in the compound. The squatters soon provided an answer.

Today, such an incursion would meet with a very shrill response from politicians and journalists. In 1946, the reaction was more measured. Possibly because the first man to move in to the squat was himself a former officer.

Especially interested in this phenomenon were those running Mass Observation, the vast social research project which aimed to catalogue the everyday life of British people. 'The squatters are half middle and half artisan class,' the MO man reported. 'One man is a master builder, another a school master and another a factory worker. All are ex-servicemen. Two of them have cars. And some could afford to buy a house but have been unable to do so. They live the typical suburban middle class life as far as they are able. There is no sign of any violent political enthusiasm among any of them.[7] Mass Observation noted that the Eastcote incursion was started by a former pilot officer, living with his family in rented rooms nearby, who noticed that the officers' mess on the site was disused, and would make rather more suitable accommodation. Word then spread among friends, and more families came to join them on the site. The electricity meter was kept fed, and the officers concerned raised rent money, should anyone ever actually ask for any. No-one did.

And unlike those instances in grander Kensington, where in 1946 squatters took over unoccupied private property, the police were notably relaxed about this incursion too. As for the codebreakers, their part of the camp was firmly and hermetically sealed, those rolls of barbed wire remaining in place. Nonetheless, it is a striking image – it is very difficult now to imagine unauthorised personnel being allowed to set up camp anywhere near GCHQ's current base in Cheltenham.

Yet this is not to say that Clement Attlee's government was perfectly relaxed: these middle-class squatters, however subliminally, were tweaking the tail of authority. They clearly could not be permitted to stay where they were. Cunningly, the matter became one not for the security services, but the Ministry of Health; in other words, were former military sites suitably safe places to bring up young children? The Ministry of Health thought not. Moreover, even though the sites concerned happened to be empty at that point, that did not mean that the government regarded them as spare. These buildings might soon be needed, it was argued, for refugees from other countries, or Polish airmen who had no desire to return to their ravaged country.

So while this was going on in one corner of Eastcote, in the other, work of the most clandestine degree was being undertaken. Although most of the bombe machines had been dismantled – there were bombes at Eastcote dedicated to chewing through codes from each region of the earth – a number were retained, and continued working in the immediate post-war period. Indeed, it has been observed that they (and their human operators) worked ever more efficiently. On top of this was the arrival at Eastcote of the machines that were to shape the future.

Captain Gil Hayward had – as a very young man – been part of the Dollis Hill General Post Office research team. Throughout the war, he served with the Intelligence Corps in Egypt. He returned in 1944, came to Bletchley and very quickly became proficient not merely with the revolutionary Colossus machine but also the Tunny. This was the astounding British re-engineering – almost a re-imagining – of the German Lorenz SZ42 cyphering machine. It was instrumental in cracking messages that had come from the desk of Hitler himself. Come 1946, and the final clearance of the Bletchley site, Captain Hayward was part of the highly delicate operation to remove two Colossus machines to the Eastcote site. Accompanying them were two of the Tunny machines.

Also involved in this move was a very young engineer called John Cane. He understood at the time that the technology was still perfectly crucial and indeed still so revolutionary that very few could have guessed at the advances. He remembered recently, however, that the Eastcote site was not perhaps as purely secure as it could have been.

'One of the blocks we installed this marvellous top secret equipment in had a three foot wide hole in the wall,' he said. 'And the [local] children used to climb through that hole and pinch our tools.' Yet John Cane understood very well the importance of that post-war role. 'The way I looked at it was that we'd done a job, enjoyed ourselves doing it and been quite safe. No-one was dropping bombs on us or anything like that.'[8]

The site at Eastcote was large enough to allow the space for such technological marvels; but was there the feeling that Commander Edward Travis and the dapper Nigel de Grey would have preferred to have been located at a rather smarter address near Westminster, a walk away from the War Office and the Cabinet? Before the war as mentioned, the Government Code and Cypher School had occupied premises in St James's Park; by contrast, this pleasant but very faintly boring suburb must have seemed – just in the obvious terms of status – rather a comedown. MI5 and MI6 would never have been based so far away from where the key decisions were being made: surely such a distance left Travis, de Grey and all their colleagues rather out of the loop?

Yet it worked the other way around too. There was in those first few post-war months a continuing tension about who should assume ultimate authority over the work of the codebreakers. MI6 still clearly felt that the department fell under their purview. Travis disagreed: his codebreakers and his worldwide network of secret listeners had to have operational independence to be effective. The department should not be subordinate to MI6 but, rather, should function as its equal. Quite apart from anything else, the new era of computers was changing the very nature of intelligence. There was an entire world to monitor. Any insistence from MI6 that it should in some way perform all analysis on GCHQ's intelligence – acting in essence as a filter before such intelligence was relayed upwards towards the War Office and the prime minister – might cloud or even distort the meanings of millions of messages.

'In the brave new world,' one hand-written Eastcote memo of the time ran, 'we have got to be prepared to follow trouble around the globe – vultures ready to take wing at the merest indication of corpses.'[9]

So, as the vultures settled in, in early 1946, some of the senior Eastcote personnel found themselves places to live nearby; there were even quainter spots not too far off, such as the village of Chalfont St Giles.

And after a few weeks spent working with the John Lewis Partnership (in that time of austerity, it is difficult to imagine that these department stores had much vim or colour), Hugh Alexander, the champion chess player and former architect of Hut 8's great cryptological triumphs, returned to the codebreaking fold. In those anonymous single-storey offices (by some accounts at least bright, nicely carpeted, and with plenty of sunlight pouring through the windows of the long corridors or 'spurs'), he, together with Frank Birch, Eric Jones, Joan Clarke, Arthur Bonsall and a range of other piercing Bletchley intellects, settled in to survey the new world before them. Within walking distance, housewives hung their washing out, husbands mowed their lawns, and the trains of the Metropolitan Line carried wholly unsuspecting locals to their rather less dramatic jobs in town. The incongruity could not have been more English.

Yet there was another consideration: next to the vast sums that the Americans were pumping into their intelligence structures, the former Bletchley personnel must now have been finding that their own funding was becoming more of a struggle in a country which was to all intents and purposes bankrupt. How could the codebreakers – listening to the creaking strains and stresses of nations around the world, and the thunderous rumbles of looming conflicts – impress upon the new Labour government the fact that the world was now, in some ways, even more dangerous than before, and needed lightning intellects to respond to lightning strikes?

Chapter Four

Mission into Darkness

Even the most squalid governments have secrets worth grabbing; and after the war, there was a scramble to salvage such treasure from the ruins of Nazi rule. Most famously, there was breathless urgency among the Americans to take control of, and to master, the German advances in rocket technology. For GCHQ and the post-war codebreakers, there were also prizes to be found amid the ugliness and dumb brutalisation. To secure them, and bring them back to Britain, would require experts more used to confining themselves to laboratories.

Nor were these men the world's most obviously qualified secret agents. One such was Alan Turing. At the time, he had been seconded to a hugely secretive research establishment called Hanslope Park, in North Buckinghamshire. This institute – centred on a handsome white stuccoed 19th-century house, surrounded with Nissen huts, and all within carefully fenced-off and frequently patrolled parkland – was an offshoot of the main codebreakers' operation. It was set up by the ebullient Brigadier Gambier 'Pop' Parry, under the umbrella of the Radio Security Service. Hanslope Park was on the face of it quite a straightforward military establishment and part of its remit was to explore and push the boundaries of interception technology. But there was also much work being done on new technological means to devise encryption methods.

The work was very much tilted towards the coming age of the computer

– the age that Turing himself had done so much to pitch the world towards. Here, in these secure Northamptonshire laboratories, were vast electronic machines, the size of wardrobes, linked with labyrinths of wire and cable. The air was thick with the smell of oil and the heat off thermionic valves. Turing – not in uniform, unlike so many around him – was working on projects such as the 'Delilah', an intended means of scrambling and encyphering voice transmissions so that, say, Churchill might be able to talk to Roosevelt on a line that would sound – to interceptors – like the anonymous hiss of white noise. The reason for the name 'Delilah' was that it was named after the Biblical figure – the 'deceiver of men'.

At Hanslope, there was none of the day-to-day intense pressure of Bletchley. Turing was able to work in calm (and rather congenial) surroundings, with his young assistants Robin Gandy and Don Bayley.

The Delilah device had some competition, for the Post Office Research Laboratories at Dollis Hill in north-west London were working at the same problem: that of encoding the human voice. The presiding genius of Dollis Hill, Dr Tommy Flowers – a supremely gifted engineer and also not an obvious choice of secret agent – had hailed from one of the poorer districts of London's East End. As a young man, he had struggled and worked intensely hard to put himself through night school to pursue his passion for engineering; this is perhaps why some of the Cambridge-educated codebreakers had sometimes treated his ideas with scepticism and occasionally open disdain. Dr Flowers vaulted above such snobbery, and he achieved stewardship at Dollis Hill at a time when telephone technology was starting to evolve dizzyingly fast.

Flowers and Turing had met often throughout the war years, and came to admire one another. Flowers had a genius for giving solid structure to the most abstruse of mathematical theories; a genius that Turing lacked. In 1944, Flowers's code-smashing Colossus had proved enormously successful and more were built. As the war in Europe ended, the East End engineer and the public-school mathematician found themselves called upon to make an unexpected journey together.

In the summer of 1945, both Flowers and Turing were quietly sum-moned from their respective establishments to travel to Paris; there, with several other British colleagues, they met with a small team of American scientists. Their onward mission – handled in part by codebreaking veteran Lieutenant Colonel Patrick Marr-Johnson – was one of the most intense secrecy. From the relative lightness of Paris, they then travelled far into the dark ruins of Germany. There was a strong perception of risk: English voices moving through some of the obscurer corners of a traumatised, nerve-shattered population, sometimes deep in the country and far from the safety of the occupied cities, may have been regarded as a provocation to desperate vanquished communities. Not everyone in those remote rural populations would have been willing to welcome such figures. But Turing and Flowers formed part of what were to become known as TICOM expeditions. These were to prove beyond value.

TICOM was the Targeted Intelligence Committee, a joint effort between the Americans and the British to send experts into the depths of former Nazi territory to acquire any scientific or technological secrets that the retreating forces had not wilfully destroyed. Different teams were sent to Peenemünde, to Innsbruck, to Heidelberg, to salvage what they could of Nazi missile technology, as well as advances in such areas as liquid oxygen, infra-red instruments and anti-radar equipment.

Turing and Flowers had their own specific mission: to examine how far the Nazis had got in terms of computerised cryptology. The areas that their team started off with – Frankfurt, Bayreuth – were under American control and there was a great deal of nerve-grating bureaucracy as the scientists had continually to prove who they were. But in that uncertain landscape – there was a prevalent and perfectly understandable fear that many German young men would not relinquish their Nazi loyalty – Turing, Flowers and the Americans travelled far up into the mountains, to a secret radio research establishment, and they made their sleeping quarters in an old hospital. The abandonment of these establishments high up in the wild hills must have lent them a slightly eerie and unsettling feel.

Turing and Flowers were, throughout, implacably silent with their colleagues about all the work that they had done, all the triumphs that they had enjoyed back at Bletchley Park. They also said nothing to those Germans that they met.

Flowers and Turing had the opportunity to meet a German cryptographer who, despite defeat, was intensely proud of the technology that he had worked with. They listened with quiet respect as he gave them a demonstration of the machine that had produced the Tunny code. It was perfectly unbreakable, the German scientist averred. He pointed to the countless millions of different combinations and permutations, the limitless complexities of its codes. Turing responded – with discretion and politeness – with a raised eyebrow and an exclamation of surprise. Neither he nor Flowers were about to tell the scientist that his unbreakable codes had in fact been shattered, and on a spectacular scale.

Elsewhere in Germany, another Allied codebreaker – an American mathematical prodigy who had been brought over to England for the war and who was to later help construct the US codebreaking efforts throughout the Cold War – was engaged in an even hairier mission. Arthur Levenson was seconded to another TICOM unit, set up to grab as much cryptological machinery and expertise out of Germany and Austria as they could. He was face to face with Nazi soldier prisoners and indeed Nazi civilians who might turn on American soldiers without any warning.

'We wanted the Tunny [encryption] machines,' recalled Arthur Levenson some years later. 'And then we had some idea of who the people were and we interrogated them and mostly they were very co-operative. Occasionally you'd get a guy and then we told him if he doesn't want to answer questions we're turning him over to the Russians. And they talked. Then when we took this group back to England with us they thought they were very lucky indeed because we passed along the way what they called dustbins. These', he explained, 'were just curious enclosures, all out in the open, teeming with prisoners, and they were much better off being with us. So Major Tester and I took a dozen of them back to England.'[1]

Given the horror of what the Allied troops had uncovered deep in the forests of Eastern Europe, how did Levenson, who was himself Jewish, manage to stay so apparently at ease with his prisoners? A distinction had been drawn, if subconsciously; for these prisoners were in essence cryptographers too. 'Then we became very friendly,' Levenson said. 'These were not combat troops, these were communications . . . They were obviously not going to run anywhere. In fact, they felt much better off with us than anywhere else, including escape. Because they'd only be picked up and terrible things would happen . . . And then we landed in London. Then one of them, a nice little old man, said he had always wanted to go to London. Just before the war broke out, he had finally got enough money and then the war came . . . I said "well, now you're getting a free trip."'

This extraordinary TICOM convoy, comprising six trucks, invaluable top-secret equipment and German prisoners of war, wound its way to Buckinghamshire, to a site not too far from Bletchley Park at Beaconsfield. It was time for the prisoners to demonstrate the machinery, and to unlock the last of the German encryption secrets. Because clearly, the principles of such technology would still be in use in a variety of other places.

'About 100 yards [90 metres] apart, we set up the antenna, they broadcast to each other, and they showed us how they set the patterns, what the whole procedure was,' recalled Levenson. 'They told us there was the death penalty for sending depths but they had sent depths [a series of messages encyphered with the same code machine setting, more vulnerable to breaking than single messages encyphered with different settings] . . . They were still alive.' And the much-desired Tunny machines did not disappoint. 'They were good, they were well constructed. They had been built when things were good . . . they had no ersatz material. They all used steel.'[2]

Levenson had his military training; but the German interlude, this exploration of a country in the throes of a nervous breakdown, must have been altogether more disconcerting for the civilians Tommy Flowers and Alan Turing. As it happened, on the days they were up in those eerie mountains in the secret German codebreaking station, Hiroshima and Nagasaki were wiped out in a flash of pure white; the military apotheosis of scientific research, the atomic bomb, had now opened up vistas of annihilation of which no-one before could have dreamed, even in the darkness of Nazi Germany.

But for both men, away from all this horror, the age held other rather more exhilarating opportunities. Turing had been wondering whether to return to his academic career at King's College, Cambridge after a six-year absence; Tommy Flowers, in the meantime, having been so instrumental in bringing the computer age into being, had a great deal more work to do in his north-west-London laboratory.

From a certain angle, it might be tempting to wonder if Dr Flowers's post-war projects might have had an element of anti-climax to them. Almost immediately, he fixed his focus on making electronic telephone exchanges a practical possibility. Certainly this was vital work: a new technologically advanced era would need lightning-fast communications between cities, countries, continents. For all sorts of commercial and political – as well as security – reasons, it was in Britain's dearest interests to keep itself at the forefront of all such developments. This is doubtless how it seemed to Dr Flowers – but how often did he allow himself to think about the leaps in computer science that he had made possible?

At the end of the war, as far as Dr Flowers knew, the Colossus machines – his proud creations – were destroyed for reasons of secrecy. Strictly speaking, Dr Flowers was not even permitted to hold on to the blueprints. He was told that no-one was ever to know of the extraordinary codebreaking feats that he had made possible, after engineering efforts that he had funded out of his own pocket. The government ensured at the end of the war that he was rewarded and reimbursed – he received the MBE, and £1,000, which in those days would have been enough to buy a house – but could the money cushion the intense distress he felt at having his beautiful creations dismantled irretrievably?

Ironically, as we have seen, any distress he suffered was perfectly unnecessary: Commander Travis had quietly decided, amid the gradual closedown and moving of Bletchley Park, that two of the Colossus machines would survive. In the chaos of post-war international politics, who knew who would end up using such technology next?

Visit the Bletchley Park Museum now and you will find an extraordinary re-creation of the Colossus, a great mass of metal, winking lights and fragile-looking white paper tape. It is barely 70 years since these contraptions were so sensitively classified that they had to be transported under shrouds of deepest secrecy from Bletchley to the Eastcote codebreaking station in Betjeman's Metro-land. And it is very easy to imagine other countries in the 1940s using Lorenz-style technology for their encryptions. For some time after the war, for instance, in the Russian-controlled sector of Germany, there were some Communists who quite blithely and unknowingly continued with Lorenz encryptions.

For Dr Flowers, there might have been the luxury of abstract speculation about such matters, but actually, he was too much of an enthusiastic pragmatist to dwell on what had been; he was drawn to the radon glow of the future. Within a few years, his work of electronic exchanges came to fruition. He can also lay claim – a lighter claim to posterity, this – to have been the genius behind ERNIE. The acronym stood (or rather, still stands) for 'Electronic Random Number Indicator Equipment'. It was invented specifically for the advent of Premium Bonds in 1956; these government bonds came with the incentive of being eligible for Lottery-style cash prizes. And so it was that Dr Flowers engineered a computer that could generate completely random numbers, to a set number of digits. ERNIE came to be frequently mistaken for a real person. In 1980, the band Madness dedicated an entire song to the machine and its promise of untold riches for ordinary people.

And what of Bletchley's other computing pioneers? William 'Bill' Tutte, the young man who had been so brilliantly instrumental in finding a lever into the hellishly complex Lorenz codes – the breaks that then led to the development of the Colossus – returned immediately to Trinity College, Cambridge after the war. There he gained his doctorate and pursued his work in the realm of pure mathematics and extremely advanced geometry. However, like many of his former colleagues who stepped out into the wider world, the links with the old establishment would prove remarkably tenacious across the years. Indeed, for some, the links were made of purest elastic, and after a few years, they would find themselves twanging back into the secret heart of codebreaking.

Then there were senior figures such as Professor Maxwell 'Max' Newman, who had headed up the department known as the 'Newmanry'. The intellectual excitement of what had been started there could not be quelled. He understood very well just how this computer revolution would unfold and he very much wanted to be at the front of developments in it. He joined Manchester University a little later in 1945 as the Fielden Professor of Mathematics, a post he occupied for many years thereafter. As well as running the department (he was a popular fatherly figure with a very dry wit), Professor Newman was determined that the university should build its own fully functioning computer; this at a time when much of the pioneering work in the field was carried out by the American military.

But Professor Newman was not completely adrift from his old life at Bletchley Park. Very far from it. As well as keeping active contacts open with his old codebreaking friends – and indeed very quietly advising them – in 1945 Newman recruited one of his brightest young colleagues, Irving John (IJ) Good to join him in Manchester for this ground-breaking computer work. The 29-year-old Good became a mathematics lecturer by day, a computer whizz by night. He and Newman and an engineer called Tom Kilburn worked towards the building of a computer called the Manchester Mark One. It was one of the world's first stored-program computers; a step up from Colossus in the sense that an electronic machine could now be said to have a memory. As we shall see later, the work carried out here was to have a direct impact on the codebreaking efforts in London.

Computer development was far from being an abstracted academic pursuit. In later years Professor Newman's work would come to be tied up very closely with wider matters of national security and defence. Theory was one thing; but there was a terrific sense of urgency about its application as well.

Alan Turing was, at this time, also thinking hard about the future of computing. Having theorised about a 'universal machine', he was now set on creating an electronic brain. And so it was that he left Hanslope Park to join a rather more open civilian outfit. As well as the GPO, and Newman's team at Manchester, there was one other site that was to be dedicated to this new realm of computer research: the NPL, or National Physical Laboratory in Teddington, in the south-western corner of London. But in those straitened days, there were also financial limits and increased competition for funding – and as it happened, Professor Newman had managed to win a Royal Society grant for his Manchester department to plough extra investment into the development of their technology.

Turing joined the National Physical Laboratory in 1946; by that time, his mind was a chain reaction of possibilities that led to the concept of ACE – the Automatic Computing Engine. This would be a machine that could calculate algebraic equations, then drop the task and turn instantly to playing chess; this would be a machine that could perform standard mathematical functions, but then be switched to codebreaking.

The machine would even, to a very limited extent, 'think' for itself it would have an ability to extend and extrapolate its own programs. The very idea of ACE initially provoked interest in departments far removed from the laboratory: there were industrialists in Whitehall who understood very quickly how such a thinking machine might change the nature of manufacturing. And there were also – as always – rather less public figures in the realm of defence and the War Office who also saw its potential. This meant particularly the chance of turning such a thinking machine to problems of high explosives, and new sorts of bombs.

The elastic that bound Turing to his old codebreaking colleagues was unusually strong, too. The masterminds at Eastcote would later try all manner of enticements to get him to return full-time to the fold of cryptography. In the meantime, vitally, Alan Turing, along with Max Newman, held on to his prized security clearance throughout these immediate post-war months and years. As indeed did Dr Tommy Flowers of the General Post Office research department. They never stopped being in on the latest cryptanalytical developments, whispered on the most unimaginably secret of grapevines.

As to the dawn of the computer age: in the early days of discussions and costings, the head of the National Physical Laboratory Sir Charles Darwin (grandson of the more famous namesake) wrote to the relevant room in Whitehall about the possibility of borrowing the Dollis Hill team and specifically Dr Flowers to bring the NPL's new computing project to life. In so doing, Sir Charles coyly referred to Tommy Flowers's previous triumph at Bletchley Park.

'Very broadly it [Turing's machine] works using principles developed

by your staff during the war for a certain Foreign Office project,' Sir
Charles wrote, 'and we want to be able to take advantage of this enlisting
the help ... in particular of Mr Flowers who has had much experience
working out the electronic side of it.'[3]

Turing's ACE computer creation was finely detailed and exquisitely
wrought – but only in blueprint form. There were huge obstacles to
bringing it into the world. Partly a question of complexity, and partly
a question of money – an enormous outlay would be needed – it also
seemed that the competition from Professor Newman's department in
Manchester might stifle it, on the grounds that Max Newman was felt to
have a shade more practicality than the supremely unworldly Alan Turing.
It has been noted by Turing's biographer Dr Andrew Hodges that when
Professor Newman's department was awarded the Royal Society grant for
its own computer development, it was a rare occasion when the machines
were not expected to be turned to immediate military or espionage use.

Yet the thread seemed always to lead back to cryptology. Another of
those who left – and yet got snagged back into the currents of codebreaking
– was the brilliant mathematician Shaun Wylie. Another of the young
men who had worked alongside Alan Turing in Hut 8 during the war,
Wylie had also enjoyed great success with the teleprinter cypher Tunny
codes that Max Newman had given so much thought to. Thirty-two years
old when the war ended, and already a foremost figure in the abstruse
mathematical realm of linear algebra, Wylie married his Bletchley Park
love Odette Murray and then went back to Trinity Hall, Cambridge. At
one point, he was to give some helpful advice to Watson and Crick who
were in the midst of researching the fundamentals of DNA; Wylie made
suggestions about the way that the double helix might lose its structure.

Naturally, Wylie said nothing to his colleagues of his wartime years
(though it must have helped that among those colleagues were other
codebreakers, such as Peter Hilton – together, they might almost have revelled in the enforced silence). Equally, though, the post-war codebreaking
operation was careful to keep up with Wylie; to the extent that, in the early
1950s, he was lured away from Cambridge to go back into the espionage
business full-time once more, this time as GCHQ's chief mathematician.

At Bletchley, Wylie had not only been a formidable cryptographer; he was also noted for his skill in acting and drama, and his very active role in the performing societies there. There was one other man – neither a mathematician nor a scientist – who agreed to stay on after the war, while at the same time leading quite literally a theatrical double life: Frank Birch. The almost preposterously colourful Birch had been one of the grand old codebreaking veterans of the First World War, who had played an active role in the cryptanalytical efforts of Room 40 in Whitehall. By the end of the Second World War in 1945, he was 55 years old and juggling careers.

An Old Etonian with a strongly academic side (and the purple-faced temper of a true martinet), Frank Birch's career had by now bifurcated to an almost absurd degree. Some years before, just after the First World War – in the aftermath of which Birch wrote an intensive history of Room 40's successes and methods for internal use only – he had become a fellow of King's College, Cambridge, and a popular history lecturer. But in 1928, he succumbed to his more artistic side, left the college, and moved into theatre. Indeed, between the wars, right the way through the 1930s, Frank Birch pursued an extraordinarily immersive acting and producing career, spanning theatre and film. He staged farces, which were enormously popular; he also took supporting roles in everything from detective dramas to drawing-room comedies and adaptations of classics.

The Second World War had drawn Birch back in full-time to code-breaking duties at Bletchley. Indeed, beforehand, in 1938 (just as he was producing a French farce for the London stage), Birch was advising the then director Alastair Denniston of the sorts of young people they would have to think about recruiting. As the war progressed, Birch's influence grew; he was increasingly involved with Hut 8 and the desperate fight to break the German Naval Enigma. Although Birch came from a different codebreaking generation to that of young Alan Turing, he saw the organisational difficulties that the Hut 8 team were up against, and how their efforts were stuttering partly because they did not get enough time with the proto-computer bombe machines (other departments made even louder demands). It has been suggested by historian Ralph Erskine that it was Frank Birch who was the man ultimately responsible for Alastair

Denniston being moved sideways from Bletchley and Commander Travis taking over.

And most notably, it was Frank Birch – the gifted theatrical *farceur* – who was instrumental in starting the historically unprecedented intelligence-sharing accord between Britain and America. He went to Washington DC with Commander Travis in 1942 and the talks they had with their codebreaking counterparts there led to the Holden agreement; this was specifically to do with the sharing of naval codebreaking of the German Kriegsmarine cyphers. This set down an extraordinary level of trust between two allies (the trust being not so much to do with intentions as with security concerns, and the crucial necessity of the secret being kept on both sides). Birch – as skilled a diplomat as he was an actor – later built on this agreement. Out of the conflicting demands and needs of the Americans and those British codebreakers working in Ceylon at HMS *Anderson* came the first seeds of the BRUSA (Britain–United States of America) agreement, which led to even more sharing of resources, knowledge and intelligence.

And now, the war over, Birch was prevailed upon to remain a codebreaker; he undertook the job of writing up a detailed history of naval signals intelligence. And yet, this man – known as an unusually stern authority figure at Bletchley – was at the same time poised to spring back under the studio arc lights in an extraordinary range of roles. Film was one thing: Birch had also spotted the exciting new medium of television, and as the late 1940s wore on, he won parts in a variety of screen productions such as *Rotten Row*, *Operation Stocking*, *Charles and Mary* (a drama about Charles and Mary Lamb) and an adaptation of *Thérèse Raquin*. He was also in the cast of a serialisation of Dickens's *The Pickwick Papers*.

Perhaps the most startling of Frank Birch's forays into the world of showbusiness – while he continued his top-secret work within the world of cryptography – was a role in the 1953 film comedy *Will Any Gentleman . . .?* in which he starred alongside George Cole and Sid James. It is almost impossible to imagine, by means of comparison, any of Birch's heavyweight American codebreaking counterparts making appearances in Abbott and Costello films. Birch, who was married to the Hon Vera

Benedicta, also contrived to live in some theatrical splendour in the swish Montpelier Walk in Knightsbridge, London. He was one of the great examples of codebreakers having unexpectedly rich hinterlands.

More importantly, Birch was also a great example of how the esoteric world of codebreaking had a particular lure of its own; that even those who left to embark upon the most wildly divergent projects could never quite resist the chance to return. It was that combination of addictive intellectual rigour and the satisfaction of being privy to the gravest of all national secrets.

On this level, indeed, the lives of the cryptographers were many times more satisfying than those of agents for MI5 and MI6. In the case of the latter, work was often grindingly humdrum, and lacking any real intellectual or even moral challenge. The point about codebreaking, however, was that one always knew that one was making the most direct and concrete kind of difference. On top of this, the codebreakers of GCHQ were wielding global clout at a time when Britain's power as a whole was starting to recede sharply. Increasingly, the codebreakers would find themselves being pushed to the front line of the nation's defences.

Chapter Five

The Remaining Jewels

The photographs of the Yalta Conference – the seated figures of Stalin, President Roosevelt and Prime Minister Winston Churchill – looked, even by 1946, like a memento of a vanished age. There was the idea of an American president seated smiling, quite relaxed, with the Soviet dictator, whom he trusted and respected, even as that dictator demanded vast reparations from Germany. Also hinted at in the composition of this image was the suggestion that the United Kingdom was the absolute equal of these two vast powers. The following Potsdam Conference had taken place in the early summer of 1945, and halfway through it, Winston Churchill was abruptly replaced: he had lost the General Election and it was his successor, Clement Attlee, who slid into that chair. Meanwhile, Franklin Roosevelt had died in the spring of 1945 and Harry S Truman, who had been his vice president, acceded to the White House.

By 1946, any idea of warmth between the US and the Soviet Union was the shadow of a memory. Naturally, there has never been any such thing as a perfectly stable world; yet in Britain, the codebreakers now had to be alert to a range of new threats. These were not just military. Britain's stature was fast dissolving like thawing snow; the empire starting to crack, colonial power stuttering. The country faced the loss not only of imperial revenue, but also valuable military and naval bases. The GCHQ codebreakers would have to work ever more nimbly to pinpoint in advance the secret intentions of hostile powers – wherever in the world they might be. Added to this was the prospect of a vast swathe of continental Europe living under an immovable Communist dictatorship. More insidious than the menace of Soviet armies was the idea – believed by some – that a young generation from Calais to Athens could become revolutionaries with no coercion at all. There were millions of children growing up who had known nothing but totalitarianism. What sort of world might they demand?

There might have been a few politicians in Washington DC who advocated continuing a friendly stance towards Stalin, but the clashing ideologies would soon make that inconceivable. The Communists were convinced that capitalism bore within it the seeds of its own destruction, and that the American way of life – soulless consumerism propped up by exploitation of the workers, as they saw it – would eventually fold in on itself. Likewise, Americans were convinced that the oppressive tyranny of Communism, not to mention the mad cycle of purges and political imprisonments, would eventually be shaken off by people yearning for liberty.

In the febrile months that followed Potsdam, the Americans had returned to their old position, that of viewing the Soviets with hostile suspicion; Stalin for his part mirrored these sentiments towards the US. But this new phase was more sharply defined by the now former prime minister Winston Churchill, and also by an American diplomat from Milwaukee. Churchill, having been invited over to America, delivered a speech in 1946 in Fulton, Missouri, in which he famously declared: 'From Stettin in the Baltic to Trieste in the Adriatic, an iron curtain has descended across the continent.' Perhaps mindful of the sensibilities not merely of former allies, but also of the many British who felt sympathy for the Russians, Churchill said: 'From what I have seen of our Russian friends and allies during the War, I am convinced there is nothing they admire so much as strength, and there is nothing for which they have less respect for than weakness, especially military weakness. For that reason, the old doctrine of a balance of power is unsound . . . I do not believe that Soviet Russia desires war. What they desire is the fruits of war and the indefinite expansion of their powers and doctrines.'

Churchill was speaking of cementing the Anglo-American alliance, of continuing that high level of liaison between all services. Again, there was a very faint element of bathos there: the idea that somehow, the British would not finish up being junior partners to the greatest military force that had ever been assembled in history. But there was at least the shared ideological commitment.

It was the American diplomat George F Kennan who, having been posted to Moscow, in 1946 wrote what was called 'The Long Telegram'; this essay set out some highly influential views on the rules of engagement between these new and vast superpowers. Whereas Churchill had looked at the new fault-line of power in military terms, Kennan brought an element of psychoanalysis, focusing on Stalin's neurosis and 'traditional and instinctive Russian sense of insecurity.' The plan of the Kremlin, Kennan wrote in 1946, was to undermine the West: to promote and encourage dissent and disunity, to turn Western workers against capitalism. Kennan proposed the idea of containment: that the way for the West to deal with this growing power was to throw up blocks and obstacles to any possibility of socialist advancement across borders, and to fence off any gaps there may be in Europe or Asia or the Middle East that Soviet allies might take advantage of. In 1945 and 1946, there were already the cases of northern Iran (where codebreaker Alan Stripp had been operating); plus, in the Mediterranean, the knife-edge political situation of Greece. The British, in that particular case, were forced to pull out and to end their financial support for anti-Communist forces there. Greece was plunged into fresh internal conflict between Communist and right-wing factions, having already been ravaged and ruined at the hands of the Nazis. From the point of view of Downing Street and the White House, it would take very little for Stalin to begin to exert influence in that corner of the world, which in turn would make the rest of the Mediterranean – including already Communist-inclined countries such as Italy – intensely vulnerable to further advance.

Could there have been a chance that the Cold War, as it came to be known, might have been averted? Might there have been the chance that Americans and Russians could still have continued smiling side by side at press conferences? Even if the White House and the Kremlin had both been filled with cooing doves, it seems profoundly unlikely: the very principle of the atomic bomb made America so manifestly more powerful than any other nation that the Soviets – whoever had been leading them – would have behaved with nervy suspicion. And from the US side, the oppressive Soviet system of government – the killings, the disappearances, the utter refusal to acknowledge in any way the indescribable horror of the 1930s, when Stalin's rule combined terror and famine and the death of millions – meant that its containment was about limiting the advance of evil.

British political sophisticates may have regarded such a view as impossibly Manichaean, and that the suffering of Russians was a part of the larger process of bringing a truly just society into being. For a very long time, a large number of figures on Britain's intellectual left were inclined to find explanations excusing the nature of Stalin's rule.

Among the codebreakers at Eastcote, however, there was a sense of conviction that had come through simply listening. Among the older members of the team, there had been for a long time a sharp sense of the deadly potential of Bolshevism. Joshua ('Josh') Cooper, one of the organisation's more notable and loveable eccentrics, had been pitting his wits against Soviet intelligence since the 1920s. His outward dotty manner – sudden exclamations of random words, falling under tables while interrogating German prisoners, throwing teacups into lakes – masked quite a serious ideological commitment to his work. At the end of the war, in the transition between Bletchley Park and Eastcote, it was Cooper who was arguing that this new phase of codebreaking work would require much greater funding to match any advances that the Soviets might make in computing and electronic encryption.

In a time when the British population was being rationed more severely than it was throughout the war, and when the nation's debts were making the administration of empire impossible, the codebreakers were going to have to extemporise. Yet thanks to the careful groundwork of Gordon Welchman and Edward Travis during the war, the legacy of Bletchley Park carried one invaluable element that, for a time, made its work as effective as any being done by the Americans; and that was the sprawling web of Y service wireless intercept stations. Many of these were first established around the time of the First World War and the early inter-war years by Britain's security services to secure an advantage in a new age of rapidly developing radio technology. They lay in or near regions that were seen as being vulnerable to Soviet influence.

The fear was not just that of Soviet rapacity, but also of the complete and utter collapse of an obliterated Europe. Assistant Secretary of State Dean Acheson addressed the US Senate in 1945 and told them: 'In liberated Europe, you find that the railway systems have ceased to operate, that power systems have ceased to operate; the financial systems are destroyed. Ownership of property is in terrific confusion. Management of property is in confusion.' Any sense of a structured working, functioning life 'had come to a complete and total standstill'. Things seemed only to get worse through the long and lethal winter of 1946–47.

So at Eastcote, Commander Travis and Nigel de Grey had almost pre-empted the Americans in their unwavering focus on Soviet signals traffic. In Britain, the listening station at Forest Moor, just outside Harrogate, which had bustled with hundreds of Wrens throughout the war, was now switched full-time to monitoring the Soviet airwaves. Meanwhile, right the way around the world, in those listening stations in Ceylon and Singapore, the codebreakers were doing the same thing. It was not simply a question of hawkish cryptographers squaring up to an implacable Soviet enemy; in a sense, these units, and also the residual military listening units based in Europe, dotted around Italy and Austria and Germany, were listening to the faltering heartbeat of a continent.

Commander Travis and his colleague Captain Hastings were also assid-uous at ensuring that their Commonwealth associates were keeping very much in step with this new world; this had meant to an extent that Travis had trodden on the toes of his Australian codebreaking counterparts – or subordinates as he would have seen it – insisting that their cypher activities be headed up by an Englishman. But there were hundreds, thousands of skilled personnel not only in Australia, but across Canada too; and Canada, of course, shares a northerly maritime border with the Soviet Union.

According to Richard Aldrich, any mismatch in wealth and investment between the British and the Americans was addressed quite simply. What the British lacked in computers, they gained in terms of scale of world-spanning coverage. And then of course, there were hundreds of young men who had a lightning flair for radio technology. The parts of the world these young people were based in were fissile. But the intelligence that they were then able to send back – intelligence shared with the Americans – was invaluable.

One of those bases – the Combined Bureau Middle East, based in Heliopolis, just outside Cairo, Egypt was still operating a comprehensive service, though the numbers working there were starting to decrease. There was a note of imperial grandeur about the intelligence-gathering setting, the glass and ironwork of the old museum HQ, a relic of unabashed Victorian cultural grandstanding amid the sands.

All of the radio intelligence gathered at Heliopolis had been relayed back to Whaddon Hall, Buckinghamshire. The immediate situation would have suggested that it was very much in Britain and America's interests to keep the operation going in Egypt: a strategic spot from which to listen in to signals from southern Russia and the Balkan countries which were already within the Soviet sphere. But night was falling on the old British Empire, and on its old imperial ways of doing things.

Having tolerated Britain's involvement in its affairs even after 1922 and the declaration of what turned out to be semi-independence, the Cairo authorities, having gained complete independence in 1936, made it quite plain that they now wanted the British to withdraw. The Anglo-Egyptian Treaty of 1936 had stipulated that 10,000 British troops could be stationed within Egypt's borders; the war had taken that number up to about 200,000. And afterwards, demobilisation was slow. There were still over 100,000 troops stationed within the country's Canal Zone. In other words, there were still populous British bases, and they were extremely unpopular with a rising generation of Egyptian nationalists. Whitehall had no wish to cause any unnecessary rancour; there was, apart from anything else, the need to think of keeping the Middle East calm and stable in order to safeguard oil supplies.

And Labour Prime Minister Clement Attlee was quite content with the idea of pulling out completely; to him, imperialism was an anachronism. In addition, this was an age of air power, and of the atomic bomb. Old strategic concerns such as keeping Mediterranean routes open to the navy, and safeguarding the Suez Canal, were in Attlee's view hopelessly outmoded. Senior military personnel from all three services argued bitterly with the prime minister about the principle of withdrawal. Chief of the Imperial General Staff Bernard Montgomery was particularly acerbic, as was former Commander-in-Chief, Mediterranean, and former First Sea Lord Andrew Cunningham. But this was the flow of history; it was obvious to all in Whitehall, for instance, that India would very shortly be breaking free from British rule.

The core of the conflict between Whitehall and the military was to do with anxiety about the Soviet Union's sensing a vacuum in the Middle East and filling it. There was also the question of Britain's self-defence. No bomber at that stage could have flown all the way from Britain to populated Russia and back again – the British needed RAF bases and runways and facilities in the Middle East, from which they would if necessary be able to strike at Soviet industrial facilities in the Urals.

And above all, there was the painful matter of national prestige. It seemed to matter less to Attlee, with his visions of world authorities acting as world policemen. To his punchy foreign secretary Ernest Bevin, though, it was vital that Britain should not be infected with what he termed 'pessimism'. And that meant – apart from many other things – maintaining a presence in the Middle East, because who else was there to do it? There was no guarantee, now the war was over, that America would not withdraw from the world stage and wrap itself once more in the blanket of isolationism. This was a moment when Britain was facing the Soviet Union and taking on the idea that if there were to be hostilities, there might not necessarily be all the help from America that was needed.

But Britain was also, to all intents and purposes, bankrupt. There was precious little money even for modest outbreaks of imperialism. And in the splendour of the sun at Heliopolis, the codebreakers and the secret listeners – some civilian – was now thinning out in terms of numbers, their base at the Flora and Fauna museum beginning to echo. In some senses, it was quite a life to give up. While for the military, the role of wireless interceptor could often be miserable (postings in the desert, with all the attendant sand and scorpions and thunderstorms so heavy that headphones would crackle and hearing would be permanently damaged), for the civilians, it was quite a different thing. Aside from the work at Heliopolis, life for many was a whirl of a defiantly old-fashioned kind of decadence: smart bars, dream-like nights on terraces, the gossip and intrigue of well-heeled expat society. Aileen Clayton, a WAAF, wrote that she stayed at 'Shepheard's Hotel, which in those days before the great post-war revolution, was sheer Edwardian opulence. There seemed to be myriads of Egyptian and Sudanese *suffragis* flip-flopping around the hotel in their heel-less slippers, clad in white *galabiyahs*, and red cummerbunds and fezes.'

'The food,' she added (and this would have been particularly true of severely rationed post-war Britain), 'after the deprivations of England, was good and plentiful.' There were 'plentifully stocked shops and gay night clubs'.[1] Egypt was still a monarchy, under the rule of King Farouk. But in the days after the war, his colourfully decadent era too was coming to the point of dissolution: the final days of an era of aristocrats dining at Cairo restaurants such as the Auberge des Pyramides, the king amusing himself by throwing coloured pom-poms around the other diners. Even for codebreakers without any of these gilded social connections, life had been a daze of scent and colour and sun.

Now some of this skilled mix of radio interceptors and cypher experts were to be relocated: some to the British base in Sarafand, Palestine; and more to the large base on Cyprus. Both were absolutely key positions to be in. Cyprus enabled the codebreakers to intercept a great deal of Russian traffic at the point when the Soviets were casting a long shadow over Greece. In Palestine, the British faced quite a different challenge: that of furious and desperate Zionism.

The Balfour Declaration of 1917 promised the Jewish people a homeland. Foreign Secretary Arthur Balfour had written to Baron Rothschild and by extension to the Zionist Federation of Great Britain and Ireland. 'His

Majesty's government view with favour the establishment in Palestine of a national home for the Jewish people,' wrote Balfour, 'and will use their best endeavours to facilitate the achievement of this object, it being clearly understood that nothing shall be done which may prejudice the civil and religious rights of existing non-Jewish communities in Palestine, or the rights or political status enjoyed by Jews in any other country.'

In 1941, with that homeland still a distant prospect, Bletchley Park codebreaker Oliver Strachey made his way into a very particular set of Enigma decrypts: the railway timetables and deportation communications that laid bare the escalating horror of the Holocaust in eastern Europe. These were the decrypts that made plain the need for that homeland. In the aftershock of war, though, the Palestinian question was, for the Foreign Office, one part of a complex interlocking structure of empire; a territory mandated since 1922, presided over by the British, and which the British were now having increasing difficulty keeping any kind of lid on.

There was a radio relay station in Sarafand, not far from Tel Aviv, that had been established in the 1920s. It had grown in size and numbers of personnel throughout the 1930s and was a key station throughout the war, sitting amid the bustle of a wider army encampment. Situated in the very heart of the Middle East, it was clear that its importance had not diminished in any way. But from 1945 onwards, life for the British in Palestine was going to prove explosive. As well as attempting to defuse the rising fury between Arabs and Jews – the Palestinian Grand Mufti had visited Hitler and made no secret of his support for the persecution of the Jews – the soldiers had to face hostility directed at them from all sides. And a younger Jewish generation – traumatised by a mass atrocity that the entire world had witnessed, and yet somehow did not want to talk about – was making ready to fight.

Then there were the thousands of Holocaust survivors in Europe who desperately wanted to leave that dark continent and make for the sanctuary of a Jewish homeland. The chief obstacles to their doing so were to be the British, as we will see later. There were many Jewish codebreakers back in England who had made incalculable contributions to the wartime cypher triumphs, and who were now looking on with some interest as the British authorities began to wriggle. In 1945, in Jerusalem, there was a graffito that appeared on a wall. It read: 'British go home.' Underneath, a British soldier had added: 'If only we f****** well could.' It was the codebreaking operatives in Sarafand who were picking up increasing amounts of traffic from Zionist groups; the local difficulties standing alongside the broader aims of divining Soviet intentions. Indeed, there was the further complication for the British that Stalin's Soviet Union was apparently in wholehearted support of the right of the Jewish people to establish the state of Israel. This was in the brief period before the Kremlin returned to its older anti-Semitic attitudes.

For British codebreakers, there were more exotic and yet more tranquil corners to which they could find themselves being posted. One such was the port of Kilindini, Mombasa, on the East African coast. From a converted school – a rather wonderfully ornate structure of pink stone – overlooking the crashing waves, operatives such as Hugh Denham replicated the non-military Bletchley approach, working in civilian clothes and thus avoiding parades and other 'time-wasting' activities. From this base, and with their receivers picking up signals from far across the ocean, the team had made brilliant inroads into the Japanese codes in the teeth of technical difficulties involving the clarity of radio reception. They had originally gone there following a Japanese bombing attack on the base of HMS *Anderson* in Colombo, Ceylon. And in the immediate post-war period, Clement Attlee was to wonder if Mombasa might make an altogether more suitable base for a range of British forces than either Egypt or Palestine or Iraq.

In the meantime, HMS *Anderson* – perched on the other side of the Indian Ocean – was still very much in business after the Japanese capitulation in September 1945 in South-East Asia. It was here that those last languid days of the imperial life were played out before disbelieving young British people, fresh from modest backgrounds in England, whose eyes were opened to a world of colour and natural luxuriance that they had thought could never have existed outside of books. The base itself – single-storey huts, roofs woven of palm, tall radio transmitters looming up – was perfectly utilitarian; the life outside was anything but. Wren Jean

Valentine, who had been breaking Japanese codes and who now had to wait a while for demobilisation after the war, was drawn deeply in: the smart restaurants, the elegant night-clubs and, away in the hills, the tea plantations, a world where all one had to do was press a small button under a table, and a servant would materialise.

And after the war, the social and cultural life of the base itself went on with some fervour. There was a string ensemble, a swing band and a thriving theatrical society. In terms of technology, this was less an age of Morse and more a time of advancing teleprinter developments. Laurence Roberts recalled one small setback: the cabling required for the machinery was too great a temptation for a few of the local population to resist. It was regularly stolen. But this in itself, he remembered, had the partial result of ushering in further advances in terms of early microwave transmissions. He, too, recalled that the great relief of such a posting was the terrific diversion of Colombo itself, which offered a great deal of entertainment to men and women alike.

There was also, quite naturally, romance, and it was thanks to her posting here – right the way around the world from her native Perth in Scotland, which she had left as an 18-year-old girl – that Jean Valentine was to meet pilot Clive Rooke. They married (though not without some initial resistance from Jean's father back in Perth, who later grudgingly relented and gave his permission when it was pointed out to him that he had allowed his only daughter to set sail through U-Boat-infested waters, and also face the unquantifiable dangers of an Asian posting). Obviously they – and countless other young people like them, men and women alike – had shown conspicuous bravery in doing their duty; but the war had had another side effect for people like Jean and Clive. It had opened up a far wider world to them than perhaps they would otherwise have seen.

For Jean, the codebreaking work was running down fast, but she could not be demobilised because the ships sailing home were filled with exhausted (and traumatised) soldiers being brought back from the Far East. As it was, she and Clive Rooke, upon marrying, decided to stay in that part of the world. She recalls vividly being in Burma on the day in 1947 that India gained its independence.

India was a particular intelligence asset that Bletchley's successors could ill afford to do without, regardless of the subcontinent's coming independence. Indeed, in the aftermath of the war, the Indian authorities and representatives of various British services executed careful little dances of diplomacy around one another. A key figure in wartime signals intelligence in India had been Colonel Patrick Marr-Johnson, who was now back in the West as part of the team working to fine-tune and formalise the unprecedented intelligence alliance between Britain and the United States. The dance of diplomacy went a few steps further: the National Security Agency has released some fascinating correspondence between Colonel Marr-Johnson and senior US cryptologist William Friedman in Washington, from 1943, after Colonel Marr-Johnson had paid a visit. In one letter, Marr-Johnson reflects on the British position in India and how others might see it. 'I wonder whether your daughter is still pondering deeply the question of the fate of India?' he asks Friedman. 'And whether I managed to persuade her that the British were not quite such evil ogres as she thought?'[2]

The listening stations in India were now absolutely key for monitoring Soviet activity, particularly in regions close to Afghanistan and the North-West Frontier (it is interesting to note how geopolitical fault lines appear to be every bit as enduring as the geological variety).

Appointed to Eastcote in late 1945 as Commander Travis's second deputy, Captain Edward Hastings was the man in charge of dealings with India and his intelligence counterparts there. The imminent removal of all British soldiers and police from the subcontinent was one thing, but he was the man trying to ensure that unobtrusive listening stations might form part of what might be termed a diplomatic legacy.

And there was something about the very business of interception that was appealing to a certain sort of intelligent, sparky though not necessarily academically trained young man. Conscription continued in the form of National Service; in order to be able to bring tired troops home from their ordeals in the east, it was necessary to train up more young men back home, many of whom had just finished school and were looking at the prospect of apprenticeships. The science of radio made many of these young men angle themselves towards wireless operator roles. As in the war itself, the job of Direction Finding, interception, and incredibly swift Morse code transcription appealed to many sharp and nimble working-class lads.

Perhaps the most famous of the immediate post-war wireless operators was a young man from Nottingham who had been doing piece-work in a bicycle factory and was destined, late in the 1950s, to become one of the defining novelists of his generation. Alan Sillitoe realised that he had a knack for Morse, even though the training course that he was sent on was gruelling and so pressurised that it made one candidate succumb to a fit during a test.

Sillitoe knew that he and a few of his fellow recruits for RAF Signals were going to be shipped overseas; but the destination was a secret. He was expecting to sail out from Liverpool, but instead these boys first found themselves packed off to Southampton, in the midst of an utterly miserable, fuel-rationed British winter, bitingly wet and grey. The world that was to come was almost hallucinatory in its contrast. Within weeks, Sillitoe was in warm, hazy air, gazing from the deck of the ship over at Bedouins walking with camels on the banks of the Nile; he watched as 'the mountains of Sinai turned purple in the afternoon light' and he found a startling recall for all the Old Testament stories that he had been taught as a child. Across the Indian Ocean, he enjoyed a dazed stop-off in Colombo which, as Sillitoe observed, took the black-and-white photographs in books his grandparents had shown him and turned them into colour.

HMS *Anderson* was not his destination; they sailed on further. And so it was that Sillitoe, then just 18 years old, found himself among the rubber trees deep in Malaya. He adapted quickly to this new life of earphones, interference and calculations of ionosphere bounces, set against an eerie nocturnal backdrop of all-night shifts in a simple hut in the middle of a restless jungle. He and his colleagues were constantly on the lookout for snakes, which could nest anywhere in their camp. The job itself, those lonely moonlit shifts, sometimes took on a hauntingly surreal tone when, in between communications between passing aeroplanes and messages intercepted from wider shores, there were sometimes bursts of music out of nowhere: classical pieces that would seem to fill the silence and the darkness.

'The music of the spheres came into my headphones,' he wrote, 'and I communicated in Morse with Rangoon and Singapore, chatted to Saigon using my bits of French, and even for half an hour after dawn made contact with such faraway places as Karachi, Hong Kong and Bangkok. Every transmitter, even if of the same make, had a different tone and, no need of call signs, one soon learned to know them and the moment of their tune-forking into the ears.'[3]

This was a brotherhood of wireless operators and the work was intensely focused at all hours; absolute accuracy was of course of the essence, as the communications would then be passed on to Eastcote for analysis. Yet, as Sillitoe noted, even despite the hours and those uncanny nights when all sorts of noises could be heard outside the listening station in the trees, there was also Tiger beer, the music from wind-up gramophones, and the serious pleasure of walking along the warm shore and watching the local fishermen haul in some bizarre-looking catches. Had it not been for National Service, this is a world that Sillitoe might never have expected to see; as it was, it clearly had an impact other than artistic, as in subsequent years he and his wife moved from Britain to Mediterranean shores.

And a little later, Sillitoe's experience was tested to the limit as another fragment of Britain's empire began to break off painfully, and he found himself in the middle of what is still termed the 'Malayan Emergency'. But there was something about the philosophy of his work, hunched over earphones, that remained consistent. Years later, he said: 'It's therapy. I like to eavesdrop, though you're meant to shred everything you take down. Once Morse has been implanted in your brain at the age of 16 or 17, it never leaves you.'[4] That was the experience of many others, though the conditions in stations in Malaya and Singapore could often be extremely uncomfortable due to asphyxiating heat and indeed the vast, terrible thunderstorms at night that – if one was wearing headphones and transcribing – would crackle agonisingly like a lightning bolt through the brain.

Others wore the burden of travel lightly as well; there were some who had spent their war years working at Beaumanor Hall and RAF

Chicksands and whose expertise was now needed out in the wider world. The winter 1946 number of *The Woygian* magazine, for interceptors past and present, contained exciting news from the Middle East. 'Bill Hayward wrote from Cairo on December 9th where he – together with Pete James, Derek Basnett, Ron Blease, Bern Norwood and 'Tubby' Fagg – was hoping to go on to Cyprus but afraid it might be the Holy Land. Also in Cairo with another draft, similarly bound, are Sgt Tyler, 'Doodlebug' Tomlinson and NL Smith. Bill sends greetings . . . and adds that he thinks Egypt "sphinx".'[5]

Of all the signals intelligence jewels that Britain possessed, the one with perhaps greater value than all the rest was a station that also proved remarkably resistant to the tide of empires; indeed, this particular territory only ceased to be British in 1997. The station was Hong Kong and the range of traffic that flowed through, was analysed and sent on was, even from 1945, quite formidable. Even before Mao Zedong wrestled his way to power in 1949 and established the People's Republic of China, the listening base at Hong Kong was of exquisite importance not only to the British, but the Americans too.

Indeed, for years the colony had been the most crucial vantage point, eavesdropping on Chinese, Japanese and also Soviet Russian traffic. This scrutiny had been interrupted by the war: having ravaged great swathes of China, the Japanese forces besieged Hong Kong in December 1941, then overran and occupied it. The British codebreakers had moved out some way in advance, having anticipated such an attack; it was always vital that their secrets should stay firmly as far from the hands of the enemy as possible. Unfortunately, in this instance in 1941, the Hong Kong codebreakers had withdrawn to Singapore, and despite the finest cypher work, no analysts predicted the assault on Singapore that was to come in February 1942. As it was, the codebreakers made it out once more, and this time ended up at Colombo in Ceylon, and then further out at Mombasa.

Back in Hong Kong, the Japanese stayed in the territory until their war ended with the atomic blasts. So in 1945 there was as swift restoration as possible not just of everyday life and commerce, but also of intelligence gathering. Hong Kong was one of the great crossroads, teeming with agents of all sorts, as well as equally smooth-operating figures moving in the (perhaps even shadier) world of high finance. There was one signals intelligence station in a small hilly outcrop referred to for some reason as 'Batty's Belvedere'. It was highly popular with some of the military and civilian operatives thanks to a nearby tiny secluded bay, hemmed in on two sides by towering cliffs. When not on duty, there were terrific opportunities for swimming and sunbathing in rich blue waters. During the Japanese occupation, the station had continued in use, but of course in the service of the Japanese forces. Come the winter of 1945, and something of its old life had been restored. 'It was a rough journey in an RAF truck to get to the summit,' recalled one veteran signals-man years later, 'but at 4am, when our shift began, the view of the surroundings was incredible, especially on a misty morning.'[6] And in time, the infrastructure around the Belvedere was to improve rather dramatically as well.

Unlike those listening stations in the Middle East, operating under a cloud of increasing uncertainty, there was something – as one operative remarked – curiously tranquil about a small outstation like the Belvedere, or the nearby listening station RAF Little Sai Wan. In those immediate post-war years, as China sought to recover, there was still a reasonably open frontier with Hong Kong; in that period, many middle-class Chinese families moved across there. In the years that followed, with the massive social upheaval of the Communist revolution, that trickle of migration was to become a torrent, and Hong Kong would end up with shanty towns on its hillsides, people living in the most desperate poverty.

The listening posts around Hong Kong naturally called for experts in Chinese linguistics; in the 1940s, the operation was a little austere, involving recruits working in pre-fabricated huts, and looking, as one signals veteran recalled, rather like battery hens. They were happy battery hens, though. And as the Americans in the 1940s became increasingly concerned about the build-up of Communist influence in the region, the listeners of Batty's Belvedere were to find themselves in one of the most secret hot spots on earth.

Meanwhile, though, the codebreakers at Eastcote were listening to the signals emanating from the unhappier corners of Europe, grimly logging the signs that the hunger and the hatred were bringing the prospect of a Third World War very much closer. On top of this, they were about to decrypt a cache of messages which would reveal, horrifyingly, the extent to which British and American security services had been infiltrated by Stalin's agents.

Chapter Six

Decoding the Soviet Heart

Any semblance of trust had been utterly destroyed. Nations looked at former enemies and allies alike – and could not fathom their intentions. There was no sense of security to be found anywhere. It was, in many ways, the ideal time to be a double agent in Europe: relatively easy in all that confusion and agitation to feign loyalty to one country while secretly working to promote a revolutionary ideology that did not recognise borders. There were men and women, long-time spies, embedded deep in the United Kingdom and America. The British codebreakers, together with their US counterparts, were soon to discover just how horrifyingly porous their security services had been.

Consider the world in which the shadowy double agents were operating. This was at a moment, in the late 1940s, when the expectation – the dread – of a Third World War was universal. Although armies were demobilised and arsenals spent, there was never for a moment any let-up in international tension, nor in cross-border hatreds, nor indeed in individual anxieties and neuroses. The loathing the Poles had for the Jews – who had been in Poland for 600 years – had in no way diminished, despite all the unimaginable horrors visited upon them; then there was the jagged suspicion and hostility that lay between many Poles and Ukrainians after a war filled with full-throated Nazi and Communist collaborations and atrocities. There was also the bitter hatred among Central Europeans

– Czechs, Hungarians, Romanians – for the German civilians who had found themselves helpless in territories that they had imagined conquered. Throughout the Balkans, meanwhile, the old tectonic fault lines of hatred gaped ever wider. Everywhere throughout the continent were millions of hideously vulnerable Displaced Persons, as they came to be known.

The most extraordinarily vulnerable of these were the Jews who had somehow survived the camps and the nightmarish death marches. After a period of partial recovery from the privations of the camps, under the horrified eyes of American soldiers, some of these former prisoners tried returning to their old villages in Poland and settlements deeper in Eastern Europe; what they found was stark inhumanity. Their houses were now occupied, without any shame, by villagers who had simply moved in as the Jews had been forcibly transported out. Those villagers had their possessions; they even wore their winter clothes and the jewellery that they had thought hidden. The emaciated Jewish people who had returned to claim what was theirs were furiously denounced, threatened, pushed away. In a few cases, they were quite simply murdered.

The Jews of Poland, of Latvia, Lithuania, Galicia, Romania, Hungary, all those forested lands, now had to adjust to a world that had been completely torn down around them. Even in a time of so-called peace, their former neighbours had passed far beyond any sense of legality, let alone decency. Return was quite simply impossible. There were parts of Poland and the Baltic states where they would never be safe.

The world that the codebreakers was listening to with anxious focus was a continent swarming with acutely helpless humanity, one in which the mass slaughter could so very easily begin again. And it was a continent which had the weight of Stalin's Russia bearing down upon it. The Soviets were eager to harvest political advantage from these flashpoints of distress. Its double agents wanted to further the Soviet cause by any means. There were a few who genuinely believed that it would make the world better.

For, as the commentator Neal Ascherson wrote, there was a time when the word 'Europe' was associated with darkness. The war had exposed something more than mindless slaughter: it had revealed one of the continent's supposedly highest cultures, Germany, to be a machine for determined, deliberate, pre-meditated mass murder. Yet the silence after the war echoed throughout the world; everyone knew what had happened in the Nazi death camps – yet very few spoke specifically of the Jews. No-one wanted to look this slaughter directly in the eye. When the Allies liberated those camps in the forests of eastern Europe – deep in the territory expropriated by the Nazis, so that the mass killings took place far from the eyes and ears of those in the heart of Germany – it might have been imagined by some that they had brought relief. Yet how could they have done? Entire families, millions of them, wiped out: for those very few who survived, what conceivable relief could there be?

At Eastcote, the listeners and the codebreakers were not merely monitoring traffic for the sake of some spy-versus-spy game: this was about checking the pulse of a sick, traumatised continent that could – at any moment – go into convulsions, and so fall deeper into the tight grip of Soviets claiming to bring stability. It has been observed that one of the intriguing philosophical conundrums for Europe in times of peace is how a continent without any discernible eastern border thinks of itself. Stalin's Russia was doing its utmost to define that border; the Americans would soon be doing the same. But with Central Europe seething with so many people who were homeless and stateless – people who apparently belonged nowhere – the potential for renewed conflict was never more than a hair's breadth away.

The agency dealing with this multitude of misery was the newly created United Nations Relief and Rehabilitation Administration, which in turn had taken over from large contingents of the American army that had worked ferociously to set up hundreds of camps for refugees. There were some Jews who were still reluctant to move too far from the concentration camps in which they had been held. As communities very slowly came back to life – courtships and marriages among the young – so there were some people who wanted to keep a hold of some familiarity, no matter how dreadful.

They were not the only Displaced Persons. For some time before the end of the war, the British authorities had known how the Czech government planned to deal with the Germans within its borders. After the war, Czech president Edouard Beneš declared that 'we have decided to eliminate the German problem in our republic once and for all'. Until 1947, that elimination was carried out systematically. All property owned by Germans was placed under state control. Then those Germans, some three million or so, had their Czech citizenship revoked. They were stateless. Then they were expelled – forced back to Germany. There was nothing orderly about the process. It is reckoned that some 267,000 Germans died.

This was just Czechoslovakia. As Neal Ascherson wrote: 'Some 12 million ethnic Germans fled or were driven out of east and central Europe . . . This gigantic act of ethnic cleansing, as we would now call it, was euphemised as "population transfer".'[1] Such a transfer on a vast scale was effected from Poland and the lands of East Prussia, country labourers and old aristocrats alike fleeing through the winter ice from the advancing Soviet forces. Stalin had declared as part of his own war settlement that these lands would be returned to the Slavs. In the aftermath of the Holocaust – where millions of people were forcibly transported to their deliberate pre-meditated slaughter – this was not remotely on the same scale. But the essential point was this: in the midst of the violence meted out to the German families heading back west (and how oddly this foreshadowed the apocalyptic violence that came with 1947's partition of India, when millions were killed throughout a similar 'population transfer'), the West had to try, however it could, to ensure that repercussions would not sow the seeds for further conflict.

The codebreakers at Eastcote were intensely alive to the advances of the Soviet Union in this time; having carefully monitored the Communists throughout the inter-war years, men such as Edward Travis knew that Soviet ambitions were not merely territorial but in a sense psychological too. There were some who believed that, given just the smallest chance, the Soviets would conquer of all Western Europe, including Britain, right up to the Atlantic shore itself.

And this was not baseless Cold War paranoia either; rather, a series of quite extraordinary decrypts made by the British and the Americans of Soviet coded messages was unveiling an utterly chilling reality: that Soviet sympathisers and agents had infiltrated themselves right into the very heart of the US and UK intelligence services. Indeed, the codebreakers were about to draw back a veil on espionage on an unprecedented and terrible scale.

The decrypting operation – known only to the tightest and most select circle of American and British codebreakers – was eventually called Venona. What had started as pulling at a metaphorical loose thread of encrypted Soviet messages had suddenly unravelled into a series of appalling revelations. The story of the Venona Project now reads in many ways as the most perfect symbol of an era; it is a story about a secret so grave that, at first, not even national leaders could be let in on it. The President of the USA and the Prime Minister of the United Kingdom were initially kept carefully out of the loop. In a blackly comical sense, Venona was almost too secret for anyone to act upon – for fear that their enemies would see that their codes had been broken. Most of all, though, it is the story of the subterranean struggle to shape the future destiny of the continent. Venona might be counted as one of the most dazzling moments of the early USA/UK decryption alliance, even if – by the late 1940s – it was accompanied by a sense of horror and impotence on the part of the codebreakers.

It was often decorously said, as previously mentioned, that throughout the war, Bletchley operatives were not reading Soviet traffic, because after 1941, the Soviets were allies. This might be the case, but Soviet messages were certainly being read elsewhere: Arlington Hall, the American equivalent of Bletchley Park, in Virginia. The reason was a most serendipitous discovery made in 1943 by Lieutenant Richard Hallock.

Whereas the Germans had favoured electric encryption techniques with machines like Enigma, the Soviets very often used a much more cumbersome system, known as 'one-time pads'. Yet these pads, with numbered tear-off sheets, were in principle much more secure than any machine cypher. The system involved identical pairs of pads or booklets, each page filled with randomly generated numbers. The message to be encrypted would be paired with a page of the pad – both agents, for instance, might agree on 'page 4'. The message would be encyphered according to the key on that page. But because only those operatives were using that key – and because after they used it they destroyed the page – it would be completely impossible for anyone else to break into that code. With no key to go on, and with no other copies of that particular encypherment procedure, there was no way to get a lever into it (unlike the Enigma which had a couple of crucial mathematical vulnerabilities).

The drawback in this fail-safe system was that the pads took a lot of time and effort to produce. Those random numbers had to be generated (not so easy as it sounds: there was a suggestion that teams of Soviet women were employed to sit in rows and shout out numbers off the top of their heads – but even this method could never be truly random; there would always be unconscious links). On top of this, those pairs of identical pads had to be printed and distributed; even the paper used had to be of a very specific quality to make it especially easy to burn or destroy. And in the midst of the German assault on Russia from 1941 onwards, it has been suggested that the Soviet authorities – buckling under the weight of Nazi aggression – were struggling, and the resources for the pads and agents were beginning to run out. Whatever the case was, the Soviets made the most atrocious error: they accidentally re-printed 25,000 pages of randomly generated numbers. That meant that the pads were no longer unique.

Moreover, these pads were being used by the Soviet diplomatic service. In February 1943, Hallock and the codebreakers at Arlington Hall – working on intercepted messages had been passed on by the US Signals Intelligence Service – realised that they were looking at a potential treasure trove. Like Josh Cooper and Nigel de Grey, the prevailing attitude among US codebreakers towards the Soviets as wartime allies was that they would cease to be allies very quickly; and so anything that could be done to get a crowbar into their communications would be a shrewd investment for the future. So, in America, a very small, very tight-knit team began work.

It would become apparent that the US codebreakers had happened upon some appalling intelligence; not merely relating to Soviet infiltration of secret departments, but also the extent to which the Soviets had managed to spy on the American atomic bomb project. In other words, out of one encryption mistake, out of one batch of duplicate code pads, were to come revelations that were absolutely key to the balance of power in Europe.

One of the American codebreakers was a young Gregory Peck lookalike called Meredith Gardner; by 1944, Gardner was breaking into the fearsomely complex NKVD (Soviet secret service) codes. Gardner was in some ways the perfect US mirror of the academically inclined British codebreakers. Born in 1912 and raised in Texas, he was an almost absurdly gifted linguist. He could read Spanish, Lithuanian, Russian, Sanskrit and German. When America entered the war in 1941, Gardner, by then a lecturer at the University of Akron, was recruited the following year to work as a cryptologist at Arlington Hall (and, some years later, he, like so many of his fellow American code-breakers, crossed the Atlantic for a spell at GCHQ in Cheltenham).

Gardner's brilliance with German was one thing; he was also swift to master Japanese. Soon, he was making a detailed study of Chinese. But in 1946, the Venona Project was pushed his way; and the deeper he became immersed in it, the more it began to dominate his every working hour. Peter Wright, the MI6 operative who wrote the controversial book *Spycatcher* in the 1980s, said of Gardner: 'He was a quiet, scholarly man, entirely unaware of the awe in which he was held by the other cryptanalysts.'[2] Gardner himself talked of his 'magpie attitude to facts, the habit of storing things away that did not seem to have any connection at all'.[3] Like many of his British counterparts, he also had a flair for extraordinarily difficult crosswords.

Yet here was a man who would prove to be partly instrumental in setting the terms of the fast-freezing Cold War. In 1946, Gardner (according to Peter Wright), using old Soviet codebooks that had been retrieved from Finland, unlocked some decrypts which contained hair-raising information. These secret Soviet messages, intended to be passed to senior NKVD agents back in Moscow, had referred to the Manhattan Project – the intensely secret testing of the atomic bomb in Los Alamos, New Mexico. That was the first horrifying glimpse that the balance of world power was shifting. Gardner's decrypts went on to reveal more, including the codenames given to Soviet double-agents, from which, with a lengthy process of cross-referencing, their real identities could be guessed at. There was, for instance, American spy-ring leader Julius Rosenberg (codename LIBERAL). Hideously, for the British, there were also mentions – still disguised by means of codenames, but nonetheless there – of the MI6 double agents Guy Burgess, Donald Maclean and Kim Philby. It took some time to narrow down the clues offered by the content of the messages passed to Moscow; but their eventual unmasking would be inevitable.

This dreadful intelligence was passed upwards – though intriguingly, not quite so far upwards as the Oval Office or Number 10 Downing Street. At first, a decision was clearly made to shield the president and the prime minister from the news. Even by the hermetic standards of the codebreakers, this was all kept extraordinarily secret; barely a handful of Americans and only the tiniest smattering of British cryptologists were allowed in on the Venona revelation. Other agencies were shut out: the FBI was given no indication; MI5 and MI6 were – apart from a couple of senior figures – equally locked out. Because of course, at the very first inklings that Gardner and his small dedicated team were uncovering unexpectedly vast secrets, the next terrific anxiety was this: how to make absolutely certain that the Soviets did not realise that their encryptions had been peeled open. Having exposed the fizzing stick of dynamite, what were the codebreakers then to do with it?

According to intelligence historian John Earl Haynes, the exquisite difficulty for the hierarchy in Arlington Hall was that these diplomatic cables also revealed that back in the early 1940s, the Soviets had made a deliberate concerted push to infiltrate agents into all corners of the American military, together with its industry and indeed its intelligence services. The Venona cables constituted only a tiny percentage of the bulk of Soviet communications; therefore it would be reasonable to extrapolate from this the assumption that the numbers of unrevealed Soviet agents still working within American society were huge.

The paranoia was not misplaced. It transpired that – rather like the Cambridge Spies – there were highly placed Soviet sympathisers everywhere throughout American intelligence and security. According to Haynes, despite the intense secrecy around Venona, a sense or a whisper of what was unfolding somehow got through to the British double agent Donald Maclean, who was then working with the British Embassy in Washington. It took years for the full consequences of the Venona revelation to ripple through the intelligence services; at first, agents could not be identified by their code-names alone. One can decypher all the messages in the world, but when faced with agent code-words such as 'Fakir', 'Dodger' and 'Grandmother', analysts were completely in the dark. Was 'Grandmother' in the Admiralty? Might 'Fakir' be attached to top-secret nuclear work?

But Venona was not simply a short-term project: as we will see, the American and British codebreakers would join forces to form a top-secret team-within-a-team to work full-time on this vast harvest of cables, these thousands of messages. And the more they worked on them, the more references and clues to the traitor agents would be thrown up.

It is a measure of the purity of the codebreakers' calling that Meredith Gardner always appeared to consider his work not so much in practical terms as a sort of work of art. He and his dedicated team were squaring up to an intellectual, mathematical and linguistic challenge that had its own inherent beauty and elegance; delving into hidden structures to bring the truth out into the open. His closest working partner was the FBI agent Robert J Lamphere, whose role was not to break codes but to chase down the spies exposed by the decrypts. Lamphere later paid tribute to Gardner, recalling how out of bundles of encryptions, he would somehow extract order out of fractal chaos and that success came with a small smile.

But it was not, it seems, a smile of triumph; Gardner later said that his own view of the treacherous agents exposed was that they at least believed in what they were doing, as opposed to being out-and-out mercenaries. There was almost a sense of a parallel between his preternatural skill and their own in carrying out their work. So much so that the eventual exposure of the agents seemed to cause Gardner some curious anguish. He saw his work as having a strange abstract purity, a freestanding cryptological puzzle, and there was something jarring about the agents exposed by his work then facing the prospect of prison or indeed the death sentence as a result of it.

Despite all the painstaking secrecy, word inevitably spread among tiny numbers of people in the intelligence community. Over in

Britain, Commander Travis, Captain Hastings and Nigel de Grey were immediately informed. Even they took something of a back seat, though. One of the main liaisons between London and Washington over Venona was Lieutenant Colonel Patrick Marr-Johnson, who had served so effectively out in India. After Sir Stewart Menzies, head of MI6, had had the preliminary discussions with his American counterparts about the sharing of intelligence, Marr-Johnson was based within the British Embassy in Washington DC to ensure that this incredibly secret transatlantic codebreaking operation went smoothly.

A little later, the transatlantic partnership would be quietly formalised. And the echoes of that alliance are still very much with us today. But for now, this window into the heart of the NKVD was unknown territory. Oddly enough, in the closing months of the war, and the months that followed, separate units of British and American signals experts had been burrowing further into the decryption operations of vanquished Germany; they wanted to know how far the Germans had got into breaking Soviet codes, and indeed what of this intelligence might be salvaged for the new era to come. They succeeded, for instance, in breaking into one particular Soviet teleprinter system with the aid of secretly acquired German know-how.

The close relationship between American and British codebreakers – one of pure mutual respect forged throughout the war – continued unbroken and indeed in some respects strengthened. The Venona triumph was not merely a matter of duplicated code-books; they had just been the incredibly narrow entry point. Meredith Gardner and his colleagues had painstakingly extrapolated from these – through mathematical and linguistic progressions involving working out Russian keys for certain English words – a wider net of Soviet encryption. They were able through pure mathematics to overcome systems of double encryption – for in most respects, the Soviets were usually extremely cautious. In Eastcote, these new leads were grabbed and worked upon by Brigadier John Tiltman and the elegant chess champion Hugh Alexander.

Meanwhile, it was not only the double agent Donald Maclean who picked up the inkling that his Soviet activities were in danger of being uncovered. His fellow Cambridge Spy Guy Burgess also managed, in his role within MI6, to catch some prickling sense of the intelligence coming over, with its references to spies with codenames like 'Homer'. 'Homer' was Maclean. Knowing that the searchlights were drawing ever closer, that the decrypts were offering clues about locations and movements which would help to pinpoint the identities of the double agents, the volcanically unstable Burgess was first forced to live in suspense, and then to make his choice: to face denouncement and prosecution as a traitor, or to defect to the land that he had worked for? A few years later, in 1951, as the suspicions around the two agents reached a crescendo, they made their escape, via the Black Sea, to the Soviet Union. For Donald Maclean, it was a form of deliverance; for the flamboyant Burgess, it was a descent into grey purgatory.

The exposure of just two double agents – with the certain knowledge that there must be more – was to deliver a terrific shock to the British intelligence services. For the Americans, though, there was another figure, who had sought refuge in Britain in the inter-war years and had grown to great scientific eminence, whose betrayal, as we shall see, was even graver.

The theft of atomic secrets from the Manhattan Project would give the coming Cold War its real edge of frost. But in 1946, the Russians were still some distance away from being able to test any atomic weapons. In terms of territorial conquest, they may not have had any need for them. Across the flattened continent of Europe, millions of freezing, hungry people in despairing queues for food and fuel in cities and towns that were barely working were pointing to quite another possibility: that so many countries lost in darkness would turn to the apparent certainties of Stalin's Communism.

From the Kremlin's point of view, the genuine popular enthusiasm for Communism in countries such as Italy and France demonstrated that a political takeover could simply mean winning over hearts and minds: much less costly and indeed much more stable than a coup involving tanks and firepower.

Europe's ragged edges were in 1946 still struggling to find definition after the implosion of empires that came in the aftermath of the First

World War. The Balkan states had a long, ugly history of bitter strife; there was also the ferocious civil war that had begun in Greece. Britain had held on to the island of Cyprus but that, too, was about to undergo bloody upheaval. Further north, Hungary, Romania and Ukraine, which had fought furious, confused wars, were still bloodied and disorientated. President Joseph Tito's Yugoslavia seemed a curious outpost of near-stability and indeed independence; that in itself would prove to be a source of fury to Stalin. Here was the epochal moment when the continent would be defined from above. Just as in the aftermath of the First World War, when the victorious powers re-drew the maps of influence, so Stalin wanted – needed – to bring as many of these states as possible under his unyielding influence.

Yet at Eastcote, there was also careful monitoring of the airwaves slightly closer to home. In political terms, France was in a state of tumult, and for a while it was looking as though the Communists there were gaining a huge amount of popular traction. More than this, the British codebreakers were detecting and reading quite a bit of secret traffic between Paris and Moscow. The rationale behind such secret diplomatic overtures was not purely one of socialist fervour; it was also to do with elements in the government of post-war France wanting to ensure no resurrection of Nazism. From their point of view, even an occupied Germany was not to be trusted; these French diplomats felt the Soviets might be trusted to give protection. This was several years before the creation of NATO – the North Atlantic Treaty Organisation. There was also a huge amount of traffic emanating from French embassies deep within Eastern Europe. In that quiet London suburb, responsibility for eavesdropping on such communications and encryptions went to the volcanic and unpredictable genius Josh Cooper. The idea of this French–Soviet dialogue now seems arrestingly incongruous. Yet France was afflicted with a form of traumatic national schizophrenia, based on the violating nature of Nazi occupation, combined with that widespread yet unspoken knowledge of countless vile betrayals; and this against a backdrop of almost medieval economic catastrophe. In 1946, deep in the French countryside, farmers were starting to hoard food, and in the French cities, the shortages were starting to sharpen the distress and anger that otherwise could not quite find expression. It was not just London watching this turbulence with anxiety; in Washington, the French were being monitored very closely indeed.

It was the American diplomat George Kennan who had written so influentially about the neurosis of the Soviet leadership – that essential insecurity, the endless watchfulness against attack. Given the horrors visited upon the USSR by the Nazis, Stalin's lack of trust was in some ways quite understandable. The Soviets had made it quite clear that in the aftermath of the war they wanted to grab back territories which they felt the Axis powers had stolen from them: Poland, parts of Ukraine, the Baltic states. Stalin also sought ultimate control over Czechoslovakia and slabs of eastern Germany too. His thinking was two-fold: the more land that any potential future German army would have to cross before it came within sight of the Russian border, the better. Also, intriguingly, Czechoslovakia and eastern Germany had deposits of uranium. Stalin was soon to acquire the secret of the bomb. It would no longer be held in the 'sacred trust', as President Truman had once put it, of the US.

Western governments, if distrustful, were not about to lift a finger to stop the Russians grabbing Eastern Europe. They could not have done so even if they had wanted to: America might have the atomic bomb – but it was not going to use it in Europe. As to land armies, the effort to bring tired troops home from around the world was still ongoing. Armed forces were being cut back, and not only on the Western side: the Soviet military, too, had its numbers dramatically cut. No-one could afford that many soldiers.

As Tony Judt wrote: 'Youthful enthusiasm for a Communist future was widespread among middle-class intellectuals, in East and West alike. And it was accompanied by a distinctive complex of inferiority towards the proletariat, the blue-collar working class. In the immediate post-war years, skilled manual workers were at a premium – a marked contrast with the Depression years still fresh in collective memory. There was coal to be mined; roads, railways, buildings, power lines to be rebuilt or replaced; tools to be manufactured and then applied to the manufacture of other goods. For all these jobs there was a shortage of trained labour . . .

One consequence of this was the universal exaltation of industrial work and workers ... Left-leaning, educated middle-class men and women embarrassed by their social origin could assuage their discomfort by abandoning themselves to Communism.'[4]

From Britain to Italy, writers, journalists, artists and playwrights were perfectly open in their Communist sympathies. Indeed, there was an abundance of sympathy, too, for all that the Russian people had suffered under that Nazi assault. This was also the age of nationalisation: formerly private business enterprises were being taken under state control. In Britain, these changes were to come in the late 1940s, with the government taking over health provision, the railways, coal-mining, electricity and gas, among other industries. In France, the process went even further. In other words, there was a conscious political effort to de-fang capitalism; a belief that only state control would make business work in a more equitable fashion for the masses.

And at the centre of this destabilising maelstrom was Germany, a country divided into chunks by the victorious powers and occupied while they all tried to determine its destiny. The Soviets had the east, and in the middle of their zone sat the capital Berlin; the city was itself carved into different quarters for the occupying powers. Germany had been flattened from all directions as the Allies had sought to bring the Nazis to their knees; from entire cities seared and melted in mighty firestorms, to the ruthless cruelty and rapacity of the Soviet army, it was startling that there was any nation left at all. In the midst of this, the British army had begun a programme of attempted 'de-Nazification', taking Germans to view concentration camps, forcing them to gaze on the gas chambers. The Soviets and the French looked at the German people and imagined that the violence could very easily begin all over again. The French wanted vast reparations, partly as a means of keeping Germany permanently on its knees. But the Americans and the British took a more pragmatic view. Under the surface, too, the intelligence agencies and Britain's codebreakers were taking a particularly practical approach to the possibilities that this new landscape was opening up.

From Britain's point of view, the proximity of the Soviets was seen as putting deliberate pressure on the West. A diplomat called Christopher Warner said they 'have decided upon an aggressive policy, based upon militant Communism and Russian chauvinism. They have launched an offensive against social democracy and against this country ... the Soviet Government makes co-ordinated use of military, economic, propaganda and political weapons, and also of the Communist 'religion'. It is submitted, therefore, that we must at once organise and co-ordinate our defences against all these, and that we should not stop short of a defensive-offensive policy.'[5]

Part of the success of that policy was successfully following and analysing the secret communications emanating from eastern Germany, and indeed throughout Eastern Europe. In those post-war years, while few may have been anticipating gun battles and tanks deployed once more, there was still the question of hearts and minds. As the perceptive diplomat George Kennan had written of the power-sharing arrangements in occupied Germany, 'the idea of Germany run jointly with the Russians is a chimera ... we have no choice but to lead our (US and UK) section of Germany ... to a form of independence so prosperous, so secure, so superior, that the East cannot threaten it ... Better a dismembered Germany in which the West, at least, can act as a buffer to the forces of totalitarianism than a united Germany which again brings those forces to the North Sea.'[6] Bolshevism was understood by the Foreign Office – and by the more senior codebreakers – as essentially an internationalist movement. Borders were an irrelevance, nation-states meaningless. In some ways, Communism was viewed as a cult; and it was in that period that the codebreakers of Eastcote found that their requests for a larger budget to widen the scale of their operations was granted.

This was more than a significant gesture; it meant that in the eyes of the government, the codebreakers had justified their status as an independent intelligence-gathering department. From this point, Edward Travis, Nigel de Grey and Edward Hastings would sharpen their efforts to recruit the brightest young minds, while also keeping a very close tab on developments in research departments in the new science of computing. The future was theirs to seize.

Chapter 7

'This Was when the Penny Dropped'

The pin-striped commuters – many still with bowler hats – who walked along avenues of plane trees to the underground station at Eastcote must have occasionally allowed themselves to wonder about all the smartly dressed men and women who were making the reverse commute and getting off the trains there first thing in the morning. But the old habits of war persisted; everyone knew that curiosity would only get them so far, and so the big secret estate, hidden at the end of a perfectly ordinary row of suburban houses on Lime Grove, was hardly even a subject for local gossip.

Codebreakers – some eager to avoid spending an entire evening in their lodging houses – repaired to the pub at the end of their day's work, and they shared the saloon bar with the commuters who had returned home from their City jobs, and were enjoying a snifter before dinner. They would have known each other by sight, and greeted each other too. But no questions would have been asked. People simply didn't then.

On top of this, wrote local historian Susan Toms, 'because of the nature of the work, staff were cautioned about mixing too much with local people, so most socialising was done with work colleagues.'[1] Two pubs in particular were greatly favoured: 'The Black Horse' and 'The Case Is Altered'.

It is now extraordinary to recall that the existence of MI5 and MI6 was never officially acknowledged in newspapers or on the television until many years after the war; but at least everyone knew broadly that there was a secret service, whether anyone referred to it or not. The existence of GCHQ was buried deeper yet in the shadows; most members of the public would never have thought that work on codes would have had its own separate department. The term 'GCHQ' was first made public in 1976 by journalist Duncan Campbell in what was then the very left-leaning London magazine *Time Out*. Before then: absolute silence. The Eastcote establishment was getting steadily more populous from 1946 onwards, yet not even the most gimlet-eyed Soviet spy could have guessed at the function of these ordinary-looking men and women.

Nor was the Eastcote site bristling with vast cloud-scratching radio aerials that might have betrayed its purpose; the signals that were being intercepted in locations all over the world were relayed on to other sites, such as Chicksands and Beaumanor, before chattering over the teleprinters of Eastcote. Still operational elsewhere was the special unit buried within Hanslope Park, North Buckinghamshire: the Diplomatic Wireless Service. To this site intercepted messages and communications were passed on from British embassies and out-stations around the world.

But the Eastcote operation had a sporting and social dimension, too, that was rather more open to the wider world. And by way of contrast to the determinedly drab and anonymous blocks and huts of Lime Grove, the codebreakers and interceptors could go and enjoy this rich recreational life at a nearby property that far outstripped Bletchley Park in terms of elegance and grandeur. Swakeleys House, near Ickenham, still stands today: a magnificent piece of 17th-century architecture at which Samuel Pepys is said to have dined. Now it sits close to the busy M40 motorway; back in 1947, it was a rather quieter proposition, disturbed only by the military flights going in and out of the nearby RAF Northolt air base. Swakeleys House, now Grade I listed, with extraordinary panelling and oak staircases, was soon to provide working and living space for a party of Americans; but it was here that the Eastcote operatives came for much-needed relaxation.

First, there was the club formed for GCHQ's rugby enthusiasts. As Eastcote veteran Geoff Hardy wrote on the occasion of the club's 50th anniversary: 'The club was formed, as the Foreign Office Rugby Football Club, in 1947 when Government Communications Headquarters was based at Eastcote ... The idea to form the club was the brainchild of Geoff Hardy and Hooky Walker while sitting in the bar overlooking the grounds of Swakeleys House in Ickenham, the home of the Foreign Office Sports Association. Swakeleys was a large mansion set in some 20 acres (80 hectares) which also had space for about ten residents. Both Geoff and Hooky were among those residents and although Geoff was playing for Wasps and Hooky for Pinner, they decided that life would be much easier if a club could be formed to play rugby in their own backyard.

'The club colours became navy blue because a set of shirts was acquired from London Scottish (a long-established rugby club) – in those days, the club had to apply to the Board of Trade for a supply of clothing coupons to buy kit which was then re-sold to the players.'[2]

Soccer was not neglected; a football team at Eastcote was soon assembled. It was called FOSA, an acronym for 'Foreign Office Sports Association'. Once again, the rather wonderful facilities at Swakeleys were an enormous help. 'The team competed in the Harrow, Wembley and District League,' states the club's history. (Incidentally, it might be noted that the club – these days in Cheltenham, along with its GCHQ members – is still going great guns.)

Another Eastcote veteran, RF Churchhouse, had fond memories of the cricket matches that were played against other government departments. In one such match, he recalled, he was close to a personal triumph, but was sadly rather let down by his wicket-keeper who missed a crucial catch. The wicket-keeper in question happened to be Hugh Alexander, who had clearly taken some time off from chess championships.

The summer brought tennis matches too; it hardly needs to be added that given the hunched, focused nature of the work that the Eastcote team was doing, any opportunity for physical exertion was gratefully taken up. Veteran Russell Barnes recalled fondly not only all the sporting activity but a reasonably lively evening life too. There were other enthusiasms, of the cultural variety. Eastcote had its own jazz club; a measure of the youthfulness of the general atmosphere. Indeed, according to Russell Barnes, jazz was a serious passion for many. His fellow signals operatives, he said, included Alexander Bennett, who was to become famous for his founding involvement with the Ballet Rambert, and Roger Hancock, later to become the showbusiness agent for the Daleks (and of course by extension their creator Terry Nation).

Swakeleys did not host all the escapism: at Eastcote, a social hall had been set aside in the complex for the codebreakers and it was here that their own jazz bands sometimes performed. At a nearby venue, meanwhile, professional jazz musicians were invited to play. A little later, a young Cleo Laine and Johnny Dankworth were among them.

There was another rather startling perk for these Eastcote operatives: and that was free tickets to see shows in the West End. (You can only wonder if today's GCHQ operatives enjoy a similar bonus.) Naturally, in the 1940s, such tickets would not have been at the astronomical prices that we see now: theatre was still entertainment for the masses, as opposed to a rare treat. Nonetheless, a journey from the Eastcote HQ on the Piccadilly Line down to Leicester Square and Covent Garden brought a range of diverting possibilities. RF Churchouse recalled on one occasion how he took himself to the Royal Opera House, and happened to do so on an unusually foggy evening; it was not too long into the performance when the stage and the auditorium were dense with the industrial fog that had seeped in from outside.

The housing situation in those rationed days of the late 1940s was never ideal; taking lodgings in peacetime was psychologically different to doing so in wartime, when the entire country was mobilised and had a sense of a common purpose. The areas of Ruislip, Pinner, Harrow and Wembley were, in the post-war years, rather on the quiet side; the younger Eastcote operatives found themselves living with landladies who were forced to scrimp and save, and who would also have had extremely strict ideas about maintaining standards of decency. The chances for illicit romance back at one's lodgings would have been vanishingly rare; and in terms of spiritual uplift, this was an age of yellowed, low-voltage lighting, carefully rationed coal, even more carefully rationed food and domestic sobriety. A couple of Eastcote veterans recalled how their landladies – good-hearted but unstoppably nosy – were always desperate to find out exactly what it was that they were doing at the vast establishment. The operatives were instructed never ever to mention the phrase 'signals intelligence'; the best thing, they were told, was simply to cover themselves with the explanation that they were working for the Foreign Office.

Yet this was also the plus side of the work, for civilians and military alike: the adrenalin shot that made each successive day uncertain and exciting. Those who worked at Eastcote knew that they were closer to the heart of the nation's vital secrets than anyone else. The dissolute Oxbridge aristocrats of MI6 might have considered themselves superior in this respect, but the altogether more classless atmosphere of Commander Travis's Eastcote was there at the true core of the fast-freezing Cold War.

Indeed, there were early outbreaks of trade union representation among the signals operatives. Given the crucial nature of their work – and the growing suspicions in the 1940s and 1950s of Communist subversion and entryism – it seems surprising that any such thing was allowed. Later, it certainly was not, as became famously and rancourously clear in 1984 when Margaret Thatcher's government banned unions at the Cheltenham HQ. Back during the war, secret listeners working in the huts at Beaumanor Hall who were appointed as union representatives were there mostly to make sure that the working conditions were tolerable; the stress of working all through the night on such painstaking work should not, they reasoned, be added to with factors such as inadequate ventilation or lack of heat.

The key to it was the nature of wireless interception work – it was tough and debilitating and the operatives were fierce about ensuring that their best interests were being looked after. There was the occasional suggestion from the authorities that a staff association might be preferable to a union; that grievances could be raised with such a body without any fears of subversion. But this idea was never taken seriously.

Certainly in the Attlee years, there was a growth of what would these days be regarded as militancy, in the sense of workers standing together to get what they wanted off their managers. It was an essential part of the post-war settlement: having worked so hard to preserve the security of the realm, the workers in turn felt they deserved better treatment and better pay.

Added to this, the wireless interceptors in particular tended not to have been drawn from the pools of Oxbridge middle-class graduates (left-leaning though many of them were in that era) but from more ordinary backgrounds. They often came from families that had seen directly how the rights of manual workers could be trampled in the absence of unions to stick up for them. Away from the relative luxury of London, there were occasions when representation was rather urgently needed. Throughout the war (and indeed before it), a naval base at the Yorkshire coastal town of Scarborough had been monitoring signals traffic at sea; come the end of the war, the traffic that was being followed – and passed on to the code-breakers – was from Soviet craft. The work was not the problem; the raw conditions inside the base were. It was (and is) a little way outside of town, on the site of the old Scarborough racecourse at Irton Moor. There was a bomb-proof bunker in which many people worked; and when it rained, those people – no matter how 'bomb-proofed' they were – also ended up getting wet. (Things are rather more comfortable these days; the base recently received a visit from the Prince of Wales.)

Another interception base that carried on throughout was Forest Moor, just outside Harrogate in Yorkshire. Londoners in particular seemed to find working at the base a shock. There were others who – in the latter stages of the war when young men were still being called up – approached it with a sardonic sense of humour. Christopher Barnes, a highly skilled secret listener who had been based in Beaumanor, Leicestershire, now found himself drafted in 1947 to Forest Moor, and in uniform too, far from the relatively genteel conditions of civilian life. He wrote to his former colleagues in the Beaumanor magazine: 'Now we are back at the old grindstone again, this time at "F.M" [Forest Moor] instead of "BMR" [Beaumanor] . . . The disciples of Karl Marx, Beethoven, Churchill, Patience Strong, Kipling and Aneurin Bevan cannot be stilled by khaki and the night air of Yorkshire is rent by their arguments just as once was that of Leicestershire. The same faces are there and their personalities have not changed much either.'[3]

In a later number, Barnes was doing his best to be stoical. It must be remembered that despite all the vaulting leaps ahead in terms of codebreaking technology, the work of these signals operatives still involved being able to track faint signals, in difficult and sometimes stormy conditions. They had to follow them, and then to transcribe at tremendous speed and with needlepoint accuracy the messages being sent in Morse. Barnes noted that the chief difference was the lack of women; in his previous posting at Beaumanor, men and women had worked side by side throughout the war. Now, in Yorkshire, he wrote, 'we are . . . a Stag Party, a fact often lamented by the Don Juan element among us.' There were still flickers of cultured civilisation though, amid the 'beds in a straight line, kit blancoed, brasses polished, uniform toe-nails etc.' There was a Choir and Music club and Harrogate offered up 'weekly record recitals' at the Hydro. 'Those preferring more cosmopolitan pleasures . . . are to be seen in less respectable Leeds,' wrote Barnes. 'Others ramble on the glorious Yorkshire Moors (I had to promise to say something complimentary about Yorkshire . . . these dour northerners are sensitive about their county.)'[4]

Beaumanor itself, after a brief post-war lull when numbers (most notably among the demobbed women) had dropped dramatically, picked up again rather smartly from about 1947. Morse expert Kenneth Carling was there during that period, when he and his young colleagues understood the shifting new focus of their work. 'Recruiting for new operators started,' he wrote, 'and a gradual flow of fresh recruits came into the job. Nearly all of these were ex-services, with varying degrees of competence in wireless operating. Most certainly they were all male and so the interesting mix of the war years disappeared, which certainly was a shame.

'My own case is typical of those joining in this period,' he continued. 'I had done my National Service in the RAF and had trained as a wireless operator. Radio communications work suited me and I found it very interesting. At the end of the 28-week course in Compton Bassett, I was posted to RAF Miho in Japan with the British Commonwealth Occupation Force . . . I enjoyed the travel, my year in Japan, and the point-to-point radio operating . . . when my [demob] came up in 1947, I found myself in civvie street back in the UK and unable to find any job associated with radio operating, and finally finished up as a welder. But I continued to seek work as a radio operator and eventually an ex-Forces employment association pointed me in the direction of Beaumanor.'[5]

As a general point, this was a period when the British government, essentially bust, was trying to rein in spending; but the point about the re-invigoration of Beaumanor (and of course Eastcote too) was that this new independent intelligence service, born from the triumphs of Bletchley, was convincing the prime minister and senior figures in Whitehall that the fast-developing science of signals intelligence and electronic surveillance was the only way in which a technologically alert enemy might be kept at bay. Added to this, the nascent GCHQ also took advantage of one thing of which Britain did have a surplus at that time: young men who were simply obsessed with radio and communications technology.

'Beaumanor had its own local training establishment,' wrote Carling, 'and most people only needed a couple of weeks to familiarise themselves with the peculiar necessities of "Y" work. Some spent a couple of weeks at the nearby Royal Signals camp, Garats Hay, to bring their Morse copying speed to 20 words per minute before going on to the Beaumanor course. This was when the penny dropped. New entrants realised there was not a Morse key in sight. The job was receiving Morse and receiving Morse only . . . we would become specialists in receiving Morse.

'The trainees went from the training room in "J" hut to the main set room where they polished up their new-found skills on what would later be called on-the-job training. We knew it as "double-banking" and would sit side by side with an older, more experienced operator to learn and/or be corrected when mistakes were made. It was a good and practical way of learning the ropes.'[6]

There were some immediately pressing issues that caused resentment: not technological, but relating to pay. The new recruits at Beaumanor were a mix of military and civilian, and it soon became apparent that the civilians were getting paid rather better than the soldiers. It became a matter for the union representative, one Fred Philips, to start chewing into. Mr Philips had been at Beaumanor for a while and was apparently skilled in discussing such matters with the authorities. There were elements of culture shock for young Kenneth Carling too. Recruits got to live at the house, which was a rather beautiful 19th-century effort set in modest parkland. But the accommodation – which was priced at 2s 6d per week – was a long way from being luxurious.

'A typical room would have four beds, with a wardrobe or cupboard allocated to each occupant's "bed-space", wrote Carling. 'Bedding was army-style: three hard uncomfortable "biscuits", two pillows, maybe a pillow case and three rough blankets . . . The living was rough but for half a crown a week could be considered good value. Redeeming features included plenty of heat [which incidentally was not to be sniffed at during one of the century's most bitterly cold winters in 1947] and big bathrooms with unlimited amounts of piping hot water. And, one extra special bathroom decorated in green and with several larger-than-life nudes on the wall. Had they been painted by an ATS artist?'[7]

Otherwise, life in some ways for these secret listeners was quite hemmed in, not least because the pay was so modest. 'Food was obtainable at the canteen and eaten in the grandeur of the spacious dining room,' recalled Carling. 'But there was not much to spend on food – or anything else out of a weekly wage packet of £3. So eating became a luxury. Living includes other important things and one had to allow for the necessities of life such as cigarettes, beer, bus fares to and from Loughborough, the cinema and last but not least, the famous dances at Loughborough Town Hall. Once in a while, for a special treat, and if prudent, a bus ride to the big cities of Leicester, Nottingham or Derby might be afforded.'[8]

The work itself, though the 'targets' for interception were new, was pretty much the same as it had been throughout the war; it required, among other things, a preternatural level of patience. As Carling and others have noted, there could be a lot of sitting around, straining to hear or follow anything in the white noise of the atmosphere. Their work could only start when their opposite numbers – Soviet radio operatives, now, rather than Germans – started their own shifts. But the interceptors had to be constantly ready and alert and, it goes without saying, with every bit as much devotion as that shown by their wartime predecessors. The young men at Beaumanor, at Scarborough, and at other out-stations dotted around the country, were now focusing not so much on a threatened invasion as on securing Britain's national defence and survival in wider terms against the backdrop of a world constantly on the edge of fresh slaughter.

Their work was not glamorous, but this system was diabolically effective, partly thanks to the ideas of Bletchley Park's great organiser Gordon Welchman. Such an abundance of communications traffic had provided the Bletchley Park – and now Eastcote – directorate with a view of the enemy that was almost like a panopticon: incredibly wide, seemingly able to see into every corner. Men like Christopher Barnes and Kenneth Carling were listening in to different divisions of the Soviet military machine, from all the different regions within Eastern Europe to which it was being deployed. The messages they intercepted, all the traffic that was then analysed, gave the authorities up-to-date intelligence on movements and redeployments among the Soviet armed forces.

At the start of the Cold War, this was what the Americans did not have in such depth: the sheer depth of Morse experts with headsets, working in night-time rooms thick with the rich smell of hot electronics and cheap tobacco, ears ringing with the white noise of the atmosphere. Even if codes were not immediately broken, the sheer range alone of messages intercepted was a treasure trove.

The prospect of future nuclear jeopardy would have particularly preyed on the minds of those working at another out-station a little further west: RAF Cheadle in Cheshire. At an 18th-century property called Woodhead Hall, the focus had moved from spying on the Luftwaffe to listening in to the Soviet Air Force. Actually, there had been – at a very low level – quite continuous monitoring of (unencrypted) Soviet signals from Cheadle throughout the war as well. Even though breaking into secret Soviet codes had been suspended for the conflict, straightforward un-encrypted communications were still quietly intercepted, as indeed the Soviets would in turn have intercepted un-coded Allied traffic. Scarborough, too, had a very small team listening in to unencrypted Russian transmissions throughout. The reasoning – very far from being cynical – would have been this: although Stalin was an ally, the fact was that before the war, he had not been, and the codebreakers had played an important role in seeking to counter international Communist subversion. Realists, not cynics, would have been able to divine that when the Allies won the war, the peace would not bring some miraculous flowering of capitalist/ Communist harmony.

Meanwhile, RAF Cheadle and Woodhead Hall played host not just to skilled interceptors, but also to a range of workshops as well, there for work to be carried out on new equipment, in the manner of Q's laboratories from the James Bond films. GCHQ itself has proudly commemorated the man who set the station up just before the war started, and who then oversaw its development and evolution as the war went on. William Green Swanborough is one of those extraordinary figures, like Nigel de Grey, who spans a period from the First World War to the 1950s, with all the world-changing codebreaking technology that period brought.

William Swanborough had been a 'Self-Trained Radio Operator' with the Royal Engineers in 1918; the inter-war years saw him voyaging to Sudan with the RAF and setting up intercept stations for the Service's then chief Lord Trenchard. Swanborough travelled out to Estonia in the 1930s, on first sight a rather abstruse place for an intelligence expert to go to share codebreaking and intercept knowledge. But it was of course to do with Estonian proximity to 1930s Soviet Russia: what Swanborough was after was a regular flow of intercepted Soviet traffic being sent on by the Estonians.

And so it was, in the late 1940s, that Swanborough turned his focus back to the Soviets. The main listening station at Cheadle was on the Staffordshire moors, under wide open skies. Now the local countryside around there is awash with millionaire footballers; for the secret listeners in the rather quieter 1940s, entertainment would have come at local hops rather than neon nightclubs.

Overall this was a world in which interceptors – who had spent the war reporting for duty in civilian clothes – now found themselves at the other end of the conflict in uniform, and tracking the signals which arose from an entirely new kind of international tension.

But they were not alone. The relationship between the British and the American codebreaking and interception operatives was more than simply warm. On a personal level, there was often great delight taken in the friendships forged throughout those years. And as much as the young British codebreakers loved being introduced to an America that they had only previously seen and dreamed about on cinema screens, the Americans who came over to Britain to help with the work at Eastcote and other sights also found their own preconceptions sometimes hilariously confirmed. The land of the tea-drinkers – damp, cold, drafty and drab – was not without its own perverse attractions. And for both sides, there was also a measure of comfort; a sense of rightness and indeed stability when facing a world that was still dangerously poised on the edge of a larger conflict.

Chapter Eight
They Gathered around like Family

By the late 1940s, it was a relationship that had become unprecedentedly intimate; and it was striking to consider that this closeness had been sparked in circumstances that were almost picturesque, if not downright romantic: that snowy January midnight in 1941 when four senior US cryptologists had arrived, in the thick darkness of the blackout, at the front door of Bletchley Park. These Americans had brought with them a technological marvel: the machine they had constructed to combat the Japanese cypher system. Bletchley's director Alastair Denniston offered his guests sherry in the quiet book-lined study that was his office. Given that at the time America was still pretty much one year away from joining the war, this initial meeting of minds was truly remarkable; doubly so given the inevitable rivalry between the two nations. After the war, there had been some in Washington DC who wanted to see this continuing romance between the two nation's codebreakers cooled down. Yet – even aside from the triumph of Venona – the relationship continued to be irresistibly fruitful.

For instance, in 1946, the British and Americans had started working together on cracking Soviet traffic under the name 'Operation Bourbon', later renamed 'Rattan'. This success was followed by an operation named 'Caviar', in which inroads were made against a Soviet teleprinter system.

After this came what was called the 'Poet' operation. The Soviet armed forces' machine cyphers were broken by a team at Eastcote, and the system of doing so was christened 'Coleridge'. According to intelligence historian Michael Smith, the equipment being used by the Russians in this instance bore a useful similarity to the 'Hagelin' electric encryption machines used by the Swedes. This was one of the moments when the American liaison officers working in London looked at the British – or more specifically, in this case, at Hugh Alexander, who had headed up the 'Coleridge' assault – and understood the depth of brilliance that they were working with. According to a communication sent back to Washington in the spring of 1947, Alexander's 'Coleridge' codebreak – which opened a window into a world of Soviet administration, which in turn yielded invaluable intelligence about military numbers and priorities – was 'the most important, high-level system from which current intelligence may be produced and is so in fact regarded here'.[1]

One of the Americans working at Eastcote who joined in with the Poet operation – branching off into another decryption project, 'Longfellow' – was a wonderfully engaging mathematician whose name is now venerated by UFO conspiracy theorists the world over. Howard H Campaigne – who had worked under Professor Max Newman and who was, later in his career in America, to do so much to push computer technology along – wrote a paper in the late 1960s which came to light several years ago. Or, at least, a fragment of the paper surfaced. It was about coded messages from a most unusual source. 'Recently a series of radio messages was heard coming from outer space,' Campaigne wrote in an enjoyably deadpan – even mischievous – introduction. The fragment of his paper does not indicate whether these messages are set as a hypothetical test by himself or not, but the way he frames the effort to decode the messages, broken into fragments, suggests a sly attention-grabbing way into a mathematical riddle as opposed to an extraordinary revelation that will alter the course of human history.

In conversation with a National Security Agency colleague in the 1980s, Campaigne was happy to muse on the rather more terrestrial concerns that he had faced in his cryptography. He was quite candid about how US codebreakers had identified the need to break into Soviet cyphers some distance before the end of the war. 'President Roosevelt had said that we were not at war with Russia and we wouldn't study their codes. But there were people down the line who thought that was very unwise.'

But the study of Soviet messages was kept extremely low-key, for understandable reasons. 'It was extremely modest,' Campaigne said. 'We did a little intercept. We had great difficulty covering up for our intercept stations. And practically all we had was a few samples of traffic.'

On top of this – and despite the unprecedentedly close relationship between the US and UK codebreakers – he also confessed that there had been some sneaky spying upon the affairs of their British friends. 'Well, we looked a little at some of their things,' Campaigne noted. 'It really wasn't an intelligence effort. It was more a cryptographic monitoring . . . the British were using an enciphered code for the convoy thing and we were convinced that the Germans were reading it. And we told them that and it was hard to persuade them that it was true.

'We also got hold of a British machine,' he continued. Professor Campaigne was referring to the Typex enciphering machine which in some ways mirrored the workings of the German Enigma. 'And of course we took it apart and examined it with great interest . . . we did do some analysis of the British cypher machine without telling them. Looking for weaknesses and we didn't uncover anything. It was a pretty secure device really.'[2]

In drizzly 1940s Eastcote, American fascination – and sometimes bewilderment – at British life continued. According to security expert Gordon Corera, one especially beguiling detail concerned official struggles with ramblers. Around Eastcote – and other listening stations buried rather deeper in England's sylvan glades – there was a criss-crossing network of ancient footpaths and rights of way dating back centuries. Under the new Labour government, which viewed the rights of ordinary man as trumping those of the landed aristocracy, there were a great number of walkers who were starting to assert their rights to use them, no matter how close these footpaths may have been to secret establishments. There was nothing in America to quite match the ferocious determination of the ramblers and their expertise on the right to march along certain by-ways;

by contrast, in the US, such people would be warned off forbidden land with guns.

Some footpaths in the most extraordinarily sensitive areas remained open, including one, dating all the way back to 1565, that ran between two blocks of the Eastcote establishment. Obviously there was security fencing and walls but nevertheless, the proximity to the secret work was startling. Incidentally, things are just as free and easy now for walkers: the site of so-called GCHQ Bude in Cornwall, featuring an array of satellite dishes, has the South West Coast Path running alongside it, the equivalent of a walkers' motorway. Meanwhile, the giant golf-ball surveillance structures at Fylingdales in Yorkshire are of themselves something of a tourist attraction for ramblers. Obviously one cannot wander around the site itself, but about ten years ago the Ministry of Defence opened up tracts of the North York Moors surrounding the installation that had, for some decades, been forbidden territory to the public. In any event, many codebreakers and secret listeners were themselves keen walkers: Christopher Barnes at Beaumanor Hall in Leicestershire relished the countryside all around; Alan Turing made a habit of running through the countryside around Hanslope Park. As it happens, that particular park is very much barred to walkers now; a most unusual defeat for the rambling community. Walking groups post complaining blogs about having to circumnavigate the estate, but there are some areas that are still deemed too clandestine to risk it.

In cultural terms, what was slightly more difficult for the Americans coming to 1940s monochrome Britain was the greatly reduced standard of living. For US cryptographers such as Joan Malone, who had been brought over to work alongside veteran British cryptographer William Bodsworth, this new world of fish paste, of processed ham, of scarce to non-existent luxury items, must have been quite an ordeal after the unthinking plenty of Virginia. This was a landscape not merely of austerity, but of rationing even more ferocious than that seen during the war. Added to this was the spectacularly biting winter of 1947: the snow came down relentlessly, never clearing. Rather unkindly, Joan Malone was given the nickname 'Sneezy'. The unconditioned air in the Eastcote blocks, together with the unpleasantly chilly weather, left her a martyr to her nose. The summer months were not much better: leafy Eastcote, with all its surrounding parks, made her hay-fever a nightmare.

Added to this particular discomfort were the wider privations: the continual shortages of coal and fuel, combined with the coupons needed to buy any kind of new clothing. This was a time when women were forced to make themselves garments out of old blankets. Joan Malone, together with her small accompanying team of American codebreakers, had come from a burgeoning consumerist paradise, where orange juice and fresh coffee were expected, to a somnolent London suburb where such things had never been known; a suburb where everything was shut all day Sunday, and on Wednesday afternoons too. The proximity of the West End would only have been a partial consolation, since the city was still a soot-smirched parade of British Restaurants and frowsy pubs.

The pairing of Joan Malone – a formidably skilled analyst and linguist – with British codebreaker Bodsworth, himself a polyglot, in some ways symbolised the entire US–UK relationship. Here was an old-school male academic, a product of the traditional English education system, sparking with a woman who in some ways represented a future of equality, and certainly a future of growing American dominance.

A key figure in forging a strong post-war partnership with these bright Americans was Group Captain Eric Jones. At the start of his codebreaking career, Jones had attracted the attention of those from backgrounds far more genteel than his own. His intellectual trajectory, when he had been recruited from Air Ministry intelligence to Bletchley Park in 1942, was strikingly different to that of the off-the-wall academics roaming the premises. Although fiercely bright, Jones was not a university man. Indeed, he had left school at the age of 15. He joined his family's textile firm and then left that by the age of 18, in order to start up his own business independently. A terrific success he made of it too; and it was only the urgency of war that made him hand it over to associates, aged just 33. He might not have been an Oxbridge classicist – Jones attended the King's School in Macclesfield – but his wider experience clearly set him up fantastically well for the extraordinary life that he was to lead. At Bletchley, he had been placed in temporary charge of Hut 3 and Luftwaffe decrypts; and this, in turn, led to permanent leadership. Commander Travis had been immediately impressed not merely with Jones's intelligence, but also by the way that he could bring a semblance of order to all the jostling, wild intellects working in that hut; an easy knack for leadership based on a charisma that many were to pay tribute to across the years.

Jones also had a gift for organising intelligence: in 1945, he had been sent to Washington DC to act as the representative of British Signals Intelligence. As in Britain, his straightforward and easy manner won him good friends – crucial to the quite extraordinary level of trust that evolved between America and Britain. Jones had both laser-beam intelligence and also a manner that was found universally pleasing. Chess champion Stuart Milner-Barry wrote of him: 'Jones was not a scholar or an academic; I suppose he must have had some knowledge of German but primarily he was a businessman coming from . . . Lancashire. He was a genuinely modest man who regarded himself as having little to contribute compared with the boffins with whom he was surrounded; in fact he was a first-rate administrator who was liked and trusted by everyone.'[3]

Codebreaker William Millward also paid tribute to Jones's awesome powers of diplomacy: 'He had the qualities of principle, strength of character, and a firm grasp of essentials which enabled him to settle most of the tiresome intrigues and controversies.'[4] Ralph Bennett described him as 'firm but understanding' meaning that everyone could concentrate on their work 'undisturbed by internal conflict'.[5]

Jones's goal in Washington was to work on cementing an intelligence liaison – and it was in large part through his efforts that America and Britain came to seal their secret codebreaking alliance, an arrangement that still holds firm today. Before then, he had worked with the US codebreaker Telford Taylor who remembered him with great fondness: 'Group Captain Eric Jones was personally impressive and, at first, all business, but eventually became a friend whom I greatly admired.'[6]

A photographic portrait of Sir Eric Jones taken in 1957 – by which time he had been director of GCHQ for some years – now hangs in the National Portrait Gallery. It shows a handsome, amused figure, slightly loud of suit but neat of hair. Sir Eric was valued on both sides of the Atlantic for his directness. Given his success in the field of commerce, it would not have been unreasonable to have expected him, after the war, to return to the profitable business that he had founded. But in 1946, he told an American colleague that he was keen 'to stay in the racket'.[7]

Initially, that top-secret UK–USA agreement excluded Britain's dominions such as Canada, New Zealand, Australia. They were not even to be privy to the fact that there was such an agreement. And they were not considered for intelligence-sharing because there was concern over how tight security could be over such wide dissemination. But by 1946, following a two-week conference, all that was to change. It was seen as perverse to lock out such formidable intelligence harvesters.

These wrangles aside, this secret alliance opened up vast prospects. Meetings took place in London in 1946, in a smart square just to the north of Marble Arch. Among those sitting in was Sir Stewart Menzies, the head of MI6; and for the Americans, Joseph Wenger. According to Richard Aldrich, when the fine print of negotiations ran into obstacles, it was Menzies who prescribed the age-old British technique for solving such difficulties: he took the American delegation to his St James's club, White's, and treated them to a wine-filled lunch. Talks got going again in a more relaxed frame. And then, afterwards, came the signing of the actual agreement: this was carried out, on the British side, by Lieutenant Colonel Patrick Marr-Johnson and on the American by General Hoyt Vandenburg.

Only recently did GCHQ finally acknowledge officially that any such alliance was formed; it was a state secret for over 60 years. There were some good reasons for this: apart from anything else, the blending and sharing of such expertise rendered it an astoundingly powerful force, whereas it was very much in the interests of both Britain and America throughout the entire course of the Cold War that the Soviets should underestimate their abilities and reach.

After the 1946 agreement, the Americans and the British and the dominions between them were listening in on every last square mile of earth. And in strategic terms, the Americans at this stage were leaning heavily on the British; thanks to the UK–USA alliance, they would have regular, secure access to the streams of intelligence being produced by listening stations from Colombo to Hong Kong to Cyprus to Sarafand. In the Indian operation, various listening out-stations were pulling in signals many miles to the north, monitoring all Soviet activity near the borders of Asia with microscopic closeness. Equally, any Soviet transmissions in the Black Sea or the Caspian Sea was being picked up by the British in the Mediterranean.

In archival terms, vast amounts are still being withheld in the UK; in America, slightly more has become available. There are, for instance, very warm letters from US senior codebreaker William F Friedman to Group Captain Eric Jones which the authorities have now placed in the public domain. The correspondence shows an ease and a lightness and a strong sense of mutual respect; there is none of the usually salty efforts on both sides to establish a tone of superiority. Particularly fruitful during this period were the regular bundles of intelligence briefings to do with Russian military movements and build-ups that were passed across the Atlantic. For while there had been some problems with deciphering Soviet military and intelligence codes – and there were far worse problems to come – there was also, by way of consolation, the great innovation of Bletchley Park's Gordon Welchman: the forensic examination of traffic analysis. That analytical beam was now turned on all corners of the Soviet empire.

For on a day-to-day basis, soldiers had to communicate with soldiers, units with units. And in listening bases across the world, the young British men working the intercepting radios were fast becoming experts in being able to tell individual Soviet radio operators; each operator had their own unique 'fist', as distinctive as a walk or a voice. And it wasn't only the individual techniques for sending Morse messages, it was also the way that these Russian radio operators would communicate with each other outside the official messages being sent. Traffic analysis also yielded up huge amounts of geographical information; by means of direction finding, one could monitor from where messages were being sent, whether certain units were on the move, and where to.

The intelligence alliance was a source of great satisfaction to the Americans. General Charles Cabell, in charge of US Air Force

Intelligence (and therefore at the heart of all planning to do with nuclear strike capability) wrote in 1948: 'At the present time, there is complete interchange of communications intelligence information between the cognizant United States and British agencies. It is not believed that the present arrangements . . . could be improved.'[8]

This was not just a new world of interception; it was also very much about the developing technology of signals intelligence gathering, and electronic methods of cracking cyphers. Gordon Welchman, at that time in London working for the John Lewis Partnership, was gnawingly aware of developments in computer technology. Compared to Britain's efforts – at the National Physical Laboratory in Teddington, and Professor Newman's department at Manchester University – the Americans were clearly striding ahead. Welchman had kept in touch with some American friends he had made in Bletchley days. It was clear to him that his future lay out there. And even though he had left cryptography behind, it was quite clear that someone with his experience would still be a terrific asset to the United States when it came to technology and questions of national security.

And at Eastcote (or the London Signals Intelligence Centre as it was still being called), Welchman's old boss Commander Travis was more than happy for him to be farmed out to the US in this way. Since Welchman had been one of the architects of Travis's new realm in Eastcote, it would have been surprising if this was not so: there was pride (and perhaps an element of healthy competitiveness with the Americans) in sending them such a fine example of British brainpower. However, for an Englishman to be admitted into the most secret spheres of the US state was quite a prospect and, as revealed by Welchman's biographer Joel Greenberg, Commander Travis provided his old colleague with an unofficial letter of reference. For while Welchman was known within codebreaking circles, he was about to enter quite a different part of America's labyrinthine defence community.

'Dear Welchman,' Travis's letter read, 'I have recently been reviewing the wartime work of this organisation with particular reference to the contribution of individual members of the organisation and I should like to place on record my appreciation of the important and outstanding part you played. Your quick mastering of a number of different aspects of the work of which you had no previous experience was most noticeable and your inventiveness and ability in the field of applied mathematics and electronics provided a notable contribution to the success of the organisation.

'From 1943 to the end of the war,' Commander Travis continued, 'your services as an Assistant Director gave you an opportunity to display your organising and administrative ability of which you took full advantage. I hope your wartime experience will be of real value to you in Civil (sic) life in which I wish you every success.'[7] While Welchman's reputation preceded him, Travis's warm words were themselves a code to do with reliability and discretion, ideal for procuring transatlantic security clearance. The Welchman family set sail in 1948, and Welchman, with that full and very privileged clearance, went to work for an organisation called MITRE.

The British and US trade in codebreakers brought romance to Eastcote. The brilliant cryptographer Joan Malone, while coping with colds, hay-fever and the delicate mores of English suburbia, got to know her colleague and fellow American Captain Harold Callaghan rather better. Love blossomed among those grey one-storey huts; marriage followed swiftly thereafter.

Incidentally, the Americans seemed as forward-looking in their attitude towards the female aptitude for cryptology as Bletchley's late Dilly Knox, who had always favoured working with women. Back across the Atlantic, at the Arlington Hall cryptography section, more US women were starting to dazzle at this time, including Gene Grabeel. Originally a schoolteacher who grew bored with that work and yearned for something a little more challenging, Grabeel loved her codebreaking life so intensely that she worked with the National Security Agency for a further three decades until the mid-1970s.

Then there was Wilma Zimmerman Davis, a true pioneer in the field. She graduated in mathematics, and, in common with a number of other female US cryptologists, started out as a teacher. But then Davis took US Navy correspondence courses that focused on cryptography. She found that she had a flair; and others had spotted this aptitude too. In the late

1930s, aged 26, she was recruited into the secret realm in Washington DC by the codebreaking pioneer William Friedman. Just months into her new role, Davis was widowed; and she later said that her colleagues at this time became part of an extended family, such was their support. 'I was a very lucky person that I happened to be there when I lost my husband,' Davis said. 'These people gathered around like family and it made life really worth living and going on.'[10]

She gained terrific experience working first on Italian codes and then on the Japanese Purple system, and even for a little time with Chinese codes. Her expertise was such that she was drafted on to the super-exclusive Venona team. Like so many others, Wilma Davis made a couple of efforts during her later career to leave cryptography behind; but she was always lured back to the work. Indeed, she didn't actually retire until 1973.

There was also Genevieve Grotjan, the woman now credited by the National Security Agency as having made the first breaks into the Japanese Purple codes. She, too, was drafted on to Venona, and once again provided the agency with an extraordinary means of levering into the codes (though exactly what is still unspecified for security reasons to this day). 'Miss Grotjan's brilliant findings in two instances enabled exploitation of communications that provided invaluable intelligence information to policymakers,' states the agency's 'Cryptologic Hall of Honor' baldly. 'This information was used by the most senior government officials for decisions in World War Two and the Cold War.'[11] Grotjan later married Hyman Feinstein and went off into academia to be a Professor of Mathematics at George Mason university.

'No two independent powers have ever exchanged as many secrets as Britain and America during and since the Second World War,' observed historian Christopher Andrew.[12] What made these exchanges even more extraordinary was the fact that they were so hermetically sealed: outside the respective codebreaking departments, not even a handful of people knew. The average MI5 and MI6 operatives were not privy to the secret.

Deep in the background, the Venona operation carried on. As well as the British traitors, that enormous tranche of Soviet codes had also ripped away the disguises of American double agents Alger Hiss and Harold Dexter White. Hiss had been a US State Department official. Curiously, his public denouncement as a spy actually came not from the codebreakers but from editor and former Communist Party member Whittaker Chambers who beat them to it at a Senate hearing; when Chambers repeated the accusation of espionage against Hiss on national radio, Hiss sued. But the tactic eventually doubled back on him and he was found guilty of perjury. The point was that even though there were levels of ambiguity and doubt to the Hiss case, it nonetheless seems certain that he was identified in the Venona decrypts. The case of Harold Dexter White was more unsettling: a very senior US Treasury official, Dexter White was among those involved in pulling together the Bretton Woods agreement that put the world's economies back onto a more stable footing after the war. Again, he was publicly denounced as a spy; more quietly, he was there in that tranche of decrypts. Harold Dexter White never stood trial – but equally, his premature death in 1948, aged 55, meant that he could never deny the successive accusations. There are a few today who maintain that Dexter White's contacts with Soviet Russia were more innocent than the decrypts appear to suggest.

The Venona messages contained other vital information as well as cover-names; in particular, they opened a significant window into the tactics and methods of the Soviet NKVD, fore-runners of the KGB, by which agents would receive specific instructions to do with conveying their own intelligence (such as how to get rolls of film to their controllers) or indeed simply meeting up – the types of places and times favoured by controllers to meet their agents. They revealed terminology used by the NKVD that these days sounds like pure B-movie spy material: if an agent was to be 'de-activated' for instance, the cover term was 'put on ice' or 'put in cold storage'.

But given the tension of the times, this went far beyond simple spy-versus-spy stuff; it is no exaggeration to say that the passing to Moscow of America's nuclear secrets was one of those acts upon which the world of future generations pivoted. Those Manhattan Project secrets – smuggled out of Los Alamos by the scientist Klaus Fuchs, with help from Julius and Ethel Rosenberg – were to give Stalin the key to true power that he needed.

The story of Klaus Fuchs seems, with the distance of time, many times more extraordinary than the treachery of the Cambridge Spies. Whereas Burgess, Philby, Maclean, Blunt and Cairncross were dealing very often in material involving other spies, Fuchs was handling secret knowledge that would change the tides of power throughout the entire world. Described by one former colleague as a thin-lipped man who never laughed, one might now argue that Fuchs had had little to laugh about. Born in Rüsselheim, Germany, in 1911, he was inspired when young to join the Communist Party. As the thugs of Hitler's Nazi party became increasingly prominent and confident, Fuchs was targeted, on one occasion being thrown into a river. By 1933, with Hitler now triumphant in the Reichstag, and the Nazis radically transforming Germany's society and its constitution, he knew that it was time to flee.

First, Fuchs went to Paris; then he came across to England. A gifted physicist, he went to study at Bristol under Nevill Mott; it was there that he gained a doctorate. Later, he moved to Edinburgh University to study under Max Born. These were extraordinary years in the realms of physics; the possibilities suggested by quantum theory were being explored. As art had modernism and futurism, so physics also came to point to a radically different kind of world.

Then, with the outbreak of war, came the official British crackdown on foreign-born nationals – most notably German citizens. Doctor Fuchs was interned along with many fellow countrymen, first on the Isle of Man, and then across the Atlantic in Canada. But the Canadian exile lasted little more than six months in the latter part of 1940; in 1941, Dr Fuchs was permitted to return to Britain.

His story from this point shows the inevitable shortcomings of both signals intelligence and human intelligence. The talented Fuchs was recruited by Rudolf Peierls to work on what sounded a perfectly ordinary war project: 'Tube Alloys'. It was very far from being ordinary. This was the cover-name for Britain's effort to develop the atomic bomb. Fuchs, having signed the Official Secrets Act, was also given British nationality; no sounder precautions were felt to be necessary.

It was a serious mistake on the part of the British. Indeed, as soon as he had been drafted into Tube Alloys in 1941, Fuchs had determined that the Soviet Union should share in this awful new power. His decision came at around the point that the Germans had consigned the Molotov-Ribbentrop non-aggression pact with the Soviet Union to the flames and launched their invasion of Russia. It is possible to see the anguished idealism that would lead a young Communist to seek to do anything to help the bloc that he considered to hold the prospects for a brighter, cleaner future.

And so it was that Fuchs had made early contact with the Soviets in London, and established regular meetings where he passed everything on. Around this time, John Cairncross, who was working at Bletchley, was also meeting up on a regular basis on the outskirts of London with Soviet agents. It seems quite surprising that Fuchs was not being monitored; what came next was more startling still.

By 1943, Fuchs and Rudolf Peierls were invited by the Americans to join forces. The scientists set sail for the US, working first in New York and then at Los Alamos deep in New Mexico, on what was being termed the Manhattan Project.

Dr Fuchs was to become more than just a valued colleague: presiding genius Robert Oppenheimer had frequent close and detailed conversations with him. And here we might see some of Fuchs's native courage, no matter where one stands on his actions. For he contrived to start getting secrets out of the most secure site on earth. Here was a man working not merely with equations on a blackboard, but next to the physical reality of the bomb itself. Obviously, security in and out of the Los Alamos site was extraordinarily tight, but Fuchs had no need to smuggle reams of documents. He had a diamond-sharp mind.

And so it was, after all those detailed discussions and debates with Oppenheimer, that Fuchs would then leave the base, travel to another small, obscure town in New Mexico, and there meet with his Soviet contact. The contact would make notes; Fuchs had the fine detail memorised – unimaginably fine, ranging from the critical mass of fissile material to the complex inner workings of the bomb structure. He simply felt it his duty: this was the technology that was going to decide the future of the world, and there was no way that the Soviet Union could be allowed to fall behind in the arms race.

His treachery would eventually be uncovered; but his unmasking would come only after the entire world had stopped in shock when Stalin detonated the Soviet bomb.

In the meantime, Fuchs returned to England after the war, welcomed closer than ever into an appreciative scientific community. Indeed, he was made head of the Theoretical Physics Division at the brand new Atomic Energy Research Establishment at Harwell. Fuchs also sat on many advisory committees, and he continually advised the need for ever tighter security around Britain's own burgeoning nuclear projects.

In the end, it was the Venona codebreakers who revealed his activities; old messages would eventually be unscrambled that made references to Los Alamos. Given the limited numbers of people who had that sort of high-level access, his identity was finally pinpointed and GCHQ helped ensure, in circumstances of the greatest secrecy, that this intelligence was passed to MI5. They would also uncover a startling postscript to the Fuchs story.

In espionage terms, the grab for the bomb was not the only Soviet gambit uncovered by the Venona programme. There was huge Soviet appetite for learning via espionage about the nascent field of jet-engine technology, for instance; or in the advances made in the area of rocket science. The Soviets were desperate to know more about the development of jet aircraft, and the new capabilities that such materiel might bring. The atomic secret was one thing; but to acquire as well the means to deliver such doomsday weapons, in a matter of minutes, either from screamingly fast planes, or by missiles that could fly across countries . . . That would instantly change the landscape of power.

But incredibly, the Venona secret itself was also compromised, in circumstances that were almost blackly comic. For among the very few who were invited in on the intelligence that these Soviet codes had been cracked were in fact two undercover Soviet agents. In the US, that agent was Elizabeth Bentley. For the British, it was the Cambridge Spy Kim Philby.

London and the south-east of England formed an extremely important axis: the Venona decrypts also revealed that there was a female agent working in the area of Oxford, who was key in passing on signals from Klaus Fuchs without her secret radio equipment being detected. In the messages, she was referred to as SONIA (and later acquired the nickname 'Red Sonia'). This was Ursula Beurton, who had managed to evade the attentions of the Radio Security Service by concealing a large transmitter within a stone garden wall.

This was not abstract paranoia, or a deliberate demonising of the Eastern Bloc. Rather, there was real anxiety. Venona exposed the most frightening vulnerability – first, as to the extent to which the Soviets had captured the hearts and minds of so many key British and American operatives; and second, the way that this capture had enabled the Soviets to acquire the gift of nuclear firepower. In Britain, even some regarded as being far to the left looked with misgivings across the Channel, into the darkness of that smouldering, smashed-up continent. They could hear the approach of the Soviet tanks from the east. Daily, they would read reports about Soviet progress in countries such as Hungary and Romania: the machinations by which elected politicians were gradually being replaced with Soviet sympathisers, making it easier for the Kremlin to absorb fresh territory without even firing a shot. And it was in Germany that all these anxieties would reach an early pitch, in the 1948 crisis that marked the start of open, formal hostilities in the Cold War. The secret listeners feeding messages back to the London Signals Intelligence Centre at Eastcote were intercepting communications that could decide the fate of Europe for an age to come.

Chapter Nine

The Torn City

The black-and-white photographs of ruined Germany are almost over-familiar now: the hollowed-out wrecks of churches, of offices, of railway stations. Such images are less familiar in full-colour. There is something quite extraordinary about seeing a photograph of a young woman in a white skirt walk along a street containing only the jagged shells of buildings, while above her, the summer sky glows with richest blue. If the Third World War was to have broken out at the end of the 1940s, then this land would have been one of the most likely sparking points. The British, Americans, French and Soviets each had their own sectors of Germany to govern and more particularly, to guard. But the Western powers had the added tension created by Stalin's desire to see Germany swallowed whole and subsumed into the Soviet Union.

This was the situation that the men and women at the London Signals Intelligence Centre or GCHQ were monitoring with particular care. They had been watching closely as so many of the smaller Eastern European states fell into Stalin's close grip. They had also been observing the situation in Germany as the process of 'de-Nazifying' the population unfolded. There were also the Nuremberg trials of the Nazi leadership. As historian Tony Judt observed, one crucial factor threatened to undermine the sense that these trials were truly just, and that was the presence among the judging authorities of Soviets. The behaviour of the Soviet army on its rampage through to Berlin was hardly a secret; but their atrocities went unremarked. As the diplomat George Kennan said: 'The only implication this procedure could convey was, after all, that such crimes were justifiable and forgivable when committed by the leaders of one government, under one set of circumstances, but unjustifiable and unforgivable, and to be punished by death, when committed by another government under another set of circumstances.'[1]

At the heart of this febrile and dangerously unstable and split nation was the city of Berlin, itself partitioned into four sectors. The city lay deep within the Soviet-controlled area of East Germany; but West Berlin was governed by the Americans, British and French.

There were already two clashing economic philosophies. The Americans, understanding quite how close Europe was to further conflict and to being engulfed entirely by the ideology of Communism, knew that it had to move decisively to restore the functioning of the continent's most productive powerhouse. West Germany would have to be put back on its feet. The US Secretary of State George C Marshall had toured the country and had left convinced that fascism could quite easily rise from its recent grave. The answer, he was certain, was vast quantities of US aid: finances far and beyond the restrictive loans that had been given to the British and the French. Europe needed a huge injection of money both for rebuilding and for firing up economies that were clinically dead.

Conferences had been held in 1947 at which the countries hoping to receive this US beneficence registered their interest. Among those countries were Poland, Hungary and Albania. But the Soviets walked out of talks. Stalin, avers Tony Judt, was suspicious. And possibly rightly so: for when looked at from the Communist angle, was this not a form of economic colonisation? The offer of such vast sums would hardly come without strict terms and conditions attached, one of which would certainly be that the recipients would have to be liberal democracies.

But this meant that while Western Europe would get the US cash, the small states of Eastern Europe would get nothing. Judt cites the case of Czechoslovakia, which would have been desperately grateful for any money. Even though the Soviet troops had long left that country, and even though there had been nothing in the way of hard menaces or threats from the Kremlin, the Czech government withdrew from any offer of Marshall Aid. Stalin did not have to point a gun. The Czechs – like the Bulgarians, Romanians, Latvians, Lithuanians, Albanians and Poles – understood that he was the power in their part of the continent.

Yet the Marshall Plan and its fallout also had a most particular effect upon Berlin, the city that was to come to symbolise all the most bitter and dangerous divisions of the Cold War. In 1948, the standard unit of currency under the Nazis, the Reichsmark, was at last replaced. The new currency had been printed under conditions of ferocious secrecy in America, and then shipped over, to be revealed. This was the Deutschmark. Citizens of West Germany – and West Berlin – were allowed to trade in limited amounts of their Reichsmarks for the new Deutschmark notes. There were economic casualties: those lucky few who had savings, for instance, found that they were wiped out instantly. But this was a preparatory move towards West Germany being re-established as a functioning economy and a nation once more. However, the Deutschmark's introduction triggered defensive action from Stalin. In response, East Germany got its own currency, from Moscow. And in Berlin, there was a city now divided more sharply than ever by two forms of currency.

This, to Stalin, was unendurable – the idea of the American capitalist Deutschmark seeping through to East Berlin and by extension, out into the Soviet-controlled sector of Germany more generally. This proved to be the trigger for the sharpest Cold War crisis yet: the Berlin Blockade of 1948.

This emergency – itself the trigger for fresh nuclear neurosis – unfolded some 13 years before the vast, sinister bulk of the Berlin Wall went up. Before then, the city's borders were rather more porous. Even so, it still proved relatively simple in 1948 for the Soviets to start cutting off the Western sector of the city. To all intents, they started strangling it.

The Blockade began when Stalin's soldiers blocked all the railway lines going in and out of West Berlin. This blockage then extended to the canals. And then the roads. The closing up of supply lines had echoes of a medieval siege: trains and lorries and trucks – bearing supplies of fresh produce, plus other food and essential supplies – were stopped from getting through. The menace was palpable. There were insufficient Allied forces in the Western sector to challenge them. But what was it that Stalin was trying to achieve? The asphyxiation of the Western half of the city? Or something even worse?

'To the Allies, this blockade seemed more than mere mischief,' wrote historian (and contemporary observer) ES Turner. 'It was a pretext for driving them out of Berlin, preparatory to consolidating and expanding Soviet power westward, which would have been seen as an open invitation to the Third World War. Those who lived through the months of the Berlin airlift need no reminding of what a nerve-fraying period it was. The Soviet presence in the heart of Europe was like one of those amorphous monsters that grip and immobilise the sleeper in a full-blooded nightmare. Was it conceivable that Stalin, who looked on Berlin as his by conquest, would hesitate to destroy any "air bridge" that the West might inaugurate . . .?'[2]

The currency had been one trigger point for this sinister crisis; but in fact, there would have been some form of hostility whatever had happened: these two cities, governed by two implacably opposed ideologies, were pushing against one another with increasing friction. In the preceding months, there had been angry gestures and signs, all conducted along fractured Berlin streets; from the Soviet planes flying insolently over British RAF bases to the equally impertinent British response, spying on Soviet military build-ups from the sky.

Perhaps the codebreakers and the interceptors should have been able to see the blockade crisis coming. (This was a little before the cryptological disaster occasioned by the Soviets overhauling their entire code system, of which more in a later chapter). In fact, some time back, the RAF and the British Army had realised that the Y Service, which had been reduced very heavily in size since the end of the war, would now have to expand in numbers once more. Professor RV Jones – the young man who had been central to so many scientific innovations throughout the war, and was later to become scientific adviser to the codebreakers – recalled this period in his book *Reflections On Intelligence*. His startling and rather contrary view – bearing in mind all the work that had been going on back in Eastcote – was that the cryptologists had not been sharp enough when it came to the Soviet Union.

'In the post-war maelstrom,' he wrote, 'signals intelligence had paid little if any attention to Russian radar and almost the only interceptions that were being made came from the unit that I had established in 1946 with Eric Ackermann near Obernkirchen . . . In the meantime, GCHQ had prepared a new charter for itself and this charter included responsibility for intercepting all Russian signals, both communications and radar. Then, armed with this charter for which they had obtained approval, without my predecessor as Director of Scientific Intelligence having the chance to comment, they proposed to take Ackermann and his unit over. I was very much concerned to be presented with the *fait accompli*, for I was sure that GCHQ, for all their ability in communications intelligence and cryptography . . . had neither the interest . . . nor the expertise to study the technical transmission associated with radar and radio navigation (ELINT) [or "electronic intelligence"]. As a quid pro quo for losing my direct control of Ackerman's unit in Germany,' Professor Jones concluded, 'an uneasy compromise was reached in which I was to be the scientific adviser to GCHQ.'[3]

And yet in West Berlin the army and the RAF and GCHQ would most certainly have been acutely aware that constant monitoring was required. Dr Jones must have exaggerated a little. Only a little later, even the rawest National Service recruits to the Y Service were routinely instructed in the basics of the Russian language. For those personnel already based in West Berlin, the city had been clearly seething with espionage and danger ever since the Nazis fell.

And for secret listeners, with their uncomfortable, almost intimate proximity to the Soviets, the events of the Blockade were only to sharpen the fervid atmosphere. Before those months, the eerie ruined night-time streets of Berlin had echoed with the footsteps of East German women, touting for business among the young British men venturing out from behind their barbed-wire fences. Self-evidently, all such encounters were sharply discouraged by the authorities, fearing all manner of espionage honey-traps. There was a clandestine black market too: civilians from the Eastern sector hoping to do trade with British personnel in return for valued Deutschmarks; quiet deals done in the shadows of hollowed, eyeless buildings deep into the night – the British coming away with Russian vodka and sometimes Russian gramophone records.

But the Berlin Blockade now saw the Western Allies' sector isolated. With roads and railway lines steadfastly obstructed by East German and Soviet troops, there was the danger of the Western side of the city swiftly being starved. Given the recent desperate conditions of the fall of Berlin in 1945, the stress this would have placed upon the local population could have provoked unstoppable unrest and violence, a trigger point for more aggression from the Soviets, and then a dreadful escalation of hostility between the Soviets and the Western Allies. The people of West Berlin had to be fed by any conceivable means. As a result, there began an enormous operation to send in supplies by air. In other words, foodstuffs would be flown in to Tempelhof airport.

This is what then unfolded: those streams of aeroplanes swooping down from grey Berlin skies, an image of resistance to implacable Soviet tyranny transmitted to the wider world. The population of West Berlin did not starve; and the Soviet Air Force did not dare to shoot down aircraft bearing food.

Even to this day, there is some confusion and speculation about what exactly Stalin's intentions were in the Berlin Blockade. At the time, there were some in the US military who had little doubt that this was the opening salvo of the Third World War. Others sensed that he was extemporising; that he had to react to what he would have seen as the contamination of East Berlin, not just economically but culturally as well.

Was it the first step to a larger objective? The swallowing of Berlin in its entirety? Or indeed the subsuming of the whole of Germany into the Soviet system? The exact signals intelligence that was being relayed from West Berlin back through to Eastcote, and thence to the Joint Intelligence Committee and the desk of foreign secretary Ernest Bevin is not yet available; yet it must have been enough to cement a firm view in Bevin's mind, because this proud left-wing politician was determined that the Americans should show their nuclear hand by 'sending B-29s over'.

The B-29s were the craft that delivered atomic payloads; this was a moment when the Americans had overwhelming superiority. (Indeed, it was a global superiority that drove some in the British government mad; it was Ernest Bevin who insisted to cabinet that the UK simply had to have the atomic bomb itself 'with a Union Jack on the top of it' if it was ever to show its face at world security meetings.)

Yet here was also the first Cold War international crisis that highlighted the need for the chess player's mentality on both sides. In 1948, neither the Allies nor Stalin's forces were in any condition to fight a protracted land war. The exhaustion was psychological as well as physical. Equally, though, if the Soviets had made a determined push, then it would have been possible, feasible even, for them to capture the whole of Berlin; after all, as noted, the city was an island in the middle of a vast red Communist ocean. And having secured Berlin, they could have gradually inched Soviet-controlled Germany's border westwards. They wanted to browbeat the tired British into leaving; they had no reason to believe that the Americans would stay in Germany any longer than they had to. In other words, the Soviet calculation might have been that Germany could be made theirs – the nation reunited under Soviet control – without a shot being fired. But the Americans were more than implacable: such an invasion would have been an outright declaration of warfare between the globe's new superpowers. And the question is: at what point would the Americans have dropped the atomic bomb on Moscow?

With even Ernest Bevin calling out for nuclear intervention (if not actual bombing), there were others in Washington DC's military establishment who felt that a pre-emptive strike on Moscow might be the way to defuse future Communist threats. Their voices, while never prevailing, grew sharper. Quite apart from the inconceivable scale of the mass murders that he perpetrated, Stalin is today also associated with twitching paranoia; yet perhaps he was paranoid with good reason.

In the case of the Berlin Blockade, it never even came to threats: the combined aviation skills of the American, British, French and Canadian air forces succeeded in making thousands of flights over Soviet territory to bring in supplies not only of food, but of fuel too. For some pilots, there were concerns that the ubiquitous coal dust above the city could get into their instruments and bring planes down; and as it happened, this was perhaps the most serious threat that the aeroplanes faced. Wisely, the Soviets forbore from making any attacks on these aerial convoys; any such move really might have been the trigger for nuclear Armageddon.

One Y service veteran remembered bitterly that even with supplies getting through, the winter of 1948 was atrocious, and life in West Berlin was uncomfortable; the freezing weather only served to heighten the sense of crisis in the besieged city. But the blockade was also an indication that signals intelligence needed a recruitment drive. It was from this point onwards that the army and air force Y services funnelled ever more young men through into the business of secret interception. And more units – not just in Berlin but throughout West Germany – sprang up. The Soviet miscalculation was that the Allies would not have the will to defend their sector of Germany. In fact, certainly in some corners of Whitehall, there were two urgent objectives. Not merely attempting to halt the progress of Communism but also – secretly – making it as difficult as possible for the two halves of Germany to reunite. Despite all the fine efforts to 'de-Nazify' an entire population, the calculation in Britain was that a reunited Germany would inevitably once more become a threat to the entire world. Frankly rather better to keep the country in two fragments: it suited the British very well to remain right where they were throughout West Germany.

Ironically, the airlift in fact turned out to be even more effective than road, rail and canal when it came to keeping West Berlin in essential supplies; far from starvation, excited schoolchildren looked to the skies to see where the next bountiful supplies of food and treats would be coming in. By the spring of 1949, the Soviets lifted the blockade. But this shaming withdrawal brought no relaxation in international relations. Indeed, it did a great deal to harden hearts; now the scale of Soviet ambitions and dreams had been exposed. As the later Labour Chancellor Denis Healey was to observe, it was clear that Soviet boots could, if Stalin so willed it, march all the way to the coast of the North Sea.

Plans for a new North Atlantic military treaty began to coalesce in talks between America and Western allies about the organisation that would become known as NATO. And as they did so, the efforts and activities of the London Signals Intelligence Centre at Eastcote were stepped up, not just in Germany but in other strategic territories in Western Europe that abutted an Eastern bloc ever more tightly drawn into the Soviet orbit.

Prague had succumbed in 1948: the post-war Czech government had been overthrown in a meticulously organised Communist Party coup and Czechoslovakia was now very firmly a Soviet serf state – one that was also in a parlous economic condition thanks to its refusal of Marshall Aid.

And these, curiously, were the economic roots of the Cold War; in a very short time, (West) Germany had gone from being an aggressor country that had to be occupied in order to quell its conquering, murdering impulses, to a nation that instead had to be protected from Soviet advances. Even more curiously, this move from taking economic aid from America to the seeking of military aid was being pushed by Britain's foreign secretary Ernest Bevin. It was he who was the first to suggest that American forces not only take up permanent residence in Europe, but they should sign an official treaty with other Allied countries in order, as he saw it, to stand firm against the Soviet threat. This would incidentally mean the siting of American weapons and missiles on permanent bases on British soil. As far as Bevin saw it, the necessity was great. It was in everyone's interests to be able to take cover behind America's protective cloak.

There was also quite an astonishing industrial phenomenon taking place at the heart of Western Europe in this period: even amid the rubble and the water-filled craters where once had been houses and shops, and even before the Americans' financial aid actually materialised, the economies of West Germany, France and Britain were humming along ever faster, and actually beginning to exceed pre-war productivity. The Marshall Plan money was certainly vital to West Germany – but not, as so many now assume, for simply keeping the lights on and getting bread into the shops. Instead, German industrialists – for there was still a very serious industrial core, even after all those RAF thousand-bomber raids – were using the money, via the government, to invest heavily in their own concerns, funding expansion and new technology.

The result was that by the time of the Berlin Blockade, the German economy, boosted by this steady and stable new currency, the Deutschmark, was taking off into the stratosphere. Obviously there were extremely productive coal- and steel-producing regions like the Ruhr – which itself was under international control – but it was more than that. Across Western Europe (even in dreary, pinched Britain), there was a post-war stirring of a furious desire for material goods. The 1950s consumer boom was a little way off, but it fizzed in the ashes of all that carnage.

The security of the continent required intelligence; and West Germany proved both for the British and the Americans a prime base for listening operations. Signals intelligence units dotted around the country could reach not only East Germany but further yet into the central reaches of Europe. As well as the day-to-day messages – those intercepted and put to use during the Berlin Blockade – there was also the element of direction finding. Fixing on the source of radio signals deep into Eastern Europe would give Britain and America an idea of the disposition of Soviet forces from day to day, hour to hour. This meant monitoring Poland and Czechoslovakia, and beyond too. This was not war, and as a result, there was not, on a day-to-day basis, that much in the way of astounding secret intelligence. The key to this period, for Eastcote, and also for its American counterparts, was intelligence in the deeper sense: the use of interception to see more clearly into the heart of the other side – what the Soviets were thinking, how they were reacting, how bellicose they were, how they viewed the life of the West as compared to the East. This was a period in which Stalin was, according to some, still perfectly confident that capitalism must fail. He had seen it implode under Hitler and the Nazis; he did not see why it should not be the case with America and Britain too.

But the introduction of the Deutschmark, the sudden revving up of industrial might, and the clear signs of growing Western wealth were a source of disturbance. Given that the chief source of any conflict is arguably economic at root, many anticipated a flashpoint developing.

From the point of view of British intelligence, there was an element of brinkmanship, too; during the Berlin blockade, there was an experimental

RAF flight over East German territory. Part of this was to do with brand-new electronic eavesdropping technology (of which more in a later chapter). But this was also a deliberate jangling of the spider's web, to see from which direction and how fast the spider would respond to the vibration. This was the new world of electronic intelligence, in which all those at Eastcote were taking a very close interest; that is, intelligence and communications gathered up by electronic means, and then analysed by the Eastcote cryptographers.

After the coup in Czechoslovakia and then the blockade of Berlin – the first concrete signs of Stalin grabbing what power he could in Europe – the work of the Cold War codebreakers was suitably stepped up. There were other corners of Europe that were particularly vulnerable, states and regions with local Communist parties that, in the wake of the conflict, seemed to attract more and more support. Greece was one of those acutely sensitive and – at the time – unhappy regions. For the Greeks, the war had not ended; it had instead been succeeded by bloody and bitter civil war. And in the swirling vortex of murderous passions, there were signs of the Soviets attempting to gain influence, eager for the prospect of a foothold in the Mediterranean. Not very far away, on Cyprus, a British listening station was focused implacably on monitoring and following every last movement of the Soviets.

The secret listeners on Cyprus were also carefully eavesdropping on Yugoslavia. Its leader Joseph Tito, while understanding that geographically it would be impossible for his country to keep Stalin's Russia at arm's length, was even so showing a remarkable spirit of independence. Very rare among Balkan and Central European leaders, he seemed not remotely cowed by Stalin's power; and this lack of fear served in turn to stoke Stalin's distrust of him. But this was to prove the start of a murderously farcical series of misunderstandings. Stalin, in his anger against Tito, expelled the Yugoslav Communist Party from the Cominform, the international Communist organisation. This, in turn, was misinterpreted by Britain and America; in Washington, it was assumed that Tito – defiant and proud – had expelled himself. And so, even though he was a devout Communist, the Americans and the British decided that he was to be supported at all costs as an anti-Stalinist. As historian Beatrice Heuser has noted, Yugoslavia was indeed to receive significant amounts of US financial aid. But not before there were further carnivals of confusion as the Central Intelligence Agency then attempted in 1949 to depose Tito and have him replaced (they failed – he stayed where he was and held this madly disparate country together even beyond his death in 1980).

But this is also an illustration of how intercepted intelligence – no matter how ingeniously sourced, how meticulously cross-referenced, how brilliantly comprehensive – is still subject to interpretation in the end. Messages and coded communications were one thing; but politics is as tangled and complex as the human heart itself, and sometimes the desires and impulses and actions of strangers – no matter if one listens to their every word – can still be difficult to fathom. In Yugoslavia, a nation that contained so many other nations – Serbia, Croatia, Bosnia, Macedonia – those ambiguities were woven deep into a living, pulsing history. Misinterpretation would be almost inevitable.

Elsewhere, Bulgaria was a focus of interest for the Allies, but again in the sense that it had little choice but to submit to the overwhelming dominance of Russia. Yet at that very early post-war stage, to some there was no such inevitability. As Beatrice Heuser has written, a great many American politicians thought it was eminently feasible that rather than becoming satellite states, these smaller countries would yearn for the freedom and comforts of the American way of life. To not want to do so, they reasoned, would surely be perverse and irrational.

In 1948, secretary of state George Marshall – whose plan in essence was the blueprint for the structure of Europe that we see today – told a group of US ambassadors: 'The ultimate United States objective toward Soviet Balkan satellites – Yugoslavia, Albania, Bulgaria, Rumania and Hungary – may be summarized as the establishment of those states as democratic independent members of the family of nations, under conditions guaranteeing their peoples effective enjoyment of human rights and non-discrimination against US interests and interests of other peace-loving states.'

More, he said, the Americans were anxious to see the liberation of these states from the 'totalitarian Soviet Balkan hegemony which has thwarted the democratic will of the majority of the peoples, infringed their independence and sovereignty and subjugated them to the domination of Moscow'. Nor were they intending to stand by passively. While the British codebreakers had been some way ahead of the Americans when it came to suspicion and dislike of the Soviet system, by 1948 the American government was very firmly framing the forthcoming struggle in Manichaean terms. President Harry S Truman – perhaps partly in the wake of Venona's uncovering of so many US agents working covertly for Stalin – now declared in secret briefings that, in essence, it was now the United States versus the threat of world Communism. In other words, there were now two mighty forces in the world – and if you were not firmly aligned with one, then you must surely be aligned with the other. There seemed little room for any kind of middle ground.

Open hostilities were to be avoided; even with the economies of Western Europe firing back into life, the situation was still terrifyingly precarious. Yet even then, fascinatingly, it was the British Labour government that proved startlingly bullish. It had been monitoring, as mentioned, the ferocious Greek civil war; and the Foreign Office and the British security services had concluded that this was in large part being fomented by Stalin's agents: the aim, squarely, was to turn Greece Communist. Was there action that could be taken to counterbalance this? The British government thought so. In 1948, it made a close study of the state of Albania, which had also fallen to totalitarian Communism under Enver Hoxha. Would it be possible to trigger a civil war there – in order to bring it into the sphere of the West? Julian Amery, who had taken part in covert wartime operations there, was one of the men asked to look into the possibilities, and how such a gambit might work.

There were a number of Albanian exiles, and had been ever since the end of the war. If members of this politically volatile group were to be dropped back in to their home country, could they spark a suitable conflict? The Americans were brought in on the idea, and they agreed. For various reasons, it all came to nothing; but it was a measure of the extent to which Britain – even while in the throes of imperial withdrawal – still felt that it had a serious duty on the global stage.

Elsewhere in the region, Cyprus had been a British colony since the end of the First World War; once 'rented' out to the British by the Ottoman empire, it was taken over completely at the dissolution of that empire and became a key strategic post for the British. The corner of the island reserved for surveillance operations – Ayios Nikolaos – was within the British military base, and its immense value was widely understood; the Americans were especially keenly interested in the material that was being produced there. They, too, set up base here; a little later on, even the FBI would have a foothold, monitoring and analysing all media broadcasts in the region. Back in England, the BBC had some involvement in this, too: its Monitoring Service at Caversham in Oxfordshire was also taking in all sorts of broadcasts relayed from Cyprus and other Middle East stations and sharing items of interest with the Americans.

As the Cold War intensified, the Cyprus base was to acquire greater weight and importance; it was from here that the interceptors could reach deep into the Soviet Union; it was from here that disturbances detected in the atmosphere would mark Soviet nuclear testing. In the late 1940s, Cyprus also acquired a much more controversial use. Jewish refugees, their families slaughtered, the survivors subsisting in Displaced Person camps in Eastern Europe, were now attempting in far greater numbers to reach Palestine; the Jews would at last, and after so many years of broken promises, have their homeland. But the British, who still held the mandate for Palestine, did their utmost to shut the gates against this influx. The Jewish refugees they apprehended in the Mediterranean were instead diverted to Cyprus. From concentration camps in Poland to prison camps in the Mediterranean; amid the outcries about insensitivity and brutality, this was also a sign of a fast-changing world, and a world in which Britain's own stature was crumbling with quite extraordinary speed. Nowhere was this more so than in the continent of Asia, where the sudden collapse of British rule was to have such immediate violent consequences, and at a time when intelligence was needed more than ever.

Chapter Ten

A Continent on Fire

The imminent collapse of the British Empire was not only a source of dismay to die-hard right-wing traditionalists. There were also those around Clement Attlee who were agitated by the prospect. Among them was his foreign secretary Ernest Bevin who, in the immediate aftermath of the war, was anxious that the nation would maintain its 'prestige' – that is, to hold on to its clout around international conference tables. But the Empire was imploding, unable to bear its own weight. It had been some time since colonial possessions had provided illimitable riches in trade and merchandise. The money required to rule was running out. From the point of view of the codebreakers, something akin to an elegant conjuring trick was needed; a means of Britain's withdrawing from its colonies with such grace and abundant goodwill that these newly independent countries would still be happy to host top-secret cypher stations.

But the slide from power occurred with breathtaking speed. The entire world was being reshaped; and to a large extent, political pressure for this remoulding was coming from America, which painted itself as being aggressively 'anti-colonialist'. It had its own reasons for its quiet determination to see Britain completely shorn of its old imperial possessions.

There was a whole new world of trading possibilities to be opened up, to America's advantage; and with them new spheres of geopolitical influence. The old British Empire was, as many American politicians saw it, a fast-emptying space, a void that would have to be filled.

Paradoxically, however, the Americans also needed Britain to maintain good relationships with its old possessions: the younger nation, though enormously powerful, was still a relative newcomer to these wider geopolitics; the elder nation had decades, centuries, of accumulated international dealings. Many of Britain's colonies and mandates were in crucial positions when it came to airfields and intercept stations. If ever the day came that a nuclear attack had to be launched against the Soviet Union via the Urals, for instance, the atomic weaponry could hardly come from Britain – no bomber could fly so far. An airfield in Peshawar (in what was then India and is today Pakistan), however, would be quite a different matter. Equally, the Americans needed signals intelligence in these places too, providing real-time analysis and commentary.

In the case of India, the question of independence – and just how speedily it could come – was causing the British to buckle from several angles. Even if there had been the will to hang on to the subcontinent – which there was not – political gravity was pressing down hard on the government. First, the Indian independence movement was terrifically powerful; allied to this was the fact that this movement had the goodwill of the rest of the world. Plus, Britain could simply no longer afford to hold on to its old jewel in the crown. It could scarcely afford to house its own population back at home. So it was inevitable that the Indian people would take control of their own destinies. Attlee's hope was that they would at least stay within the Commonwealth.

He wanted to bargain: independence in return for certain favours. India could go its own way so long as British (and by extension American) forces and intelligence could continue to operate discreetly within its sphere.

The codebreakers and the secret listeners had been in India for almost as long as the original British merchants. Even though the technology of the 19th-century Great Game with Russia had obviously transformed – no more codes drawn into etchings of local butterflies, for instance – the principles of the contest remained the same. Now, strategists realised, the gradual British withdrawal from the Middle East might make Stalin

think of striking through a newly vulnerable India, to get at the treasure
of the oilfields that lay west of it. So in terms of early Cold War paranoia,
India was right at the forefront of intelligence anxiety; the British and the
Americans needed it dearly, not least for help to keep the Middle East
secure for their own requirements.

One of the most prominent codebreakers in India throughout the
war had been Lieutenant Colonel Patrick Marr-Johnson; though he was
experienced and clever, he was also an abrupt figure with a sharp temper
who seems to have been cordially disliked by many. However, like so many
of the codebreakers, he had a startlingly rich hinterland. Whereas other
code geniuses tended to have great aptitudes for music, Marr-Johnson's
talents lay towards poetry. Indeed, some years later, he had several
volumes of poetry published: not what one would immediately expect
from an abrasive military intelligence man who had spent so much time
losing litres of sweat in remote jungle intercept stations. Marr-Johnson
– who as we have seen had made valuable friends in Washington DC –
had travelled out to the Wireless Experimental Centre in the salubrious
suburbs of Delhi, from where he and his colleagues could see another
great danger looming.

Independence for India would clearly not be enough: the subcontinent's
Muslim population wanted to be certain of their own security, and the
obvious means of achieving that would be a form of secession. A state
within a state was one possibility – but a full separation of Muslims and
Hindus was gathering momentum.

The codebreakers and others in intelligence could see very well
what the possible consequence of this would be: bloody civil war, with
millions of casualties – an entire continent tearing itself apart. For some
colonial British figures who were still there, this might have seemed a
distant and abstract prospect; for instance, in some intercept stations,
the officers still had their Indian servants who made the tea, obeyed
the signs on certain doors that declared 'No entry – to anyone at all'
(these were the most secret decryption rooms) and made their beds.
The officers and their wives still dined out in very smart restaurants,
went dancing at the smartest, coolest clubs. All these luxuries were

supremely attainable, in a way that they most certainly were not back home; not just the material comforts, but also the languorous evenings of rich sunsets and the pale glow of dancing fireflies. The fight to get a crowbar into the Japanese wartime codes had been as exhausting and even more monotonous and mentally tough than the struggle against Enigma. Yet for many, including men in the Intelligence Corps who had never before left England, India had been a new world of colour and strangeness and splendour.

Young Peter Budd – just 19 years old when the war against Japan ended – had been monitoring Japanese signals all over the subcontinent (including an astonishing 18-month stint in the remote paradise of the Cocos Islands). He was now conscious, as this chapter of empire began to close and the targets swiftly began to change, that he was a witness to history. Budd, a naval signals man for the Y Service, was being transferred to a defiantly landlocked intercept station near the North-West Frontier. He arrived by rail at Delhi. 'A lot of Indians lived on the station under cover,' recalls Budd. 'We were sitting there waiting for the Bombay train to come in. Suddenly about a thousand Indians poured in. I was pushed right up to the edge of the rails.' The reason for the commotion? 'Closer to me than you are was Gandhi,' says Mr Budd. 'And next to him was Nehru.' Both had just come from talks with Sir Stafford Cripps, the British president of the Board of Trade.

Budd's journey took him to a base just outside Karachi where he soon settled down to a life of intense work but abundant material awards. He and his colleagues were allowed to wear civilian clothes. And owing to a tangled bureaucracy resulting in unexpectedly high wages – they were assumed to be officers, when in fact they were not – Budd and his friends 'lived the life of Riley', as he says. 'We had tailor-made suits made from our own tailors, we ate out in restaurants.' When all of this came to an end, and Peter Budd found himself back in late-1940s Britain, living in the pinched suburbs of west London, he knew that he would always look back on that period of secret signals interception with exceptional vividness.

The push for Indian independence had gathered incredible speed, presenting new challenges. How could any authority, any nation, no matter how ingenious, plan the re-ordering of an entire landmass, overnight? And given the 1946 Soviet manoeuvres in Iran and close to the borders of Afghanistan, what was there to stop the territory fast moving into the Eastern bloc's sphere of influence? What of all the MI6 agents still stationed throughout India? There was one more security issue on this checklist: a mineral called thorium, which was bountiful in certain areas of India. Thorium was one of the prime ingredients needed for the new generation of atomic bombs. There was very little chance that the Americans were going to allow such a precious prize to lie unprotected and fall into the hands of Soviet atom bomb scientists.

On top of this, despite all the accusations of oppression and repression, the war had forged a strong visceral link between British colonial administrators and their subjects; two million Indian men had served in the armed forces and 87,000 men had been killed. Certainly, Britain owed India almightily; but was a swift withdrawal really the best thought-out means of repaying this debt? Lord Mountbatten was made Viceroy of India in 1947; plans for the partitioning of the country – with the Muslim populations granted the creation of Pakistan – were drawn up. Jawaharlal Nehru's Indian National Congress and Mohammed Jinnah's Muslim League had become convinced that this was the only way that Hindus and Muslims would co-exist in peace.

As it happened, not even that was enough. And while maps were being drafted by British officials, civil servants elsewhere were packing up all signs of their administration. This included intelligence: sensitive files concerning dealings with Muslim and Hindu groupings in various parts of the subcontinent were carefully destroyed.

During the war, the entirety of India had been peppered with Y Service stations sending invaluable material back to Bletchley Park about the Japanese. A number of Indians were being introduced to the latest techniques in signals intelligence and interception and now, as India prepared to slough off suffocating British rule, those sharp codebreaking operatives were beginning to move in.

But independence came seemingly before all sensible plans had been acted upon; for instance, the new maps showing what was to be Hindu and what was to be Muslim territory had not even yet been published. Partition was to turn into a mass stampede of panic and of terror.

Word spread through communities large and small, whispered by untold numbers of people, right across the subcontinent. The fearful rumours raged like a contagion; entire villages told themselves the exodus had to be made now, before religious enemies came to slaughter them. This, in turn, seemed to spark some form of homicidal hysteria, as murderous Muslims and Hindus alike set about fulfilling the others' worst fears.

In the north of the country particularly – the most sensitive in terms both of local hostilities and the wider geopolitical picture – the land was soon soaked with blood. At first, sick with apprehension and bewilderment, and then frantic with fear, millions of people, hearing word that their land was to become either Hindu or Muslim, began to pack up and flee. But they were not permitted to do so unmolested. These vast numbers of people, seeking to rush across these new borders that no-one had told them about, became the targets for criminals, desperadoes and for murderers who hated them for their beliefs. In some parts of the countries, there were columns of refugees 45 miles (55 kilometres) long making the dangerous journey towards sanctuary. So many of these people – especially the women – were targeted. Rape, murder, massacre; there were desperate, sickening scenes and there was no-one to offer help.

Railway trains were packed with terrified refugees. They would get held up by bandits and killers – and every single passenger on board would be murdered, leaving only the driver and guard alive so that the trains would then arrive in distant cities filled from top to bottom with corpses.

Amid this terrifying butchery and seemingly unstoppable anarchy, there was little in the way of useable intelligence; another complicating factor in the hasty handover. MI6 had tried to make some mutually satisfactory arrangements with the Indian secret authority that was to replace it. And indeed some progress had been made until Clement Attlee insisted that the Secret Intelligence Service withdraw from the country altogether: independence meant independence and the British had a duty to stay true to their promises.

But the widespread re-organisation of signals intelligence was one of the reasons why there was little prior indication of the horrific violence to come. In truth, even if there had been all the signals in the world available, what realistically could have been done? Added to this, Indian and Pakistani signals intelligence now had to start focusing on one another, in an atmosphere of rancorous and frightened suspicion, especially in disputed territories such as Kashmir. Across a mighty continent, everything appeared to be being made up on the hoof; and the mass suffering this caused was unstoppable and unimaginable.

Yet despite the carnage in the countryside, the handover of intelligence responsibility in the cities eventually became more orderly. British Army signals officers had been training up their Indian counterparts in various degrees of encryption and decryption. Some operators found that when partition came, they had to move swiftly. Norman Logan recalled: 'I was a member of the South Staffordshire regiment but was attached to 2nd Indian Airborne Division Signal Regiment after being converted to cyphers in 1946. The regiment was at that time situated in Clifton, which was part of Karachi . . . under the command of Lieutenant Colonel David Horsfield.

'Towards the spring of 1947,' Logan continued, 'the unit relocated . . . to Quetta and it was here that it saw the independence of both India and Pakistan in the August of that year. 2nd Indian Airborne Division Signal Regiment was designated an "Indian army unit" and moved very quickly from Quetta (Pakistan) into India. The British army contingent . . . moved to the transit camp in Karachi from where we were repatriated to the UK.'[1]

While MI6 had had to pack its bags, its sister service MI5 had made more subtle arrangements, and forged a close bond with the Delhi Intelligence Bureau. Despite all the horror of the mass migration, the British government held on to good will for having been willing to keep its promise to leave. To this end, Viceroy Mountbatten was to stay on another year until 1948.

And what of the Wireless Experimental Centre in New Delhi? The prospect of Indian independence meant a certain amount of precautionary spring-cleaning before a new wave of secret listeners came in. Codebreaker Alan Stripp remembered how the base was systematically purged of all sensitive material. 'Whole truckloads of paper', he wrote, were shovelled into a 'poorly designed and hastily built incinerator, from the chimney of which, as we watched, Top Secret documents wafted, half burned, over the astonished western suburbs of New Delhi.'[2]

Yet for all the turmoil that was to come to the region, there was a great deal of continuity, British officers working hand-in-glove with their Indian and Pakistani successors. Curiously, one reason for this was not anxiety about the Russians, and their ever-looming shadow over the mountains of Afghanistan, but actually about the Americans. Even at a time when the codebreakers were working with such unprecedented closeness, there were a few officials in Whitehall who feared that the Indian and Pakistani cypher bureaus would be lured into forming much stronger relationships with the US than with themselves; the US, after all, could hand over huge sums of money in return for all sorts of security investment. The British had nothing like that to offer. Added to this, the Americans had during the war established a large signals intelligence base for their own purposes in Delhi.

It is striking to think that even now – in fact, particularly now – the topic of American and Pakistani co-operation in matters of communications and codes is a subject of the most exquisite sensitivity and official silence. It has sometimes been said that the disputed region of Kashmir – bitterly tugged between nuclear-armed India and Pakistan for decades – is where the next world war will be ignited. These are places in which interceptors and codebreakers have always had to tread most lightly.

And no matter how much Lieutenant Colonel Patrick Marr-Johnson may have argued for the essential benevolence of British rule, there were recent catastrophic events in the subcontinent that appeared to prove otherwise, including the hideous 1943 rice famine which Britain had done little to help alleviate and which – even now – some suggest darkly was partly engineered by Churchill at a time when the Indian Nationalists were at their height.

And whatever Whitehall and indeed the codebreakers in Washington DC might have thought, Nehru and some around him were not at all convinced that a close security relationship should continue. Indeed,

Nehru considered that 'entanglement in the power politics of Great Powers' would only sharpen the hazards and dangers that India would be exposed to. He felt that the main threat to India was posed by the Soviet Union; and that if the Soviets chose to annexe India, Britain would not have anywhere near the strength to even begin to help. So why then provoke the Soviets by continuing a cosy relationship with the former colonialists?

Over in Ceylon, the vast listening base at HMS *Anderson* in Colombo – an onshore concern teeming with smart Morse experts and codebreakers – continued its work even as the country reached towards its own independence. Partly there was a sense that the Ceylonese government allowed its continuance as a way of avoiding finding itself subsumed within India's politics. There was also an element of subterfuge on the British part: most of the activities within HMS *Anderson* were top-secret, and indeed were to remain that way for some time after the war. The government of Ceylon simply did not know that this naval base was being used for surveillance purposes.

Nor did the Ceylonese authorities know just how vital this base was considered to be by Whitehall. The site was vast, the personnel boasted impressive numbers, and part of the incredibly secret work being done there was as a Far East branch of the Diplomatic Wireless Service, which made its focus the communications and traffic of foreign diplomats. The intercepts and decrypts would then be sent back to Eastcote.

Like the Wireless Experimental Centre in New Delhi, HMS *Anderson* still seemed very much steeped in the old empire. The base itself had been sited on a golf course. Those who came to work there marvelled at the lushness and occasionally startling diversity of the local wildlife; snakes were encountered frequently. Although white naval uniform was strictly adhered to, the less constricted out-of-hours life was alluring: Colombo itself was an attractive town with enough night-clubs and restaurants to keep young sophisticates happy. Then there was the world beyond, up in the hills; a world of incomparably rich tea plantation owners in sumptuous villas, attended by numerous servants. The atmosphere in those immediate post-war months cannot have given any indication that any of this was to change; the British were still in charge not merely politically, but culturally too.

The spirit of the base remained youthful; the young Morse experts and teleprinter operators loved putting on shows: cabarets, musicals, comedy revues. And indeed, the recruits kept coming: radio-mad boys, spotted as they reported for National Service, the combination of their intelligence and enthusiasm for a new generation of communications technology marking them out for the voyage into the colourful tropics.

One such young man, recruited in 1946, was Laurence Roberts. In fact, he had trained just before the end of the conflict at the secret station in Leighton Buzzard (then in Buckinghamshire), just a few miles from Bletchley Park (it was also at Leighton Buzzard that WAAFs learned about plotting and filtering for RAF Fighter Command). Laurence Roberts was a deft hand with technical issues such as Single Side Band Transmission, used in high-frequency radio circuits. He had also done some teaching at the nearby radio station base in Cardington, Bedfordshire. But in 1946, his expertise was required right the way across the world. He recalled: 'This time there was no secret destination. It was the Far East. After getting as far as Singapore and two weeks at a transit camp, it was back on a troopship and I finished up at another signal centre – Gangodewella, Ceylon (now Sri Lanka), five miles (eight kilometres) inland from the capital Colombo. This was peacetime overseas service and miles away from the "Active" job a few years earlier.'[3]

It might have lacked that immediate sense of urgency, but the stations in Colombo – as well as those in other colonial spots – were keeping an hour-by-hour watch on the larger picture unfolding in the region; so much was still uncertain, so little could be guessed about what the real Soviet intentions might be in this part of the world. And despite Roberts's sense of 'peacetime', some rules were still strictly observed. 'We even had to wear a proper uniform on duty, nothing like the Western desert,' he noted wryly. 'The one big plus sign was being able to get into the old colonial town of Colombo when off duty. By the time I got to Colombo,' he continued, 'a lot of the high speed W/T Morse circuits had converted to Radio Teleprinter Operation. It meant a whole new procedure system had to be learnt; a means of routing a message from originating station to its final destination by typing the instructions on to the original punched tape. It was slower than automatic Morse because the limiting speed of a teleprinter was 66.6 words per minute. But the saving was in not having to type the message out from the receiving Morse tape. It was a good system.'[4]

Life was not entirely friction-free in this rich paradise: secret though the work was, some of its technical aspects were of enormous interest to certain entrepreneurial locals. 'At Colombo . . . the transmitters were a few miles from the receiving station (which was at the main campsite) and they were connected by landlines for keying the transmitted signals,' remembered Laurence Roberts. 'The native population took a liking to the cable between the two stations and would steal lengths of it and turn it into profit. This would mean a shut-down of the W/T link until it could be repaired.' Happily, technology was making further jumps forward. 'The situation was resolved by the introduction of a microwave radio link between the receiving and transmitting station,' recalled Roberts. 'A special party came out from the UK (the radio branch of RAE Farnborough). I believe this was one of the first uses of microwave technology and it was very successful.'[5]

Incidentally, the Soviets had been working on similar technological lines – and the deployment of microwave lines to spy on Western embassies became the bane of many a politician's life, requiring military, security and political figures to zip themselves up in soundproof tents before talking.

Roberts's life in Ceylon was less fraught, although Indian independence in 1947 brought a new, slightly more fervid atmosphere to Colombo. Ceylon's own independence was not too far off. 'My stay at Colombo was at the time that India and Ceylon gained independent status . . . and later, when Mahatma Gandhi was assassinated [in 1948], resulting in a lot of tension among the local population. Colombo was out of bounds and lots of extra guards were posted and at one time nobody was allowed out. But gunboat diplomacy was still a means of restoring order in those days. A Royal Navy cruiser came into Colombo harbour, disembarked the Royal Marine band and all available hands and marched through the town to the naval barracks.'[6]

The days were fast approaching when such an attitude would be utterly unthinkable. Laurence Roberts was, not too long after this incident, posted back to Britain; the last problem he had wrestled with in terms of signals intelligence was sun spots: in that part of the world, such astronomical phenomena could cause very real difficulties, resulting in black-outs and signals having to be sent back to Britain via submarine cable.

Ceylon's independence came in 1948, just as India and Pakistan were being confirmed in their own new status. But the work at HMS *Anderson* continued without any stoppages. It has been suggested that the Americans were very keen to set up a listening station outside Colombo, which would have been run under the aegis of the US Navy. Their desire was, however, thwarted. The Ceylonese government was content to see the British forces continue in place; the presence of the Americans would have seemed too much of an unwelcome intrusion. Of course, neither they nor indeed any other nation-state would have known at that time the startling extent to which the British and Americans were in any case sharing information and intelligence. The positioning of the Colombo base was particularly advantageous and fruitful in the intelligence that it continued to provide to both allies.

Yet in strictly technical terms, HMS *Anderson*, parked as it was between a busy railway line and a vast farm of electricity pylons and beneath the landing path of a nearby airport, was never the most ideal location from which to listen to faint signals in the first place; during the war, it had been a matter of extemporisation (the base had first been evacuated across the Indian ocean to Mombasa after a Japanese attack; on its return in 1943, the underlying structural difficulties had never been fully addressed). But the camp stayed where it was for the next couple of years, the British personnel continuing to be drawn from bright young lads, and all members of the camp remaining enthusiastic for Colombo's bright and exotic life. Eventually, the base was asked by the Ceylonese authorities to move a few miles away (the reason was that the government had now earmarked the site for extensive property development). The British happily – and gratefully – complied. An extensive and extremely expensive new secret interception complex was built a few miles away in the hills of Perkar (eliminating all the old annoyances to do with electricity pylons). The Ceylonese authorities were still not told that the main role of the base was interception.

But then, several years later in the mid-1950s, Britain's attempt to seize the Suez Canal back from Egypt's Colonel Nasser, resulting in the country being roundly humiliated on the world stage, led to a turning-point further east. The Ceylonese authorities – infuriated by what they had seen as a contemptible imperial manoeuvre, and doubly furious that British naval ships had refuelled in Colombo – announced that they no longer wanted the British in their territory. Britain tried in vain to protest. The post-colonial slide seemed inexorable.

Elsewhere in the region, that process was rapid and abrupt; particularly so in Burma, where so many had fought such horrific battles in the humid jungles against the Japanese. It had been a war of filthy, terrifying forest skirmishes, of monsoons, vampire-like insects and suffocating heat, of untidy gunshots and bayonets thrust deep into guts. For the secret listeners of the Y Service, tracking and monitoring every last Japanese transmission, the territory brought all kinds of technical difficulties. Dennis Underwood recalled how, as a young Y Service operative in 1945, Burma was a prospect of 'constant damp, always sweaty, plagued with prickly heat, message pads sticking to hands and wrists etc'. Then there were the tropical storms – many secret interceptors had hearing problems in later life. 'The lightning would blow the fuses in the antennae feeds so that we lost our stations,' recalled Underwood. 'Better than having the sets burned out though.'[9] The facilities proved a little more reliable (and better protected from the pervasive moisture) in the post-war years.

Strikingly enough, one codebreaker – Jean Valentine, the Wren who had been posted to HMS *Anderson* to work on Japanese codes – had in the interim returned to England with Clive Rooke, her husband-to-be; they married, lived in a London pock-marked by bomb-sites – and decided to move back east once more, to live in Burma's capital Rangoon. Clive Rooke had flown with the RAF; and now, as a commercial pilot with BOAC, the couple could transfer to this new territory and enjoy, in comparison to the general population, quite spectacular luxury (certainly when compared to the soot and the cold of London). Jean and Clive lived in a house with servants, which was handy for when it came to dealing with some of the local wildlife. 'I remember going into my bedroom one evening and between the bathroom and the dressing room, there was a snake coiled up,' recalled Jean. 'So I yelled for the boy [a servant] to come and deal with it – which he did – and then when I went off to bed, I found the snake's mate coiled up in the dressing room.'

But Burma was wildly volatile: there was the simmering genesis of a civil war between the (largely) coastal- and lowland-dwelling Burmese and the Karens, communities who lived in the hillier territories and who were often Anglophile – to the extent that it was said that they received help from former British officers when it came to planning insurrection. Developments in India had led a charismatic young Burmese soldier called Aung San to take up the cause of independence with Britain, and he did so in the full expectation that he would be able to take full control from that point onwards. According to some, the British had done an unusually bad job of governing Burma; indeed, the authorities had, through neglect and ineptness, contributed greatly to poverty and crime. Unlike India, the civil service was ramshackle, there was little in the way of public transport and even though food was plentiful, its distribution was frequently ropey.

Nonetheless, it was convenient for the British to try and maintain some kind of a toehold, and the Burmese and the Foreign Office were able to negotiate an understanding. After the signing of an independence agreement, Aung San's newly elected government would enjoy the protection of the British military for three more years. In return, of course, the British would have continued use of air bases and related stations. But this post-colonial agreement soon turned to bloodshed: in 1947, during a meeting of Parliament, Aung San and six of his cabinet colleagues were assassinated. The man behind the mass murder was swiftly identified as Aung San's chief political rival U Saw, who had a few years previously met with Winston Churchill to discuss Burma's future. The British authorities, in their last few weeks of colonial rule, put U Saw on trial. He was found guilty and sentenced to hang. It later emerged that U Saw and his political allies were being supplied with arms by renegade British officers, who were also giving weaponry to members of the Karen community.

But Burma, despite its border with China, was not quite so crucial to British interests as the territory of Malaya and Singapore, both recently wrested back from the Japanese. Indeed, Malaya was particularly important to Britain not just in defence terms, but also economically. Unlike India and Pakistan, this region, which was rich in rubber as well as other materials and minerals, still contributed hefty sums of money to the UK Treasury.

And the new-found independence of India and Pakistan was also to bring a fresh and unexpected difficulty to British security: both nations, utterly hostile to one another, were asking Britain to provide protection in various forms. It was an almost impossibly knotty dilemma for the Foreign and Colonial Office. To persuade India to stay within the Commonwealth – and thus at least spare a hole being punched in Britain's economy – it would be necessary to apply a great deal of charm and generosity and practical aid: specifically, of a military nature. Yet at the same time, Pakistan – with its hyper-sensitive borders, and its extreme proximity to the Soviet sphere of influence – needed to be kept happy, too. Supplying help and expertise to both sides, without the other knowing, would not be an ideal solution.

For Edward Travis and Nigel de Grey back at Eastcote, all these were matters of the highest seriousness, and they also in part illustrated the growing importance of their particular espionage speciality. One could fill Pakistan – from its mesmerising cities to its remotest rural communities – with secret agents on the ground, but there would still only be a limited amount of useful intelligence that they would be able to report back. Intercept stations, on the other hand, would enable the codebreakers to listen to Stalinist Russia's every heartbeat, across the vast plains and wastes with their industrial centres, particularly in the sensitive region from Siberia to Kazakhstan. Just as the West was beginning to become increasingly aware of its dependence on Middle Eastern oilfields, so too the Soviet Union would want to open up fresh lines of fuel to facilitate its modernisation. The job of what was still the London Signals Intelligence Centre was to listen out for the first indications of any incursion or infiltration, first into Pakistan, and then into the oilfields to the south and west of it. The process of decolonisation would have had an inevitable untidiness whatever happened: how does one dismantle a century of institutions overnight? But India and Pakistan were in what the Foreign Office termed the 'north tier' – countries adjoining Stalin's empire whose integrity was now under constant threat.

Travis and de Grey also had an additional pressure: a growing conviction among British and American military figures that the Third World War was a matter of months away. There were many who thought that it would happen no matter what: there were cracks and fissures, geopolitical fault lines stretching right the way around the globe. One of the agonies for the personnel at Eastcote at that time was that – by comparison – the Second World War itself had been simple. There had been a central problem to solve – either in the form of Enigma, Tunny, the Japanese JN-25 – and though the intellectual gymnastics required were awesome, the results were immediately effective. Here, in this suburb at the end of the Piccadilly Line, receiving bundles of transmissions from agitated, angry regions far across the world, the codebreakers were looking not so much at a Cold War as a kind of Ghost War. This was not like tracking the movements of U-Boats, or eavesdropping on Panzer divisions. This was trying to keep tabs on a mighty empire, that of Stalin's Russia, without ever being entirely certain what the intentions of that empire were.

This was a world of new regimes and new governments, many of which were far from being stable. And between 1947 and 1948, they also faced something of an unexpected internal development, to do with the culmination of an ancient Middle Eastern conflict.

Chapter Eleven

Exodus

It has been pointed out that one of the dark ironies of the codebreaking effort during the Second World War was that if the Germans had recruited their country's finest Jewish minds – as opposed to murdering them – then their cryptological departments would have been rather more successful. Certainly, Bletchley Park had been boosted by a great range of hugely talented Jewish recruits; many stayed on after the war to help found the new GCHQ. And many of those who left still maintained contact with the world of cryptology. But that is not to say that the experience of the Jewish codebreakers was universally comfortable. For some, the post-war landscape was to bring unexpected complications.

Yet the ethos of this new GCHQ – as well as its approach to the most intransigent problems – would much later find a powerful echo in Israel's extraordinarily effective modern equivalent: the intelligence department called Unit 8200. Indeed, some of the key philosophical lessons of the British codebreaking operation are still very much in place in Israel.

Among the first Jewish recruits to have been drawn to the codebreaking effort in 1939 had been Miriam Rothschild, a brilliant biologist, sister of Jacob and a member of the famous banking family. There was Professor Max Newman, the Cambridge mathematician who had been a tutor to the young Alan Turing. Among the Wrens was Ruth Bourne who, after having sat an intelligence test, guessed very quickly what line of work she was going to be ushered into. 'I had read enough spy novels,' she said. She added that for her, the urgency of helping the war effort had an extra dimension: the prospect of the Nazis invading Britain literally gave her nightmares.

Among the young undergraduates lured in from university were Walter Eytan and his brother Ernest. They had changed their name from Ettinghausen; and they had the distinction of being the only German-born men to work at Bletchley Park.

'The security clearance must have been singularly perceptive,' Walter Eytan wrote, 'since such antecedents might so easily have disqualified us for BP, and in the United States certainly would have done. I suppose the responsible officer, knowing or discovering that we were Jews, must have concluded, correctly, that we had an extra interest in fighting Hitler, and therefore might be even more ardent than the others at our BP work.'[1]

The nature of the war work was such that Eytan's dramatic post-war destiny was formed in that crucible. 'I may be the only one', he wrote, 'who will recall a peculiarly poignant moment when in late 1943 or early 1944 we intercepted a signal from a small German commissioned vessel in the Aegean, reporting that it was transporting Jews, I think from Rhodes or Kos, en route for Piraeus '*zur Endlösung*' ('for the final solution'). I had never seen or heard this expression before, but instinctively I knew what it must mean, and I have never forgotten that moment. I did not remark on it particularly to the others who were on duty at the time,' continued Eytan, 'perhaps not even to my brother – and of course never referred to it outside of BP, but it left its mark – down to the present day.'[2]

At Bletchley, Walter and Ernest had formed a Zionist society, and held many meetings and discussions over dinners and drinks. The overarching theme was, of course, the necessity of forming an Israeli state after the war: how it was to be achieved, how the mass immigration could be managed. Strikingly, these discussions – and the passions fomented – were to affect the careers of both brothers in profound ways.

With the war over, the Eytans elected to stay on with the codebreaking operation. With the move to Eastcote, Ernest became what was termed an 'intelligence librarian'. This was, in part, the crucial role of building up a codebreakers' library, to help pinpoint certain technical recurring terms emerging from decrypts. These could be anything from abstruse military details to the richer corners of cultural life. Meanwhile, his brother Walter Eytan's own life was very shortly to take a turn for the more dramatic.

In 1946 – as the wider world absorbed the horror of what had happened in Europe, and the abject conditions that the survivors were living in – Walter Eytan left GCHQ and took himself to Palestine. There was a state to be founded and he was determined to be in there at the very beginning of it.

In wider terms, the increasing tension and outbreaks of violence in Palestine created a fascinating fault line for the codebreakers and interceptors both in Britain – which of course still had the mandate over the territory – and in America too. Ever since the Balfour Declaration of 1917, the British government had been committed in principle to the establishment of a homeland for Jewish people. Yet in the intervening years, it had struggled – with the help of the military and the RAF – to try to keep the peace in the territory between warring Jews and Arabs. Sometimes the British methods – implemented against both sides – were both clumsy and casually brutal: for instance, the aerial bombing of settlements using increasingly sophisticated aviation and firepower. The result was that the British were ardently hated. Come the end of the war and it was clear that to a great many Jewish people, there was simply no time to be lost. Millions had been foully slaughtered; the Nazis had aimed to murder every single Jew. Now, in this new era of Soviet control of Eastern Europe, the world was scarcely any safer.

Yet the British were equally determined to try and halt the Jewish exodus that was fast gathering pace, the fishing boats setting sail across the Mediterranean from French ports, heading for the Palestinian port of Haifa. What the government wanted above all else was stability – not least for its own interests. The Chiefs of Staff had stated that 'it was essential to the security of the British Commonwealth to maintain our position in the Middle East in peace and to defend it in war'. There was paranoia about Soviet infiltration across the region through agents in Egypt's capital Cairo; and others lurking in Jerusalem. On top of this, Britain was fast running out of money. The foreign secretary Ernest Bevin had suggested moving military and air force operations from Cairo to Mombasa – air technology had greatly improved, it was argued, so there was scarcely any more need to maintain a costly army in Egypt. The idea was abandoned, not least because it was at the same time becoming increasingly apparent how bountiful the oil-fields of nearby Saudi Arabia would prove; the Middle East was becoming indispensable to the economies of Europe and America.

And this was another reason why the British started behaving so viciously towards Jewish refugees: it was in part the diplomatic need to keep the ever more powerful Arabs on side. And so, as the refugee boats approached the coast of Palestine, British naval vessels headed them off, and took all those on board prisoner. These unfortunate refugees were then conveyed as previously mentioned, to a prison camp on Cyprus. The symmetry with the concentration camps was hideous; but to the British government, it was a problem seemingly without an answer. Before the war had ended, Attlee's Labour Party had largely been committed to the idea of mass Jewish immigration of around 100,000 people and the creation of a Jewish state. Now, all was in confused flux. There were some Jews calling for a shared 'motherland' for two Semitic peoples – Jews and Arabs alike. There were even some Arab scholars who were calling for a Jewish state, though one in which Arabs had full rights. But all this was against a decades-long backdrop of violence between the Arabs and Jews. And with British intransigence, it was a group of Jewish terrorists who were to step that violence up.

The Irgun group was responsible for the 1946 atrocity of the blowing up of the King David Hotel in Jerusalem, in which 91 people – Arab and Jewish and British – were killed. The British army stationed in Palestine went after Irgun and three of the group's operatives were executed. Their comrades had little doubt what to do next. Two British sergeants were kidnapped by Irgun – and were themselves hanged. The atmosphere in Palestine, for Arabs, Jews and ordinary British soldiers, was razor-edged.

America, and President Truman, were not helping. Truman had demanded that Palestine be opened up to hundreds of thousands of

Jewish refugees. This led to a rare explosion of exasperation from Clement Attlee, who pointed out, in a pained fashion, that America would have no responsibility for then trying to keep the peace between Arabs and the increased numbers of Jews. The foreign secretary Ernest Bevin went rather further, insisting that Truman had only made this declaration because he did not want thousands of Jewish refugees turning up in New York.

In the midst of all this violence and hatred – the Zionist Stern gang terrorising Arabs, Arabs murdering Jews – arrived Walter Eytan. After all those years decoding German messages of horror, and after the evenings of Zionist discussion with Joe Gillis and others, he could at last see where his destiny lay. Indeed, of all the Jewish codebreakers at Bletchley, Eytan's subsequent career was the most spectacular.

On arrival in Palestine, he joined what was in essence the Israeli government-in-waiting, called the Jewish Agency. Among Eytan's intellectual gifts was a dazzling flair for languages; and it was not long before he was becoming indispensable on the diplomatic front. He secured a position working for future Israeli premier Golda Meir and – as the British began their helpless and angry withdrawal – he started working with UN commissioners on issues such as the peaceful dividing up of Jerusalem. And indeed, as soon as the state of Israel came into official being in May 1948, Eytan became director general of the newly formed Foreign Ministry.

And in this role, he was not only furiously energetic, but also witty and inclined to understand that there could be no simple answers. For instance, at a time when many of his colleagues held little but the darkest contempt for Arabs, he himself was in favour of Israelis and Arabs meeting halfway in terms of economic co-operation to help build up the entire region. He went on to engage Egyptian diplomats in talks; these were doomed ultimately to failure but again, Eytan was open to the wider world, with a healthy respect for his counterparts. He took this engaging, open skill around the world, seeking to establish diplomatic ties and full recognition for Israel everywhere from Burma to Iran. While Israel's first premier David Ben-Gurion was implacable about the need to demonstrate strength at all times, Eytan was there to prove that the new state of Israel had a lively, functioning intelligence. Indeed, Israel swiftly developed a lively, functioning codebreaking unit, too, doubtless with the help of a few top tips from its expert foreign minister.

This had an unexpected repercussion for his brother back at Eastcote, though. Ernest Eytan was highly thought of – his work during the Battle of the Atlantic had been admired – and it had seemed natural that he should carry on doing what he was so good at. But his brother's growing stature within Israel proved troublesome to a few in authority; it was suggested that Ernest might even pose a security risk. Now possibly there was a case to be made before the establishment of Israel that the family link might be construed as awkward. Afterwards, though, and it is difficult not to recoil at a tang of straightforward anti-Semitism in the implied suggestion that the ties between the Jewish brothers were far stronger than any sense of national loyalty or indeed the strictures of the Official Secrets Act. On top of this, it took the relevant authorities a long time to reach a final decision. It was only in 1952 that Ernest Eytan, ensconced quite happily at Eastcote, was moved. Another – rather less intense or secretive – civil service berth awaited at the Inland Revenue.

Other Jewish codebreakers forged beguilingly varied lives. The brilliant Rolf Noskwith carried on for a bit at GCHQ Eastcote but he left in 1946 to attend to the family business. His father had been very successful with a lingerie firm and Noskwith wanted to ensure that Charnos, as it was called, kept thriving. A rather longer stint was put in by Squadron Leader Nakdimon Shabetai Doniach. Within those grim, plain grey pre-fabricated buildings at Eastcote, his innate elegance with languages made him a natural tutor to other codebreakers. According to historian Martin Sugarman, he 'was in charge of teaching Russian and overseeing the teaching of Chinese to Foreign Office officials'.[2] Even more vitally, at Eastcote, Doniach continued the technical expertise of the cryptanalysis operation; in an evolutionary step forward from Bletchley's exhaustive card index system, he oversaw the creation of a complete technical Soviet dictionary. Any terms that came up – military, mechanical, avionic – would be logged, registered and monitored closely, the repetitions helping terrifically in cracking future codes and also sizing up military potential in different regions.

There were other notably brilliant Jewish codebreakers who found a sort of lifetime vocation in cryptology. Indeed, there were several American recruits who, after the Park wound up, returned to the US and continued with codebreaking efforts, working in close union with their UK counterparts for many years afterwards. Among them were Arthur Levenson, Captain Abraham Sinkov and Major Solomon Kullback. Sinkov was a mathematician, born in Philadelphia and educated in New York, who had been recruited into William Friedman's US cryptography efforts the year before the war broke out. Months before Pearl Harbor, Sinkov was among the small, incredibly secret party who travelled across the Atlantic via battleship to visit Bletchley Park, and to share German and Japanese codebreaking secrets and techniques.

He was later posted around the world, pulling off dizzying feats in cracking Japanese codes at astonishing speed. On his return to the US, Sinkov became closely involved in the growing computerisation of the field; and he became a pillar of what was later to become the National Security Agency – GCHQ's transatlantic cousin. As is traditional, Sinkov's family had no idea what it was that he actually did, either in the war or afterwards. His son said that whenever Sinkov was asked, he would reply 'I am a mathematician.' On the occasion of his 90th birthday, President Clinton sent him a letter thanking him for all the work he had done on so much vital cryptography. That must have rather let the cat out of the bag; but then, who better to finally reveal Sinkov's true achievement than the President himself?

An even more ebullient Jewish figure in Britain during the war and afterwards back in the US, where he continued the signals intelligence work in partnership with GCHQ, was Solomon Kullback. He was a Brooklyn boy, educated in New York. Like Sinkov, his talents had been spotted early on by William Friedman. Enrolled in cryptography courses, the men were encouraged by Friedman to continue their more straightforward education by attending night classes and working extremely hard Kullback, like Sinkov, attained his doctorate in mathematics. He and Sinkov then progressed further in the code game. Before the war, code-generating machine manufacturers would try to persuade the US government into buying up their systems. Kullback was one of the men appointed to test these machines and their breakability. He invariably did break their codes, and the machines in question were not taken up. 'We solved them for our own amazement and amusement,' Kullback later said.[4] As a result, according to the NSA, he and Sinkov did a great deal between them to ensure that US codes were as watertight as possible, at about the time when they were starting to get a serious lever into the Japanese codes.

In 1942, Major Kullback (the military ranking came with the codebreaking) made the voyage across the Atlantic to join the cryptology revolution; throwing himself into the hut system at Bletchley, the beguiling atmosphere of 'near anarchy' and the concomitant startling brilliance of its successes against Enigma. He was embedded deep in Bletchley's secrets, having also been made privy to the diplomatic codebreaking operation – spanning the globe – that was operating from Berkeley Street and which from 1942 was headed up by Commander Alastair Denniston. As well as focusing specifically on diplomatic cyphers, the operatives at the Berkeley Street premises in central London had also set about decrypting commercial communications from around the world.

Major Kullback formed an admiration for his British counterparts. 'I found the British most helpful and co-operative,' he later said. 'They were completely frank, open and above board with me and kept no detail of their operation, procedures, techniques or results from me.'[6] After the war, and firmly back in the US, Kullback became the chief scientist of the National Security Agency, staying with the codebreakers and liaising with the British until the 1960s before moving into academia at George Washington University. Colleagues recalled with fondness how Dr Kullback would respond to codebreaking triumphs with the exclamation: 'We dood it!' This was a catch-phrase used by Hollywood comic entertainer Red Skelton. It may have sounded more beguiling coming from the master cryptographer.

One other brilliant British codebreaker, who might have stayed on, instead followed Walter Eytan in his determination to help forge a new nation. Michael Cohen had left the Eastcote codebreaking operation by

1948; it was then that he started coding messages for the Jewish Agency Offices in London to be sent across to Jerusalem. Thereafter, with the state of Israel newly declared, he set sail for the port of Haifa. It was there that Cohen helped set up the 'British kibbutz' in the Upper Gallilee region. There followed years of intensive agriculture; and in cultural terms, the start of a period in which the British political left as a whole looked across at this burgeoning Israeli life of communal farms, with communal dining and family facilities, and sighed for what looked like the establishment of a form of utopia.

As a result, Cohen left the codebreaking far behind him and, when later pressed to recall any details of that life (by the 1980s, numerous books were being published and the secret was out), he simply smiled and mentioned the two beautiful Wrens that he had worked with.

It was not always perfectly easy to be Jewish in Britain during the middle years of the century, and there were codebreaking veterans who recalled minor outbreaks of anti-Semitism; cries from military men about the requirement for everyone to go 'kosher'; and sly suggestions that Whitehall did not want to see too many Jewish people getting into positions of high authority within the codebreaking establishment. Frankly, it would be surprising if there had not been any such tensions: British society as a whole was scarcely free of prejudice – this was an era in which certain golf clubs would not admit members with Jewish-sounding names. But on the whole, the memories were positive – and this indeed was to prove crucial to the future. One such man who could reminisce very fondly over his codebreaking days was Arthur Levenson.

Levenson, like Solomon Kullback, was a Brooklyn boy, and also like Kullback, almost preternaturally intelligent. Indeed, it was Kullback who gave him his introduction to the world of cryptography just before the outbreak of war. After training – both in codes and in the military life – Levenson was shipped out to Bletchley Park alongside figures such as Bill Bundy. In conversation years later, Levenson was very wry and witty about the world that he found there.

'We were treated like, oh, marvellous,' he said. 'I mean Americans were very few and we were supposedly integrated but we were treated as

Top: In 1946, the codebreakers moved from Bletchley Park to Eastcote, a base in north-west London – John Betjeman's 'Metro-land'. Despite the pleasant leafy surroundings, William Bodsworth described the Spartan new HQ, seen from above, as 'shattering'.
© *National Collection of Aerial Photography (Published through Google Earth)*

Right: Bletchley's suave Hut 8 veteran Hugh Alexander (much swooned over by female codebreakers) was a crucial figure in the new, regenerated GCHQ – but he continued to pursue his parallel brilliant career in chess.
© *Bletchley Park Trust*

Top: The 1948 Berlin Blockade – Soviet troops ruthlessly starving the city of food and essentials, and Allied airlifts being sent in – proved a tense Cold War test for the codebreakers, and the secret listeners posted throughout Germany.

© *Charles Fenno Jacobs/Getty Images*

Left: With post-war Germany in ruins – even the grandeur of the Reichstag was destroyed – the codebreakers were in a race to seize advanced Nazi cryptography technology, and also to establish secret bases to intercept and crack Soviet traffic.

© *Popperfoto/Getty Images*

Top: A gleaming new age of computers and codes: Bletchley veteran Professor Max Newman became a post-war computing pioneer at Manchester University, and maintained close links with GCHQ as the Cold War froze deeper.

© *School of Computer Science, University of Manchester*

Right: One of the twentieth century's most pivotal codebreakers, Nigel de Grey, who had decrypted the First World War's crucial Zimmermann Telegram, bringing the US into that war, was a key post-war architect of the new GCHQ. He had a deeply sardonic wit and an acidic impatience with military brass hats and trades unions alike.

Crown Copyright, reproduced by permission Director GCHQ

Left: As the British Empire began its speedy and sometimes bloody disintegration, far-flung codebreaking bases such as HMS Anderson in Colombo, Ceylon, lost none of their vital strategic importance, and their secret work went on.

© *Martin Sharman [Flickr: Kalense Kid, https://flic.kr/p/9jy8An]*

Left: Post-war National Service pulled radio-mad young men into the realm of secret wireless interception; many were sent out to countries such as Malaya, deep in jungles, monitoring burgeoning unrest and revolt. © *National Army Museum, London*

Bottom: Wireless interceptors were posted all over the Far East, and many revelled in the amazing new worlds that opened up. Novelist-to-be Alan Sillitoe recalled eerie tropical night shifts with inexplicable snatches of classical music coming through the ether. *Crown Copyright*

Right: Sir Edward Travis, the much-admired – if sometimes bellowing – director of both Bletchley Park and its new post-war incarnation. He ensured that the newly regenerated GCHQ won proper respect from Whitehall and rival secret agencies.
© *National Portrait Gallery, London*

Bottom: Frank Birch (second from left), another brilliant Bletchley veteran, who went on to help forge the momentous Cold War codebreaking alliance between Britain and the US. This secret life didn't hinder his love for acting; he appeared in many early television dramas at that time.
© *Kings College Archives, Cambridge*

Top left: The fierce demands of monitoring the Soviets meant an increase in numbers – and a move for the codebreakers out of Metro-land. There was a site at Cheltenham that had been partly developed for the military during the War which seemed the perfect choice. © *GCHQ*

Top right: When the codebreakers considered the move from London, other towns – including Oxford and Cambridge – were considered. Cheltenham was rumoured to be a popular choice because of its race-course. © *GCHQ*

Above: A new world of ingenious US/UK surveillance innovation was encapsulated by the American submarine USS *Cochino* and its on-board technology; but pursuit of Soviet vessels was hazardous and in the 1950s there was a hideous fiery tragedy at sea. © *Public Domain, https://commons.wikimedia. org/w/index.php?curid=688136*

Right: The Americans produced some dazzling codebreakers, many of whom came over to work with GCHQ. One such individual was Meredith Gardner, an intensely modest genius, who was partly responsible – by breaking into key Soviet codes – for unmasking the Cambridge Spies.
Courtesy of the National Security Agency

Top: America's answer to Bletchley Park: Arlington Hall in Virginia, not far from Washington DC. It was here, in this crucible of codebreaking, that the activities of atomic spies at Los Alamos and other double agents were uncovered.

© *Library of Congress, Prints & Photographs Division, HABS VA, 7-ARL,12A--8*

Bottom: The men and women of Arlington Hall and GCHQ worked together incredibly closely; like the UK codebreakers, Arlington Hall's experts were drawn from all over, such as schoolteacher Gene Grabeel and Brooklyn prodigy Solomon Kullback. The relationship between the US and UK was – in this instance – genuinely special.

© *Library of Congress, Prints & Photographs Division, HABS VA, 7-ARL,12--1*

Top: The Berlin tunnel – a terrific ruse to tap into Soviet communications – had an equally ingenious forerunner in Vienna, when young wireless interceptors such as diplomat-to-be Sir Rodric Braithwaite entered secret passages through false shop fronts.

© *AP/Press Association Images*

Left: Unfortunately, thanks to traitor George Blake, the Soviets knew all about the Berlin surveillance tunnel; they staged a serendipitous 'discovery' of the British interception equipment in 1956 in order not to give away their double agent.

© *Gnter Bratke/DPA/PA Images*

something special. They were very nice to us. The Director would invite us out, give us pink gin.'[5]

After the war Levenson stayed on a little longer, working, as he said, 'on a few problems' – one of which, as we have seen, was plunging into the darkness of Germany to salvage Tunny machines and to question German cryptographers. Following these extraordinary experiences, he returned to the US, and after several years in Army Intelligence, became one of the key figures in the National Security Agency. The continued harmonious relationship between the Americans and the British reached a sort of good-humoured apogee in Levenson; and the Lewis Carroll-like eccentricity of many of the key British codebreakers – and their enthusiasm for fighting their way out of thickets of mathematics and language – also found an echo in Levenson's huge love for the works of James Joyce.

Indeed, his love for Joyce is a superb glimpse into the aesthetic tastes of codebreakers: novels such as *Ulysses* and *Finnegans Wake* were written, in part, as gleefully encoded texts, the meanings hidden deep within. *Ulysses* is more straightforward, though abounding in puns, reversals and indeed the recurring mystery of the postcard (coded) message 'U.P: up'. *Finnegans Wake* was Joyce's deliberate exercise in cryptology: the language constantly dissolves and reforms, entire paragraphs resemble cryptic crossword clues. Above it all is the sense of the author devising this enigma, an explicit, witty and mischievous tease for even the most intellectual of readers. Levenson – who in later years was assigned some of the knottiest cryptographic problems by the National Security Agency – must have adored wrestling with the novel that is composed of the swirling dreams of one man, penetrating the poetry and half rhymes and the baffling absurdist knockabout comedy routines to fish out its true themes of sex and death and the oppressive nature of history.

One of Joyce's great preoccupations, threaded through *Ulysses*, was that of a nation strangled and oppressed by colonialism and seeking to find its own voice and language; to recover a true sense of nationhood. Similarly, some of the Jewish codebreakers had an almost spiritual passion about the need for Israel to come into being as a 'kingdom'; throwing off both the British and the Arabs. As with other Zionists, there were the pragmatists and moderates who sought some way – as Winston Churchill had suggested – to partition the land so that it could be shared among Arab and Jew alike. Then there were others who burned with a holier zeal; these believed that political violence was justified to establish the state. What sort of state it would be was merely window-dressing, fine detail. As a result, when the British effectively threw in the towel in 1947 and announced that within a year, the territory would be left under the watchful eye of the United Nations, events turned ugly.

The codebreakers and secret listeners based in Sarafand were among the many British personnel who were going to have to pack up sensitive equipment and incredibly confidential paperwork amid an atmosphere of escalating anarchy. The Irgun guerrilla group was attacking British soldiers and Arab Palestinians; the Arabs were attacking Jews; and the streets of Tel Aviv and Jerusalem were beginning to crackle with gunfire. But there was a sense among some British soldiers that it was very important to hold back in terms of fire: a moral imperative that Jews should not be attacked after all the unimaginable horrors visited upon them in Europe. This was also a point when the world had little sympathy for the British position. There were still haunted, emaciated Jewish refugees living in European Displaced Person camps. How could they be denied the safety and security that everyone else took for granted?

Signals officer Peter Davies, based in Sarafand, recalled the atmosphere as the time came for him and his intercept colleagues to try and ship their entire operation out. Some were headed for Cairo; other bits of equipment were to be shipped back to Britain; yet further items were to be consigned to the flames. In terms of interceptors and codebreakers, some of the operation in Jerusalem and Sarafand was being moved over to an ever expanding base on Cyprus.

Startlingly, the copper wire used in their wiring systems became sought-after treasure: in the aftermath of war, there was a worldwide shortage. And so the signals officers found themselves racing against Bedouin raiders to get to remote desert installations to clear them out. Added to this, British withdrawal was fraught with the possibility of random death;

soldiers climbing to the top of telephone poles became tempting targets for snipers.

In May 1948, the British mandate in Palestine came to an end. But it might be noted that there are those in today's Israeli equivalent of GCHQ – the world-beating Unit 8200 – who, even in the midst of technology scarcely conceivable to many, cheerfully reflect one of the key approaches to cyphers set down back in Britain, at Bletchley and GCHQ: that of the work being carried out in an atmosphere fizzing with free-wheeling free-thinking. One former Unit 8200 officer recently told the *Financial Times* that operatives are expected to be argumentative, to question everything and at times to disobey their senior officers. 'In intelligence, you can't only work by rules,' he said. 'You need to be open-minded. We teach them [new recruits] how to work out of the box.'[7] Edward Travis and Nigel de Grey would have nodded vigorously at this.

By 1948, the British still had a foothold in Egypt, with operations continuing at Heliopolis, and still assiduously monitoring Russian communications. But that foothold was growing shakier by the week; Egyptian nationalists were growing angrier about the idea of foreign soldiers patrolling their streets.

A great deal was being asked of the codebreakers at Eastcote. The startling and rapid dissolution of the British Empire – the extinguishing of its power in Asia and key regions of the Middle East – punched a hole in the gathering of intercepted communications. A sudden Soviet switch in encryption techniques was going to present the cryptologists with another crisis, on the face of it insurmountable. Yet at this crucial moment in the late 1940s – when Britain's influence was melting, and the influence of America growing – their work carried on as feverishly as ever. And while political relations between Britain and the US became rather scratchier, the codebreakers themselves not only continued their unusually harmonious arrangements, but also were by now allowing others into this warm embrace too. Eastcote and Arlington Hall were forming, with Canada, Australia and New Zealand, a codebreaking superpower: a global team of some of the most towering intellects, pitting themselves against the savage complexities of Soviet secrecy.

And in the midst of this kaleidoscope of inter-continental change, one senior Eastcote codebreaker was set the task of plotting out the future of GCHQ; what could the codebreakers learn from their own history, and most particularly from their own mistakes, that would make them a more formidable force in the difficult years to come?

Chapter Twelve

'The Signs and Portents Will Not Be Lacking'

The village of Iver, in Buckinghamshire – about 20 miles (30 kilometres) from central London and about five miles (eight kilometres) from the Eastcote HQ of the codebreakers – had the faintest tang of show-business about it. The wealthy hamlet was very close to the Pinewood film studio which, despite the pinched nature of the times, was producing dozens of dramas and comedies, often with imported Hollywood stars. Home-grown stars such as Sidney James and Roger Moore were to acquire properties there. In the late 1940s, the neighbours of Nigel de Grey must have wondered if he had missed his vocation, and whether he should be working at Pinewood too.

As far as they knew, this unassuming man was a civil servant of some sort by day. But he was also a hugely enthusiastic amateur actor who threw himself into a variety of different amateur productions. De Grey had been a member of the Old Stagers, and the rather upmarket 'Windsor Strollers' too. Surely this quiet chap in his early sixties should have been working for producer Michael Balcon or director Basil Dearden?

The pleasing incongruity of Nigel de Grey's story is that, of course, every day in that period he was right at the heart of the Cold War, fighting to break into Soviet cable traffic, as military and intelligence experts all around declared that the next world war was about to begin. De Grey had a kind of unnatural calm that was also extremely apparent when – at the behest of Eastcote's director Commander Travis in 1948 – he put together a top-secret document looking towards the future of the codebreakers, laying the foundations of the new GCHQ by examining their recent history. The organisation was about to expand in numbers once more. So, learning from both successes and failures at Bletchley, how were the codebreakers going to continue to adapt to this new world of daily atomic jeopardy? How were they going to keep one step ahead?

'Dear Eric,' begins a neatly handwritten note at the top of this (now) de-classified document. De Grey was addressing this thesis to his colleague Group Captain Eric Jones (who was later to succeed Travis as the head of GCHQ). 'A point I meant to make somewhere in the notes I sent you did not I think find a place after all.'[1] This prefacing point was to do with the numbers of men needed for Y Service units dotted around the world. These brilliant radio experts were attached to army, navy and Royal Air Force and their staffing levels were dictated by the needs of those services. De Grey's point was that the Y Service personnel should in fact match the enemy's numbers – if the enemy had multitudes of trained wireless operators sending out illimitable signals, then similar numbers were needed on the British side to counter them.

'No attempt was made prior to the war to estimate what the probable scale of enemy communications would be,' wrote de Grey, adding that the resulting inadequacy of transmitters and personnel was an example of a 'hidebound' Whitehall. De Grey was thinking about the structure of this new GCHQ; and his friendly note to Eric Jones was about how to give it the investment it needed in the face of what must have seemed inevitable Whitehall cheese-paring. Although codebreaking was in some ways a much cheaper source of intelligence than having agents on the ground, the advent of the computer age meant that it would have to spend significant sums on innovative hardware. It also needed to fund the essential scientific research into new technological means of cracking codes and eavesdropping on the enemy. How were they to match the brilliant success rate of Bletchley?

'Seventy-five percent of the justification for the existence of GCHQ in peace time is that it should be ready on or before the outbreak of hostilities,' wrote de Grey. 'It is obvious therefore that its mobilization plan must conform to the national or international military plan. It must assume, however problematical the situation may appear, that it will be successful, as it was in 1914–1918 and 1939–1945. Moreover, it is probably fair to say that its value in both wars was greater for strategical purposes rather than tactical – which does not imply any lack of "operational" importance. All the weight of the evidence goes to show that concentration of effort on the technical production side was the more successful policy.'[2]

This new age was at once nuclear and electronic; in the space of a heartbeat in the summer of 1945, there had been a dimensional change in the rules of engagement. De Grey knew that for the codebreakers to enjoy fresh victories, they, too, would have to embrace and get some way ahead of the computer era (as indeed their colleagues across the Atlantic were busy doing). But that did not necessarily mean a budget nightmare for the Ministry of War, setting up vast computerised codebreaking departments in stations across the world. De Grey and his fellow codebreakers were adamant that such things were more effectively handled when centralised.

'There is not, provided communications are adequate, the necessity to set up large technical processing organisations at overseas commands for strategical codes and cyphers,' he wrote. 'There was considerable confusion of thought over this in the Navy,' de Grey added. 'What Commanders in Chief really wanted was a concentration of all the intelligence relevant to their command for their own staff to assess, what they thought they wanted and demanded was that the technical processes also should be carried out at their Fleet base.' It might have worked for local issues, de Grey conceded, but even then only as long as all intelligence – no matter how seemingly unimportant – was sent back to the main codebreaking centre. The point was that the codebreakers' strength lay in the fact they remained at the centre of the web.

'Where more than one country is involved, the clear cut division of responsibilities and the closest integration of staff at all possible points in the common task were the two outstanding lessons of the American alliance,' de Grey wrote. He forbore to add at that point that this particular alliance with the Americans was still going very strong. 'This ensures the complete sharing of all technical knowledge and intelligence, avoids misunderstandings and determines who controls what.'

The other issue of course was the relative independence of the codebreakers; at Bletchley Park they had answered to MI6 and the Foreign Office. After the war, and following the split from MI6, this independence increased their determination to point out that they knew best 'who controls what'.

The next war would be radioactive. Nigel de Grey, thinking as he wrote in that somnolent leafy west-London suburb of where the codebreakers would be best located when the sirens started crying out once more, posed the question: 'First of all then, it has to be determined whether GCHQ should on mobilisation: 1) Stay put; 2) Move in the UK and if it do so, should it move to a) the heart of a populous city; b) a suburban area; c) a country area; d) below ground – eg the bottom of a coal mine or a clay pit.'

Drastic though the bottom of a coal mine sounded, even that might not have been sufficiently far from harm's way in the event of an atomic attack. So de Grey also thought further afield. (Incidentally, his reference here to 'GCHQ' was part of increasingly common usage by the late 1940s; though many were still referring to the London Signals Intelligence Centre, those at Eastcote were now more frequently using the GCHQ acronym.) If they were to move abroad, Nigel de Grey wrote, should it be 'to a) British territory, Canada, Australia, South Africa etc; b) Mandated territory – north Africa etc; c) Allied territory – America, Benelux etc, bearing in mind the proposed seat of the conduct of the war as a whole, or of any specific theatre of war. It is assumed that the main conduct of the war must necessarily be sited in conformity with the expected risk of disruption of communications (not merely telecommunications of course).'

De Grey was drily understating the prospect of nuclear Armageddon; but he added with more mordant wit that if international tensions were moving inexorably in that direction, 'the signs and portents will not be lacking'.

The most important thing was to avoid improvisation; any moves made hastily in a crisis could imperil the entire operation. 'On a lower level,' de Grey wrote, 'there is always a fatal tendency to regard any important cryptanalytical success as a special case requiring special measures to handle it. Success', he added rather magnificently, 'is the common form of GCHQ, it is to be expected, there should in a well organised establishment be no special cases or mistrust of a well-tried, well-seasoned staff.' His suggestion here was that 'dummy runs' should never be overlooked. That way, de Grey wrote, things 'should be all right on the night'.

And what about recruitment? Where were the new generation of codebreakers to come from? De Grey, it will be recalled, was an Old Etonian who had been recruited from the business world, at a time – before and during the First World War – when many codebreakers were either naval men or classicists drawn from Oxford and Cambridge. De Grey noted that very clearly at Bletchley, the idea of recruiting from Oxbridge – and pursuing gifted mathematicians – had been perfectly effective. So how should they now proceed at Eastcote and how many should they take on?

'It is for decision', de Grey wrote, 'whether GCHQ will use one or more of the following channels for raising staff: 1) Direct contact with Universities, secondary schools etc. In general, this method produced not only the original 60 high grade people [for Bletchley Park before the war] but also considerable numbers afterwards. As national recruiting became more methodical,' he continued, referring to Bletchley, 'this system tended to clash with the proper authorities. There were also diminishing returns as men and women joined the Services. Government Code and Cypher School [the pre-war term for GCHQ] had no Establishment and these people were automatically taken on to Foreign Office books – the first 50 without "friction to the Treasury"'. Could such an informal recruiting system be tolerated by the bean counters of late-1940s Whitehall?

And what of the less glamorous, less intellectual vacancies that the new organisation would demand? Again, de Grey thought warmly back to the war: 'For lower grade labour,' he wrote, 'especially girls, large numbers were raised through the Foreign Office, in contact with the Ministry of Labour, who directed the more intelligent types for interview by the Foreign Office (Miss Moore).' This, incidentally, is a throwback to an old Bletchley Park memo, equally breathtakingly sexist as it seems now, in which then director Commander Denniston complained about some of the 'girls' being sent his way; he wanted fewer of the 'cook and messenger' type, he said.[3] Added to this, many 'girls' – including the absurdly glamorous debutantes such as Osla Benning – were recruited directly through smart social connections. In the new post-war world, with its radical Labour government, such an idea may have had a little less appeal.

There were other roles too to think about – the 'lowest grade', which might have included maintenance engineers and drivers. De Grey noted a little sourly that at Bletchley, some such workers came from local recruitment but that on the whole, the town and surrounding area had proved 'mainly unproductive'. Wherever the codebreakers found themselves moving to in the event of a Third World War, it would have to be somewhere with streams of potential (and competent) manual and low-grade-clerical workers quite close by.

There were other skills to think of too, and de Grey analysed the men and women – linguists, traffic analysts – who had served in the huts and blocks, trying to pinpoint the factors that made them a success. 'GC and CS did initially very well in securing a high grade team of young dons etc,' he wrote. However, he added, 'few women reached the highest levels.' De Grey did not speculate on why that might have been the case; but his colleague Joan Clarke, attached to this new organisation having proved so brilliant at Bletchley, might have had her own views on the subject. Of course, it was much more than simple old-fashioned sexism; in cultural terms, there was at the time an overpoweringly strong bias in education in steering girls towards the humanities, and away from science and mathematics. Even if girls demonstrated high aptitudes in these fields, the cultural expectations of them – added to the social expectation that when they married and had children, all work outside the home would cease – meant that very few broke through. (Joan Clarke stands out today as much as Margaret Hilda Roberts, the young chemist from Grantham who studied at Oxford and later of course became Prime Minister Margaret Thatcher.)

And had Alfred Dillwyn ('Dilly') Knox – a brilliant classicist codebreaker central to the cryptographic effort in the First and Second World Wars – still been alive, he might have had rather a different view on the contributions of women. At Bletchley Park, Knox seemed overwhelmingly to prefer working with them. One of his most dazzling young colleagues was Mavis Lever, just 19 when recruited. After the war, she had married fellow codebreaker Keith Batey (both sadly died not too long ago), and had left the cypher game, first to raise a family and then to return to academia. Her background, crucially, was in linguistics rather than mathematics. Now, in the late 1940s, Nigel de Grey, in setting out the template for the new GCHQ, was giving thought to the kind of ways such experts could be best utilised in the future.

'Linguists: the pure linguist without other qualifications was not of great use,' wrote de Grey. 'Recorded opinion favoured 1) sound grammatical knowledge; 2) current idiom; 3) power to apply knowledge as a basis for guess work. Honours degree in Modern Languages not necessarily a sufficient linguistic qualification,' he added. 'Some additional test recommended.'[4]

He also explored the talents required by those working specifically on traffic analysis; here, it was more a question of 'deductive faculty' and a lithe intelligence, as opposed to any specialised gift. 'In all of the above,' de Grey wrote of the dons, the linguists and the analysts, 'accuracy, quickness of work and some degree of puzzle-mindedness considered necessary.'

'From the general point of view,' he went on, 'speaking "managerially", there was [at Bletchley] a lack of men sufficiently experienced to take charge of sections where problems such as the handling of large volumes of paper arose . . . There was also a lack of commercially trained leaders eg women who had run typing pools in banks and insurance companies, accustomed to organising output up to a given rate per day, or men

who had been sub-managers with a team working under them. The
bank clerks, while excellently methodical, did not entirely fill the bill.
No emphasis was laid in recruiting upon obtaining this type. Time was
wasted by "talented amateurs". Very many of the tasks were of a plain
"factory" type.'

This fascinating view of codebreaking being an industrial activity,
which first germinated with Gordon Welchman, was now finding its
full voice in Nigel de Grey. At the time he wrote this, with the numbers
of people working at Eastcote still a fraction of the crowds who had
teemed around Bletchley Park, he was clearly planning for a future with
a purpose-built environment, as opposed to a collection of slightly drab
long pre-fabricated blocks abutting an American air force station outpost.
For the expanding field of signals intelligence to be truly effective, it had
to be able to operate in the way that Bletchley Park operated. And that also
meant with the full backing of Downing Street.

Incidentally, de Grey was not completely sexist; having witnessed some
of the miracles performed at Bletchley Park, he envisaged a key role for
many women in this proposed establishment. 'It was astonishing what
young women could be trained to do,' wrote de Grey. 'EG Fish and bombe
Wrens, Typex operators, in an incredibly short time with wonderful
accuracy, although quite untrained to use their hands or apply their minds
to such work.'[5]

So: these bright young women, unused in normal circumstances to
applying their minds, and these bright young men, some potentially to
be hauled straight out of their Sixth Forms: were these the most suitable
people for the new codebreaking establishment to be going after?
Funnily enough, although there was the sharpness, suppleness and
adaptability of young brains to consider, de Grey also had experience
of the potential setbacks of focusing mainly on youthful recruits. 'Age,'
declared de Grey. 'Recorded opinion lays emphasis upon youth because
it is more trainable, more prepared to accept direction, better able to
stand the strain, more flexible in mind – all obvious considerations.'
But, he continued, there were less obvious considerations too. 'There
are facts to be set against this: 1) Experience has a value and was none

too prevalent [at Bletchley]; 2) cases of mental breakdown occurred equally between young and middle-aged; 3) both men and women are often tougher in middle age than in youth; 4) flexibility is not always so valuable as judgement.'

The mention of mental breakdowns was important: at Bletchley Park, a few such cases had been seen. Part of it was the huge pressure of the work; but another factor was the very nature of the work itself, that combination of dizzying intellectual pirouettes combined with often cruelly dull and laborious checking and re-checking. Modern electronic encypherment techniques reduced language to a vortex of anarchy; just a few years previously, one of the Polish mathematicians who had first cracked the German Enigma had stated that where there is arbitrariness, there is always – somewhere – a certain regularity. But the new computer age made such regularities almost invisible, generating cyphers with many thousands of millions of potential combinations. Angus Wilson (who in the 1950s became one of Britain's most prominent and acclaimed novelists) had been a codebreaker at Bletchley Park; and there, his mind had buckled. The authorities had offered him a spell of recuperation in a special government institution. He turned it down, on the grounds that he was better off sticking with the madhouse he knew. The codebreaking mind was a distinctive thing – leaping laterally, able to hold the vastest abstract ideas. But clearly it was also prone to fragility. The coming of computerised cyphers was not going to ease that sort of pressure; especially if those codebreakers found themselves staring into the abyss of a Third World War.

And what of the Y Service – the brilliantly nimble men and women who had listened deep into the ionosphere, tracking crackling signals in deserts and jungles and on lonely mountains? Nigel de Grey noted that during the war, this had been one arm of the codebreaking process that had been slow to get going; part of the reason was the complexity of the job that required interceptors to translate Morse at the brain-burning rate of 30 words per minute. So it was difficult enough to find and recruit sufficient operators from among the young army, navy and air force conscripts. Here, the recruitment of women to work in establishments such as Beaumanor and Forest Moor eased a lot of the pressure. But – as de Grey noted with a dash of vinegar – when it came to civilians, there were fresh problems presented, one of which, in his view, was their tendency to belong to trades unions.

'Trade union regulations were restrictive,' he wrote, 'and all GPO [General Post Office] and ex-GPO operators were unionists and stations manned by them were never 100% efficient: mixing of ex-GPO operators with War Office civilians led to trouble and ex-GPO men were segregated into a separate station. Union never forwent their restrictive practices.'[6]

There were Y service operatives who would have snorted with indignation at that assertion (and de Grey never made it clear which of the Y Stations had to be segregated). Certainly, there had been some flashes of ill-will at Beaumanor in Leicestershire. This was not so much down to the operators wanting to establish 'restrictive practices' as to simply improve the conditions in which they were working. Union representatives had protested to the station's Commander Ellingworth about the bitterly uncomfortable huts in which the radio equipment was housed; the impossibility of concentration in the winter when the huts were so cold; and the near suffocation of the summer months, combined with the thick, un-air-conditioned fug of tobacco smoke. Nonetheless, codebreakers of Nigel de Grey's generation (he had been born in the final years of Victoria's reign) clearly had little time for what they obviously regarded as domestic Bolshevism. (And funnily enough, the relationship between GCHQ and union activity was a sore spot that would flare again in the years to come, most notably in 1982 when Prime Minister Margaret Thatcher attempted to have unions shut out of the institution.)

And in the event of this new conflict, would the codebreakers be civilian or military? Bletchley Park had always operated in a kind of twilight zone. Wrens, ATS women and WAAFs were all required to wear their uniforms on duty, and were explicitly under service rules and discipline; yet they were working alongside men who – even when conscripted – had the choice of wearing the uniform or not. Many did so only for the purposes of obtaining free rail passes on their days off to London. In the Bletchley directorate, Colonel Tiltman consistently wore his uniform (always involving rather natty tartan trews), but joked with younger male recruits who insisted on wearing theirs. But behind these sartorial dilemmas had been a more philosophical problem: for instance, were codebreakers who were then sent off to stations like Heliopolis outside Cairo or the Far East Combined Bureau in Colombo under the sole command of their military superiors? What sort of weight would orders from Bletchley Park have? Indeed, in Egypt, this very fault line of authority had caused some venomous disputes: codebreakers accused by military colleagues of making Bletchley Park their priority, and not instantly sharing intelligence before Bletchley Park could analyse it.

But there was another fault line too: money. 'Mixture of service and civilian produces gross inequalities of pay,' observed de Grey. 'Parliament always agitates for the services to be properly paid, indeed highly paid. No-one agitates for civilians.' (Except perhaps trades unions, one would have been tempted to tell him.) He continued of the Bletchley Park experience: 'While most civilians accepted their position equably, there were monstrous cases where men were doing the same (not similar) work and some getting nearly double the others. Such violent inequity tends to sap enthusiasm at times. Service officers in the Government Code and Cypher School were not in danger and some got staff pay . . . Decisions will have to be reached therefore on numbers duties and types of service officers . . . which the services propose to attach 1) on mobilisation; 2) subsequently.'

There was a note on the fresh difficulties that new technology would bring. For instance, de Grey observed, at Bletchley Park upon the outbreak of war, recruits preferred 'preliminary training courses' as opposed to learning at top speed on the job. The declaration of war had made that a practical impossibility for many; but de Grey noted, in the future, 'a more highly developed organisation' might be able to cover that gap. What was important in the wider context was to avoid some of what de Grey perceived as the deficiencies in the wartime service. This applied especially to the Y Service interceptors out in the field. 'Many British and American Y units were sent overseas with expeditionary forces, untrained and useless,' he wrote. 'A bad operator is rather worse than useless eg RAF unit sent to Singapore, units sent with Torch to north Africa.' Incidentally, it seems eyebrow-raising – even in the context of a 'top-secret Ultra' document circulated only among his close colleagues – that de Grey was willing to blame the 1942 fall of Singapore, and its capture by the Japanese, on hapless Y Service secret listeners; the intelligence failure was most assuredly rather larger than that . . .

Nigel de Grey's point was that the skill of the Y Service operatives was specific and had to be nurtured; the army imagined that gathering intelligence in this way could be done by any old operator. It could not. De Grey's answer was that such operatives should be spotted early, recruited early and trained early, and that their unique speed and talent and sharpness should be recognised accordingly. On top of this, when it came to recruitment of codebreakers in the future, the new GCHQ should have the authority to pick out the best candidates and exempt them from military conscription. 'Great importance attaches to GCHQ being a party to if not the sole constituent of selection boards,' observed de Grey.

'If as has been said [signals intelligence] dances to the enemy's tune and the saying is true, it is provident to guess the enemy's programme before the band begins to play,' he continued.[7]

And so to the gleaming technological innovations: what would the regenerated codebreaking department need, how many and how much? 'High speed calculators – not much is here relevant,' wrote de Grey. 'It is no use thinking small on this subject. Preparation for, experimental work on and production of the first 6 bombes cost roughly £100,000. The large "Fish" calculator [that is, Tommy Flowers's innovative Colossus machine] embodied 2400 valves of a type reckoned practically unprocurable. Experience', de Grey added, 'was that each new problem tended to require modification of existing machines or the devising of new ones. When a factory is geared up for large-scale production, any redesigning or modification throws the whole organisation out of step.'

'Government Code and Cypher School had three main sources of supply: a) British Tabulating Machine Co, bombes and some subsidiary machines; b) GPO engineering research at Dollis Hill.

Recourse when BTM was fully occupied was had to the Government's Telecommunications Research Engineering establishment. The first device which they made far exceeded their powers of production and had to be farmed out to Mawdsleys for manufacture. It was far too long (18 months approx.) a process before it came to perfection. On the other hand, their work on Fish and a Japanese machine were most useful. But clearly, Government Research Departments, unless they embrace production (as at Dollis Hill whose work consisted in the main of assembly of standard parts and only a small amount of engineering) are not of more than limited use.'

Again, there might have been a personal bias against state-run concerns that led de Grey here to underplay the rather magical contribution that Dr Tommy Flowers and his GPO team at Dollis Hill had made; regardless of the amount of time needed to perfect these revolutionary machines – admittedly not an ideal factor in war – the fact was that they had moved cryptology into an entirely new dimension of possibility.

So where would this magical machinery come from, if not from the stolid and lumbering government departments? Like so many of his colleagues, Nigel de Grey got a flash of enthusiasm in his eyes when he looked across the Atlantic towards the work being done in America. 'Very great assistance was afforded by both Navy and War departments in America,' wrote de Grey. 'The Navy contribution was outstanding in research on electro-mechanical devices. Their resources of manufacture were of course larger than ours.' They still were, too – as we shall see, former Bletchley codebreaker Gordon Welchman was now over on the east coast, helping to usher in more of these electronic leaps.

And decoding brought with it a number of equally important subsidiary tasks – many to do with the secure transmission of the intelligence. Nigel de Grey was wondering how many copiers – ie early photocopiers provided by the company Roneo – would be required in a time of heightened international tension? There were other required items that would later become mainstays of the entire spy-fiction genre: microfilm cameras and microfilm readers. In the late 1940s, such things were just about available, but the special pleading in view of the cost was presumably very loud.

And unlike the slick ease with which James Bond and Avenger Emma Peel swiped, snapped and read their microdot documents, de Grey was less than impressed with the huge amounts of behind-the-scenes labour that the technology required. 'Dealing with microfilm,' he wrote, 'which as a method of conveying large quantities of documents about the world should have been ideal, saving the burden on cables and air bags, proved particularly tiresome. It was easy to make 35mm and 16 mm film. But to enlarge them upon receipt was beyond the resources of most centres. 35mm was possible though lengthy and expensive. Only two automatic plants for enlarging and printing 16mm existed, one in London, one in America, both belonging to Kodak. They were both in demand for airmail letters for the troops and were very expensive to operate, let alone possible risks to security. Recourse', he added, 'was had to film projectors and a copying staff which, although the work was of the dullest, achieved a fair output, but it was obviously a one-horse method. Staff of six girls.'

De Grey mused that the demand for photography and copying was so large that Bletchley had to install its own specialised department; and presumably would have to do so again at Eastcote – or indeed, wherever the codebreaking was carried out. 'It is obvious that considerable development of a photographic copying department should form the subject of study and the organisation be kept informed of the latest apparatus and its suitability. Apparatus should be earmarked and supplies assured.' Incidentally, it is rather sweet to consider that this super-secret proposal was essentially about a photocopying department. The world turns with unforgiving speed.

It is also worth bearing in mind – when we all have the books and monographs of the world's libraries digitised at our fingertips in our homes – that the codebreakers in the late 1940s were scrabbling around trying to procure for themselves reference books and atlases. Expensive, detailed reference works were rare; facts could not be verified, as they can now, within the blink of an eye. 'No large scale maps or charts existed in Government Code and Cypher School on mobilisation,' wrote de Grey, eyebrows raised. 'Hut 3 had none until the Battle of Norway. There were no existing channels for obtaining them.'

Indeed, given the highly esoteric nature of the codebreakers' work – the need to grasp every last syllable of the enemy's communications on subjects from local politics to topography – the omission was startling. 'The only reference books were chiefly concerned with diplomatic activities eg *Statesman's Year Book, Almanack de Gotha* etc,' continued De Grey. 'A few dictionaries – largely private property – practically no atlases. No technical literature whatever concerning the enemy armed forces save British blue books. No address books, telephone books, railway guides, tourist guides, motor maps. No vocabularies, no modern technical dictionaries, or standard works.

'While the official publications on enemy forces were well informed on the aspect of standard weapon equipment, endurances, speeds and such like, they were not informative on organisation, structure or subordinate formations. It cannot be too strongly emphasised', said de Grey, 'that the need for such guidance was a paramount requirement in the early stages for the existing staff and later for instruction of new entry.' And so for the new-look GCHQ? 'It is suggested that unofficial handbooks or guides to the potential enemy forces, with emphasis on organisation, should be compiled on a loose leaf principle and constantly revised by GCHQ,' stated de Grey. 'Into them could be embodied official statistics etc where regarded as germane. Every effort fair and foul', he added, with underlining, 'should be made to acquire foreign service handbooks and manuals of instruction for the sake of information, idiom and technical equivalents. In this respect, GCHQ has quite different requirements from the Ministries. Compilations of this nature would save much time on the arrival of reinforcements.'

Funnily enough, the Bletchley Park database – which at that time was a vast number of cards, handwritten and cross-referenced, bearing information on enemy technical terms, and weapon jargon – had been maintained and added to by a platoon of highly dedicated debutantes, whose boredom thresholds had been stretched beyond imagination by the tedious nature of their work: every deciphered German message had been filleted for concrete terms – propellers, engine parts – and names, too, of as many officers and subordinates as could be contained on shelves in one big room. As Alan Turing and Professor Max Newman continued to struggle with the possibility of endowing a machine with a memory, information and knowledge was still a matter of physical hard copy.

It was highly unlikely, in the event of nuclear war, that Britain's high-society debutante army might be raised again: many of them, such as the Honourable Sarah Baring, were married off and settled on grand estates. On top of this, there had been a shift in the global axis since the outbreak of war in 1939. By the late 1940s, it was no longer an automatic truism that aristocratic girls were ideal recruits because their social class meant that they were more disposed to loyally keeping secrets. The new GCHQ was clearly not going to be established on a base of cosy social connections.

Added to this was a new nervousness following the unwelcome revelations of the Venona decrypts; the hermetically sealed departments of dedicated codebreakers – American and British – were still unlocking the secrets of these messages, and still in the process of identifying those who had betrayed Allied secrets to the Soviets. But it was painfully clear that the Comintern (the body that united Communist parties internationally) had succeeded beyond perhaps even its own wildest dreams in infiltrating the most extraordinarily guarded US and UK areas. For GCHQ, recruitment in a new age of lethal atomic science would have to be even more circumspect than it had been before, and the threats and warnings given to those embarking on a career of cypher-cracking would need to be even more dire than those issued to personnel at Bletchley Park.

Added to this was the insight in de Grey's monograph that – certainly at the time – signals intelligence could not quite operate at complete effectiveness without an accompanying element of human intelligence. The nature of the information de Grey required to have at his fingertips was traditionally the type obtained by human agency: from the humble tourist guides, to the more sensitive and detailed lists of personnel and senior commanders, and the innovative weaponry that they were to deploy. But de Grey – perhaps as a result of his wartime experiences – seemed to have limited patience with the idea of the codebreakers having extensive dealings with either MI5 or MI6.

'It was a mistake to interpose SIS [MI6] between the ministries, service or civil, and the Government Code and Cypher School,' observed de Grey. 'There was no point in it, save possibly some obscure and long forgotten loose thinking about security . . . In the Japanese war of course, the India Office was a vitally interested customer but Government Code and Cypher School relations were never clarified quite satisfactorily owing chiefly to the long-standing interposition of SIS, difficult by then to set aside.'[8]

This was about more than a simple inter-service rivalry; more than a sense of clever codebreakers viewing MI6 agents – back then largely recruited, like the early days of Bletchley, through the smarter social echelons and Pall Mall clubs – as faintly incompetent. De Grey – and with him the codebreaking establishment – had clearly learnt the lesson from the war that prized intelligence should not be scattered about; that only the absolute bare minimum of people should be receiving such briefings, and certainly without any of the intelligence being filtered by agents from quite another discipline. 'Experience of the war was always that direct reporting to the user was the cleanest and safest method,' said de Grey, 'for both sides knew exactly where they stood, could discuss problems direct, and Government Code and Cypher School could control security of use.'

But there was an unexpected security risk that de Grey mused upon, and in so doing, he threw a most intriguing light on the future relationship of the codebreakers with the wider government and the Westminster establishment. It was all to do with delicate matters of money. He noted that when it came to extremely expensive bombe machine production back in the early 1940s, the cost was covered first of all by MI6, and then, thereafter, by the Admiralty. It was 'non-audited', meaning that Bletchley did not have to make special representations to politicians or civil servants.

'Another very useful arrangement was the "pool" fund of the GPO, established to cover service requirements,' wrote de Grey. 'Out of all this the work of the GPO Dollis Hill establishment for Government Code and Cypher School was financed and no special Treasury sanction was necessary. This relieved GC and CS of considerable labour and the necessity to violate security to obtain the required money.'

In other words: such financial secrecy was good for the defence of the realm; the fewer interfering and carping Whitehall types who knew what the codebreakers needed to raise money for, the better. This was perfectly sensible in a jumpy age, but there was also a hint of passive aggression too. De Grey knew very well – from British liaisons and from the sparky American codebreakers stationed at Eastcote who were puzzling their way through that mountain of Venona Russian encryptions – that the US was pulling away fast in technological terms, awash with money from a grateful and uninquisitive Congress.

'In dealing with secret equipment,' de Grey wrote for the benefit of his director Edward Travis, but also his business-minded colleague Eric Jones, 'it is all important to have open doors to finance and not to have to go through the hierarchy pleading and explaining the necessity . . . A preliminary study of this whole subject is necessary and agreement with the Treasury as to what liberty of action GCHQ should be granted in time of war.' But the sentiment from de Grey could not have been clearer: in time of war, GCHQ should be given what it wanted with absolutely no questions asked; for the questions themselves would throw up concerns about national security.

He illustrated the point with some facts from Bletchley concerning the British equivalent of Enigma, the Typex machines. They 'were almost always in short supply', de Grey noted. 'Many important plans for communications were bunkered by shortage of these machines and the people to work them. Their gravest disadvantage was that they produced only a single tape copy. More time and staff were wasted in GC and CS duplicating by typewriter and duplicating machines than any other single thing and since an enormous proportion of the total traffic handled . . . when the Far Eastern war was in full swing passed through the Typex machine the lack of i) a page print and ii) any mechanical duplication was a really serious feature.'

The consequence was that backlogs developed; with all the thousands, and then millions, of messages pouring in from every theatre of war, and with the need for British units in the field to receive that intelligence, the system would come close to logjam. The result, de Grey said, was that they had to resort to 'factory methods' to get the work done.

'This was done chiefly by keeping careful records of output per watch, per machine and per girl,' said de Grey. 'This showed up weaknesses, peak hours etc and enabled the manager to adjust numbers and skill per watch, additional training for slow workers and additional servicing of machines . . . Properly constructed chairs were found to minimise fatigue and increase output – but were seldom available.' The time-and-motion techniques at last allowed Bletchley and its outstations to work out the optimum number of 'girls' needed to work the optimum number of machines. Some women appeared to have a natural knack for the work; others did not. It was not a precise science. In the various huts and blocks, other methods were tried to improve 'productivity' including the playing of 'music while you work'. This did not improve speed; and de Grey noted that generally among Typex operators, morale was often low. With any new war – and the many emergencies that it could bring – such issues were far from being personnel trivialities; this was the very heart of intelligence and it needed to be working at peak condition.

And where should they all put themselves? Again, de Grey reached to the past for inspiration as he sought to outline the new sort of institution that would be needed. In 1939, he said of the move to Bletchley from St James's Park, 'central space was always lacking from the first mobilisation of 137 people in accommodation for 80. Building was always therefore against time.' The blocks that were built, he said, at least constituted 'an asset' to the government, in the way that the 'wooden hutments' did not (although one wonders what the shade of de Grey would make of Bletchley Park's exquisite restoration of said 'wooden hutments' for today's modern museum – an English Heritage 'asset', no less). 'It was a definite advantage', wrote de Grey, 'that we had on the staff a man who had had long experience in public works [actually water and drainage]'. This allowed him to override civil servants from the Ministry of War who in many cases were 'amateurs'. This man, said de Grey, now dead, had left behind a legacy: 'He left on his death complete plans for an underground building to house GC and CS in war-time.'

Even at the first stirrings of nuclear neurosis, many government departments were starting to think in subterranean terms. In the event of war, it was starting to be believed, everything on the surface would simply disappear in a scorching instant flash. There had been suggestions for underground housing of codebreakers before; prior to the move to Bletchley, one idea was to put the cypher experts in quarters and offices beneath the St James's Park HQ of MI6. Hitler's bombing, many assumed, would start the very minute war was declared, and the Luftwaffe attack would almost immediately leave the entire city shattered and in flames. But the underground notion was abandoned; delicate brainwork – and fissile personalities – meant that the chances of any startling innovations emerging from such close quarters was low.

But it was clear that Eastcote, on the outer fringes of London, could not be a permanent home. For some of the codebreakers, it was maddening to be stuck in suburbia: they wanted the neon and the rush of town. Others hankered for rural peace. It would not be too long before an inspirational compromise was suggested.

And what then of the larger number of recruits who would be needed to be drawn in at speed once Britain went to war with Stalin? Indeed, even without conflict, the spreading global reach of the Cold War mean that the codebreaking was poised to expand further. De Grey was concerned about human happiness (and its knock-on effects in the workplace); having seen the low morale of many women who worked in those cypher factories, he wondered how things might be improved for their successors.

'It should not be forgotten that new entry will be entirely unfamiliar with Civil Service rules, regulations etc', he observed. 'They are accustomed to payment on the knocker and unaccustomed to mistakes in deductions of income tax and subsequent recovery. They do not understand Civil Service jargon and circumlocution. They want to know exactly where they stand and actively resent delays in getting answers. Nothing saps new entry's morale quicker than dilatoriness in dealing with their troubles.

'A very large number, especially girls, have no other resource than their weekly pay', he added, a nod to the independent means of the smarter young women and an acknowledgement of the new generation of young working women coming through. At Bletchley, he said, 'a very large number were badly treated – chiefly by blunders – and redress took months to obtain. Establishment can do a very great deal to make life tolerable to new entry, by clear explanation of conditions and prompt and accurate attention to hard cases.'[9]

Any feminist cheering that this might have evoked would, however, have been choked by his next point. He said of some new entrants that 'they may appear and may be stupid but they need all the more to have humane handling.' This unfortunate phrasing made many of the Typex operators sound like cattle. De Grey's progressiveness only went so far. Of these badly treated Bletchley women, he said, 'hardship cases were by no means confined to the lower decks'.

So much for the human factor; but the codebreakers were running a global operation in a world shifting dizzyingly fast. The ambitions of Nigel de Grey were evidently shared by his colleagues in the directorate, but could they ever hope to achieve them? They would have been all too aware how overshadowed they were by their one-time parent service MI6; and even more piercingly aware of the battles ahead to compete for ever shrinking sums of cash.

As we have seen, the Eastcote establishment had already been writhing under a number of financial frustrations, even down to the vexed question of whether the Middlesex setting entitled the staff to a few shillings extra of London weighting in their wages. But on a broader canvas, the impotence that de Grey – and doubtless many like-minded colleagues felt – was palpable. America was effervescent with innovation, a future filled with reel-to-reel tapes and flashing lights; there was little doubt that the lumbering Soviet empire was fast catching up. And here was Britain – the greatest and most creative of all codebreaking innovators – gradually suffocating in the grey sludge of austerity debt and Whitehall inertia as, across the world, vast chunks of empire snapped off, bringing a diminishment that was very hard to adjust to.

That said, there were still 'overseas centres', and the question of how they should be used in the forthcoming Third World War was also addressed. De Grey was anxious for clarity (a contrast to the opening months of the Second World War, when various separate departments appeared to be gainsaying one another). This new-look GCHQ would have very well-defined lines of communication with the military. Also, it was not just a matter of sending through thousands of decrypted messages; there had to be clarity in terms of who did the filtering of the military intelligence. De Grey's preference was clearly that this should also stay within the realm of GCHQ. The whole set-up was cleaner that way.

And what about the Dominions, which were, at the time that de Grey was writing, being pulled into the unprecedentedly wide embrace of the UK/USA agreement? How things had changed! Canada, noted de Grey, had had a rather mixed codebreaking war. It was 'part service, part civil, very active in interception but small and inexperienced in processing'. What about ebullient Australia? Quite apart from the fact that it was just about to suffer its own Soviet double-agent drama, it too had had an up-and-down war. 'From the American standpoint,' observed de Grey, 'it had no intelligence reporting function, merely the production and circulation of decrypts.' That said, the Australian authorities were proud of their signals intelligence operation, which was so active in the field units of the Australian army and air force.

Then there was the Indian elephant in the room: at the time that de Grey was writing, the Indian Congress had achieved independence, and Jinnah had his Pakistan. The weight of British signals and codebreaking work was based on that golf course just outside Colombo. Nigel de Grey harked back drily to the days when the Experimental Wireless Centre at Delhi had generated dramatic amounts of 'acrimony'. This was partly a conflict of seniority – who got to control the flow of intelligence through Delhi and Colombo. It was, de Grey said, a 'persistence of the traditions of the bad old days', by which he meant that the military was inclined to sideline Bletchley Park's overall centralised dominance. Added to this, the man in charge at Delhi, Lieutenant Col Marr-Johnson, had a notably corrosive manner. Codebreaker Alan Stripp, while not naming him, observed that 'too often administration relied on authority rather than professionalism'. Of course, none of this was the fault of the Indian codebreakers, or those based in Ceylon; they had, said de Grey, done a splendid job against the specific complexities of Japanese codebreaking. What concerned him was that lack of centralised control; this new age would change all that. No matter how congenial the idea of anarchy may have been to the thought processes of cryptologists, the organisation behind them had to be strong and rigid and in complete charge at all times.

De Grey could not pronounce on the future role of the Commonwealth: the whole thing was 'in flux'. But when it came to allies, he said, 'all the evidence points one way . . . There cannot be a successful partial liaison – all or nothing.' And the codebreaking centres, wherever they might be, had to resist the excessive demands of military brass-hats. All had been well 'save for financial starvation' in the 1930s, wrote de Grey. But then, with the war, the senior military hierarchy started to take a sharper interest in codes and in building up their own Y Services with ever expanding numbers of their own officers taking control (or trying to take control) of cryptanalysis. This, to de Grey, was an intolerable invasion. It 'diminished the scope' of the codebreakers. Moreover, each service 'was a law unto itself'. Intelligence got duplicated – and this carried the danger of reflecting endlessly in a mad hall of mirrors.

Worse, Bletchley Park had been 'none too clear on its principles and rather took the line of limiting its responsibilities'. In other words, it had offered itself as a batman or valet to the military, rather than maintaining the strict integrity of its own independence. That would have to change. 'While it is obviously necessary to set a limitation on the responsibilities of any organisation . . .' wrote de Grey, 'GCHQ should not hesitate to pursue any course that may lead to better signals intelligence and better use of it, whatever the theoretical objections. Had GC and CS halted in its stride every time objections were made, there would have been no Naval Section, no intelligence work in Hut 3, no combination of sources in the BMP and no task control from Hut 6 or Hut 3 or Naval Section . . . On the other hand,' he added, 'GC and CS was a laggard in . . . military field code work and many other respects. It deserved a good deal of what it got.'

The magnificent conclusion de Grey was steering towards would have delighted his colleagues. 'All this points towards clear thinking and plain speaking with GCHQ customers,' he wrote. 'It points too towards the lesson that the peace time organisation should be the skeleton of the war organisation – "the image of war without its guilt" [de Grey was quoting Robert Surtees on the subject, strikingly, of hunting] . . . so that on mobilisation it is a well-running machine. If that is done and GCHQ avoid the great mistake of GC and CS which was to create at the very first emergency an anomalous complex in its internal system entirely contrary to its planned and accepted organisation, friction and dangerous complications should be avoided.'

But perhaps the most startling aspect of this blueprint for the future was that it was being drawn up by a civilian with seemingly no consultation with any member of the armed forces that it would be dealing with, its 'customers'. The codebreakers may have transformed Bletchley from a cottage industry into a worldwide factory; but the men running GCHQ seemed as defiantly quirky and eccentric as their forebears. In America, the mighty army and navy had contributed cryptanalysts such as Telford Taylor and Bill Bundy and the meshing of military and civilian personnel carried with it a feeling of determined military discipline; this sense – of an advanced and complex establishment deeply and inextricably intertwined with the military – continued and deepened after the war. With the nascent GCHQ, there was a faintly maverick flavour: not in any political sense (the codebreakers if they could be characterised at all in such terms were profoundly conservative) but rather that they did not welcome intrusion into their territory. Brigadier John Tiltman and Lieutenant Colonel Marr-Johnson were among the few to continue with their military careers. In contrast were figures such as the bearded sandal-wearing Highland-dancing expert Hugh Foss and the chess champion (and regular chess correspondent) Hugh Alexander. There was a sense of continuity with Bletchley – and with the First World War Room 40 operation – that verged on the defiant. Cloak-wearing Nigel de Grey – by day analysing the terrifying lurches in geopolitics that threatened Europe with further bloodshed and by evening appearing on stage in amateur productions with the Windsor Strollers – seemed somehow to symbolise this unashamed left-fieldedness.

Two key developments from Russia – viewed with horror by the British and Americans – combined with a torrid period for MI6 – would also come to mark the British establishment's understanding of just how vital the new GCHQ would be.

Chapter Thirteen

The Emerald Labyrinth

During the winter months – and the British winters of the late 1940s were particularly unforgiving – Forest Moor could be shrivellingly bleak. Based a few miles outside the prosperous Yorkshire town of Harrogate, in a landscape that the Brontë sisters would have thrilled to, was a vast aerial farm: a metal forest of tall antennae covering many acres which, since the end of the war, had been picking up huge numbers of transmissions from the Soviet Union. The intelligence harvested at Forest Moor was shared, automatically, with the Americans. The base stood as a symbol of the remarkable relationship. In terms of working conditions, gradual improvements had been made since wartime days, when Wrens remembered the very specific discomforts of working shifts in rickety structures buffeted by blade-sharp winter winds.

As with all other radio establishments, those who worked there did so under conditions of direst secrecy. It was a base that the Americans found particularly helpful, covering as it did so much of East Germany and Eastern Europe. But it was also the very easiness of that alliance between the US and the UK that led Commander Travis and Nigel de Grey to propose an even snugger proposition to their Washington counterparts: a joint code-generating system.

Effective though Typex had been for the British, this essentially Enigma-like machine was pretty much obsolete by the late 1940s. It was not just a matter of technology: the fact was that it was also looking increasingly vulnerable to enemy codebreakers. The system could be cracked. But money was desperately short; how could a new system of code-generating be brought in without crippling the entire nascent GCHQ operation?

According to Richard Aldrich, the British codebreakers, in making their pitch to their richer American colleagues, picked a curious means of doing so. They chose to reveal dramatically to their allies that the US needed to update its own system – because the British codebreakers had levered their way into it, analysing the workings of the Sigaba system. In essence, the directorate at Eastcote let the Americans know that they had been blithely – and secretly – burrowing into their most closely guarded cryptological machinery. This was not to say that they had been actually reading their messages (though of course one way to tell that one had really understood encoding machinery would be to unravel its efforts). Such a thing would have been considered an outrage – even though each side must have assumed that enemies and friends alike were always worth eavesdropping on.

The British point was to tell the Americans that a new, joint code-generating system – an Inter-Allied mechanism, used interchangeably, and with complete trust – would be fantastically convenient, cost-effective and diplomatically attractive to all concerned. There was one setback: the Americans reacted to this British revelation of the penetration their Sigaba system with complete horror. As personally close as many of the codebreakers were, the idea that the British had had the potential capacity to read their secret traffic went quite beyond the boundaries of rudeness. It opened up new vistas of neurosis, especially in the face of the ongoing Venona Soviet decrypts, which were unmasking British and American Soviet double agents alike.

There was a slight dash of spicy hypocrisy in that reaction too, of course, for the Americans had been quite blithe about poking around in British diplomatic communications as sent via the Typex system; it had not taken Washington codebreakers long to master the principles of that encoding technology. But the essential fear about security remained perfectly valid. Even by 1948, there were still bumps and spats between

London and Washington. One such had come with the British behaviour over the Palestine Mandate. Some in the US establishment took a bleak view of British treatment of Jewish refugees attempting to make landfall in Palestine. Equally, though, there were staff at Eastcote – and throughout Whitehall – who were mistrustful of handing Middle Eastern decrypts over to the Americans.

This was the dawn of the Central Intelligence Agency in the US, and there were those in Whitehall who suspected – without any particular evidence – that this new organisation contained 'Zionist sympathisers'. There was also a jumpy conviction that sensitive decrypts had already been leaked, thus aiding the more ferocious Zionists in and around Jerusalem. But, according to Professor Aldrich, Whitehall was unaware that American codebreakers had in fact been picking up signals from Zionist groups in the region, to do with the supply of arms – and then failing to pass such news over to their British allies.

These outbreaks of friction between friends were perfectly understandable though: such an intelligence-sharing arrangement was still very new territory, just a matter of six or seven years old. It was reasonable for both sides to expect a few boundaries. Britain's wider interests in the Middle East at that time were going to be crucial to its future prosperity. In the absence of empire, and with the country's need for oil growing, it was already teetering along a very high tightrope. On top of this was the sure awareness that America had somehow, and invisibly, become by far and away the dominating partner in this alliance. And America's own global interests were seldom going to be to the advantage of Britain's material wealth.

Against this backdrop – the British fast fading in grandeur, the unstoppable rise of American power – the news that the British had in principle cracked the American coding system did not result – as Eastcote had hoped – in a renewed sense of joint purpose. If anything, it made the Americans shrink back a little. Added to this was a sense that American research into encryption was now pulling ahead of the resource-starved British. Although in American terms, the US codebreakers were themselves operating on slender budgets, they were still a galaxy away from the threadbare operation at Eastcote. Those laboratories in New York and deep in the Virginia countryside were producing a whole new race of computers. For this, they had scant need of expertise from London. They were sharpening their focus upon a Soviet Union that had already blockaded Berlin, and mounted a Communist coup in Czechoslovakia, and which was embedding itself yet further from the Baltic to the Black Sea. The Americans, meanwhile, were establishing a very strong presence in more northern areas, listening to every Morse dot in the airwaves above Finland and the borderlands of the Soviet Union.

What the US did need from Britain though – and very strongly – was manpower and ingenuity when it came to keeping tabs not only on those hazardous fringes of Europe (the material that Eastcote gathered from East Germany, for instance, was passed on to grateful counterparts in Arlington Hall), but also on the more inaccessible regions of the earth. Conscripted British youngsters in National Service were being sent to remote territories where British rule, far from ending smoothly, was resulting in a gruesome long-drawn-out mess. The Malayan Emergency, which started in 1948, was an illustration, among many other things, of the limitations that the Eastcote codebreakers were now slamming up against.

Malaya, like so many other lines on the world atlas, had been a construct, drawn up in the 19th century in order to best exploit the area's vast economic potential. The British had moved in and established control over local sultanates; in this region of vast rainforests were huge deposits of tin. The land was also rich in rubber. As the mercantile 19th century brought a revolution in industry, so the resources of Malaya were harvested and sold at fantastic profits. The local people, it was felt, were too proud to work on rubber plantations; and so to fulfil the vast economic demand, great numbers of Chinese immigrant workers were imported. The idea, according to Neal Ascherson, who served out there as a young soldier, was that these Chinese incomers would return to their own territories once demand dropped off and their work was done. But they did not.

By the 1940s, Malaya had a sizeable Chinese minority population; but the native Malays had no intention of giving them the same constitutional rights as everyone else. And when Attlee's government set about after the war working out how best to pull back from the region – while avoiding jeopardising Britain's still hugely lucrative supplies of tin and rubber, which were doing much to keep the Treasury afloat in those times of financial hardship – it became grindingly obvious that the result could instead be bloody civil war and revolution.

Facing the Malay sultanates was a new grouping, largely composed of Chinese people. In its first incarnation, it was the MCP, the Malayan Communist Party. Following some dirty dealings involving a high-ranking double agent called Lai Tek, this party was banned. Many young men and women who had been members fled the cities and towns to begin new lives of resistance in the teeming, sweating jungles, and in the savage hilly landscape where, only several years beforehand, Chinese and British had fought side by side against the Japanese.

The Communists were now the Malayan People's Liberation Army. They began a campaign of guerrilla warfare that, at first, the British were confident of dealing with. Yet it soon became clear that an enemy that could disappear at will into the dense emerald labyrinth of the forest would not be one against which conventional military forces would be much use. So began the MPLA campaign: their targets were plantation owners, wealthy British and Malays alike. Young inexperienced soldiers such as Neal Ascherson were sent on patrols into 'ant-swatting' jungles of infernal heat.

And then there were the wireless interceptors, like the young novelist-to-be Alan Sillitoe. 'The four-engined Lincoln bombers of 97 Squadron flew to Malaya from the UK and began pounding suspected bandit hideouts in the jungle,' he wrote in his autobiography. 'All twelve would take off from Singapore Island and head north-west, their wireless operators competing to be first in getting a bearing. As each string of Morse came hammering on the air, I noted his call-sign and told him to wait and when they were in the correct queuing order I would go down the list until all were dealt with. Every bearing was sharp and therefore accurate though it was hard to think that their bombs hit much in the kind of jungle I knew about.'[1] Some weeks before the Emergency began, Sillitoe and some wireless interceptor friends had indeed mounted an expedition deep into the forest, a holiday of sorts, the aim being to climb a local mountain. After days of laboured progress – of hacking back plant life, and stumbling, and climbing with the green canopy above all but blocking out the sky – they had at last climbed so high that they could look out over a vista that seemed to have come from Arthur Conan Doyle's story *The Lost World*: a land of forest and paddy field, unconquerably remote. Such was the exhaustion occasioned by this expedition – not just the labour of moving through such terrain, but also the impossibility of sleeping out in this alien wilderness, alive with running water and the croaks and cries of animals and insects – that Sillitoe had a near out-of-body experience, switching, as he said, from the jungle in front of him to his family front parlour back in Nottingham, the two alternating as fluidly as a dream.

If straightforward war was not possible in this sort of terrain – even efforts to cut supplies to the MPLA were consistently thwarted by a guerrilla resistance that simply knew the land and its secrets so much better – then any prospect of useable signals intelligence seemed also a forlorn hope. Young men like Sillitoe were expert at seeing that their own side's communications got through; less accessible were the coded communications of different cells of the MPLA.

Yet the signals effort was key to the struggle, as indeed was the clever dissemination of propaganda throughout the country. In 1948, the Colonial Office sent this memo to the joint intelligence operations in Malaya: 'It has been decided that the criminal elements engaged in acts of violence in Malaya should be referred to as "bandits". On no account should the term "insurgents", which might suggest a genuine popular uprising, be used.' As historian Philip Deery pointed out rather acutely, the terminology used on the airwaves was also a means of making sure that the insurance cover on Malayan plantations was not invalidated; banditry came under the heading of 'riot and civil emergency' which the owners were insured against. A full-on colonial war was not covered.

But this policy had an unforeseen knock-on effect, as it rapidly became obvious to everyone from military commanders to wireless operators that the MPLA were not merely 'bandits' but highly organised, well-equipped, well-trained and lethally effective. Added to this, Britain would at least need the moral support of the United States if it was to declare to the rest of the world that it was justified in trying to fight the uprising. These 'bandits' also had to be portrayed somehow as viciously motivated tools of a rapacious Communist empire seeking to topple freedom and liberty.

'It seems to us very dangerous', stated a British intelligence memo at the time, 'to pretend that the troubles in Malaya are not caused by Communism but only by a kind of local banditry. As we saw in the case of Greece, where the Greek government were for long anxious to describe the Communists only as bandits, international public opinion in the United States . . . is inclined to take the line that when wholesale military operations are required to suppress mere internal unrest, it is in some way due to bad government. This is especially so in a colony; and instead of receiving sympathy and support from American public opinion in our praiseworthy struggle to combat the well-known international Communist menace, we shall be merely regarded as a bad colonial power coping with rebellions.'[2]

The chief reason signals intelligence could only go so far – and the Malayan Emergency continued for 12 years until 1960 – was that the insurgents themselves at first only had rather limited access to radio equipment that could stand up to being hauled through wet warm jungle. There were, according to Leon Comber, some radio sets that, ironically, had been an unintended gift from the British: leftovers from the war, when British special forces had tried to equip the anti-Japanese guerrillas deep in the lush forests. But these heavy-duty wireless transmitting sets required a lot of maintenance amid conditions such as violent rainstorms; and to move them, together with their generators, was awkward and time-consuming and required a lot of manpower.

Elsewhere, there were more congenial spots for young expert wireless operators to find themselves tracking enemy codes. One such was Christopher Barnes: a gifted and intelligent veteran of Beaumanor Hall and the rather more austere Forest Moor station. In 1948, he had managed to swap the biting winds of Yorkshire for the politically lively – yet atmospherically congenial – British base at Cyprus, which was soon to become a kind of Clapham Junction of signals intelligence in the sensitive Mediterranean region.

'Those . . . who found themselves in Cyprus will be left with a host of memories, pleasant as well as unpleasant,' Barnes wrote mid-way through 1948. 'Memories of the long days of sunshine and great heat, of bathing in the royal blue Mediterranean, of the ancient churches of Famagusta, of Bill Hayward arguing with all-comers into the small hours of the morning. Of Bellapais Abbey and the ruined castle of St Hilarion in the summits of the purple Kyrenian mountains, of "Curly" Hendley after the demob party . . . the colourful peasants with their mules and donkeys, the old ships from the fishing ports, mountain sheep and armies of goats . . . Of the gothic cathedrals of Famagusta and Nicosia now used as mosques, the countless little windmills that watered the plain . . . the camp cat eating the night duty fish ration . . . little cafes, black coffee, wines and the inevitable egg and chips . . . oranges and many other fruits, though mainly oranges, the Turkish bazaars and oriental pageantry of many parts of Nicosia . . . night duties, fatigues, blanco-ing and loud-mouthed sergeant majors.'[3]

Barnes was being commendably discreet (this short memoir was published in Beaumanor's staff magazine); he certainly gave no hint about the frenetic amount of work that was being done at the intercept station on Cyprus. From Israel declaring its statehood, to picking up volumes of encrypted traffic from Iraq and Egypt, day and night shifts were intensive, with the wireless interceptors expected to work at peak levels of concentration and accuracy. Certainly at that stage in the Middle East, access to the kind of encypherment technology fast being developed by the Americans and Soviets was very rare; in most cases, the communications that Barnes and his colleagues were picking up would have been using the sort of wartime code-making machines that Bletchley had turned into a sort of factory-line process for cracking. A little later, Cyprus would become even more important; especially to the Americans, who came to understand what an amazingly vital foothold it was in the region. But in the late 1940s, these close Allies were still dancing around one another a little. No-one could doubt the commitment of Clement Attlee's government in seeing Communism as an existential threat to be fought in all territories. But just how close would the Americans allow the British to get?

The question, in 1948, took on a wider dimension too, one involving the ever-closer cryptological union of the British Dominions. Canada, Australia and New Zealand each had their own formidable teams of cypher-crackers; the teleprinter lines to Melbourne during the war against the Japanese had been particularly hot. However, by 1948, there were a couple of serious security scares that made the Americans look askance at their friends.

Thanks to the ongoing horror that was the saga of the Venona decrypts – those tiny hermetically sealed teams of US and British codebreakers were still working at them to unveil the names of Soviet agents infiltrated everywhere – leaks in the Australian codebreaking department had been found. Now, Commander Travis at Eastcote had already made moves to ensure that the Australian cypher operation was closely watched over, inserting his own man, Teddy Poulden, as head of Signals Intelligence in Melbourne. Poulden's previous post had been as deputy to Bruce Keith at the Far East Combined Bureau in Colombo.

The Canadians, too, had had moments of huffiness when out from Eastcote came codebreaking veteran Geoffrey Evans to be deputy head of their signals intelligence operations. This was balanced with prickly offence caused by their American neighbours. Canada, given its vast territory, and its own proximity to the borders of the Soviet Union, expected that the Americans might have been a little more generous in the matter of sharing out encrypted intelligence. But the Americans held back, and there was a whiff of imperial snobbery there that outdid any insult that the British codebreakers could have offered. The Americans, for a while in the late 1940s, wanted Canada to be only marginally in the loop – to be given intelligence and leads on a strictly need-to-know basis.

There was a reason for this other than simple disdain, according to Richard Aldrich: in the view of the US codebreakers, the Canadians appeared to be relatively lax about their own coding security. The proximity with Russia went both ways. Just as the Canadians would be straining every sinew to listen to the Kremlin, so the Soviets would eagerly be rifling through Canadian traffic to pick out the fruit not just of Ottawa's diplomacy but also of American and British communications.

Even so, it now also seems quite remarkable that the allies were willing to share quite as much as they eventually did; for in the realm of cryptography – as everyone at Bletchley learned – the overriding, ever-present anxiety was that as few people should know the secret as possible. At Bletchley, this had extended to not even allowing many operatives of other secret departments to know. So for America, Britain, Australia, Canada and New Zealand to come closer together – even with strict boundaries being set on the type and nature and volume of intelligence shared between them – was quite remarkable, and also a formidable counterblast to what had clearly been terrifically effective Soviet infiltration at all layers of the secret service.

By 1948, after several incredibly confidential convocations between these allied nations, a much more comprehensive agreement was reached. It was still known as the UKUSA alliance and it is still very firmly out of sight of anyone but accredited personnel. According to the political analyst and historian Peter Hennessey, that agreement became the foundation for many decades of intelligence work against the Soviet bloc, an alliance that spanned the planet. Yet even with the might of all those combined intellects, there were still gaps and weaknesses. In the still fast-shifting landscape, from Europe to the depths of China, new forces were stirring. The codebreakers of Eastcote and Arlington Hall were fast and brilliant; but they were not psychic. Convulsions in the Far East would show how easily blind-sided they still were.

Yet next to this was a sense that, even as its strutting imperial power declined, Britain's codebreaking creativity was still world-beating, with as much of the old eccentricity and swashbuckling individualism as before. Of the men and women who typified the operation at Eastcote, Hugh Foss (sent to America to help there and described as a 'Lend-Lease Jesus'), Hugh Alexander (who seemed determined that his top-level secret work should not interfere too heavily with a fascinating and authoritative chess career) and Joan Clarke (persuaded after the war not to return to her mathematical studies at Newnham Collage, but to continue and help to construct GCHQ) were key. Their stories in the late 1940s open a window into how the nascent GCHQ was being formed out of very fine and recognisable British traditions.

Chapter Fourteen

Highland Reels and Drawing-Room Comedy

Of all the many wonderful figures that somehow made their way into this shadowed, esoteric world, Hugh Foss might be said to have had the most colourful background. He had been a codebreaker since the 1920s; born in Kobe, Japan, to an Anglican minister father, Foss had been educated at Marlborough school and Cambridge. After he graduated from Cambridge, he was recruited to work for the Government Code and Cypher School; his formative years in Japan would prove a particular advantage over the years and decades to come.

Yet Foss was marked out not merely because of his dazzling intellect and good humour; he also led a life that might have fitted nicely into one of novelist EF Benson's social comedies. When we refer to espionage figures leading double lives, the expectation is usually of a dark and ironic dichotomy. Foss was the reverse: his parallel life involved an all-consuming passion for the pastime of Scottish country dancing. It was completely pervasive; and by the time he got to Eastcote, helping to construct this fresh approach to a world of signals intelligence, it had almost become an alternative career. It also had the most extraordinary effect upon his personality.

Hugh Foss was married to Alison; she was a little on the short side, whereas he was a looming sentinel of a figure at six foot five inches (1.95 metres).

He had russet hair and a straggly beard. In the early 1930s, as Foss was making careful studies of the complexities of Japanese encryption techniques, Alison had a novel idea for an evening out: she took her husband along to a private house in Chelsea, west London, which was playing host to an evening of Highland reels. It is difficult to know how Alison Foss must have responded to his almost instantaneous obsession. That evening, he had declared himself enchanted; but he found the instructions for each dance seriously lacking in the sort of detail he thought they required. In the following few days, Foss had acquired himself a scholarly book on the history and techniques of traditional Highland reels. This was a world he had to enter.

So it began: cypher-cracking by day, in the rather shabby offices of the Government Code and Cypher School in Queen's Gate, Kensington; seeking out reels come the evenings. This fascination was to continue upon the outbreak of war, and after the move to Bletchley Park. Obviously, the defeat of the Axis powers was the daily priority – but given the crushing pressure this was putting upon some of the youngest new recruits, how best was the experienced Foss to help them relax and let off steam?

Thus it was that the main mansion at Bletchley Park began hosting evenings of Highland reels. In the summer, these occasions would sometimes be moved outdoors, on the lawn in front of the lake. Naturally there were no pipers to hand; music was provided via the gramophone player. As a means of diverting anxious young minds, it certainly proved effective for one particular couple. Oliver Lawn, then 19 and working in Hut 6, and Sheila MacKenzie, also 19, and working as linguist, joined Foss's society. Sheila, a native Scot, had had some prior experience from her Aberdonian upbringing. For young Englishman Oliver Lawn, it was exotic escapism. Their eyes met across an eightsome reel. And they became one of Bletchley Park's many romances, and their subsequent marriage lasted for a great many decades.

It was around this stage that Hugh Foss, himself squarely English, began to transmute into a more Caledonian figure. Perhaps it was the influence of his Scottish wife. But he began to wear a kilt. Like many things at Bletchley Park, this was taken in various people's strides. He also became noted for his militant addiction to sandals. He would never wear anything else. This is how this straggle-bearded sandaled figure came to be known by his beguiled American colleagues in Washington as 'Lend-Lease Jesus'.

Foss's mind could move with as much elegance and intricacy as any of the dances that he spent his spare time devising. His work burrowing into the heart of Japanese communications was invaluable. But Foss, like so many of his senior colleagues, also maintained personal habits of great particularity. At a time when women were expected to be proficient housewives, his own wife Alison was said to be spectacularly and comically bad at it, with the result that Foss would interrupt his day to go and make sure that the children made it to bed. The washing of dishes became a fraught routine for both husband and wife; they both developed an obsessive-compulsive mania for ensuring that it be done in a very precise way. Saucers had to be washed first because, apparently, they had had the least 'contact with human lips'. One guest, on offering to carry out this chore, was told with a shriek from Foss, 'Oh! You mustn't do the cups yet! Saucers first!' Yet against this was balanced the involvement of the Foss household pets. 'The dogs are a great help!' announced Foss of their role in the washing up routine.[1]

The end of the war brought Foss back from Washington, and also a return to London, to embark upon the daily Piccadilly Line tube commute to Eastcote. The Foss family lived in Chelsea, about an hour's travel away. By this time, he and Alison were back in with their Chelsea Highland reel enthusiasts. Naturally, none of the Foss family friends had the faintest clue what it was that he was doing for a living. They could have no idea that he was at the very nerve centre of the Cold War. Indeed, if there had been any suspicions of spook activity, these would surely have been thoroughly dispelled by Foss's great 1947 coup, when he took over the editorship of a magazine devoted to Highland reels. The fact was that it was not enough for him to enjoy the dances. He had to devise them too, and find the music to set them to. His reeling legacy – now fondly remembered by Highland dance enthusiasts – includes such routines as 'Black Craig of Dee', 'Duncan MalCalman" and 'Who'll Be King But Charlie?'. Incidentally, the step moves that serve as instruction for these dances are slightly reminiscent of chess problems: letters and arrows and numbers, tightly formed around one another, elegance in a sort of mathematical shorthand. Indeed, we might almost say that they are a form of hermetic code in themselves; the natural shorthand of a remarkable mind.

Before the war, Foss's enthusiasm had pulled in one rather spectacular convert to the pursuit: Alastair Denniston, the head of Government Code and Cypher School, and the architect of Bletchley Park's founding successes. Denniston had an aptitude and a taste for Highland reels; perhaps as a former Olympic hockey player, he had the correct muscles and stamina to serve on the dance floor. He implored Foss and his wife to find him a suitable female partner, though. Denniston was married, but there was no suggestion of impropriety: it was simply that Mrs Denniston could not stand the idea of spending her evenings in such a fashion.

After the war, in the soot-smirched city, the skies grey with drizzle or sleet, it is easy to see that Highland reels might have offered a joyous, colourful escapism; the tartan, the pipes, the swirls and circles. In those early days of GCHQ, just as at Bletchley, the furious intensity and pressure of the work would require an equally strong pressure valve. But for Foss, this was nothing less than love. The dances presented new sorts of challenges for him. 'A reel of three comprises three people dancing a figure of eight in the same space at the same time,' he once declared, adding a quote from Macbeth. 'Be bloody, bold, and resolute!'[2] And he had to find new converts to this terrific activity too. So it was that – in his spare time – he assumed editorship of a new paper of somewhat limited circulation: the *Chelsea Reel Club Intelligencer*.

The first issue contained a variety of delightful items. There were instructions for a new dance that Foss had worked out. There were detailed step moves for more established routines that Foss felt could be taught a little more effectively. Added to all this was a bonus: a logic puzzle for his readers to solve.

In that puzzle lay the only public clue to the twin delights of Foss's life: that irrepressible, unstoppable, insanely enthusiastic urge to share not only the dances, but also vaulting intellectual challenges. There was a pleasing and curious innocence about his desire to impart the intricacies of logic problems.

Of course, that is one way that sanity is preserved; otherwise, years-long immersion in cyphers would surely have had a profoundly distorting effect on the way that one looked at the outside world. Yet this idiosyncrasy also feels peculiarly British; it is difficult to imagine such vivid eccentricity among his US counterparts, who gazed on Foss with amused delight.

Also rather distinctive was Eastcote's openness to women at a socially conservative time. Of course, right across society, war had brought women into the workplace; but now, in peacetime, they were expected to resume their old roles as home-makers when the young men returned. For this reason, GCHQ was forced to say reluctant farewells to hugely talented young women like Mavis Lever and Sheila MacKenzie. One woman who did stay on – doubtless to the immense relief of Edward Travis and Nigel de Grey – was Joan Clarke.

Clarke had been recruited for Bletchley Park in 1940; like many of the men, she was contacted directly by her old Cambridge tutor Gordon Welchman. Clarke, a mathematician, had been supervised by Welchman for the geometry section of her degree. At that time, female mathematicians at Cambridge were rare; equally, there were not that many at Bletchley either.

Not that there was anything madly unconventional about Clarke's upbringing. She came from a family that was both religious and rather academic: her father and other relatives had taken holy orders, and had also been fellows of Cambridge colleges. Her formative years were spent close to the glittering giant of Paxton's Crystal Palace in a genteel suburb of south London called Upper Norwood. She went to Dulwich High School for Girls, and from there won her scholarship to Newnham College, Cambridge.

Her mathematical flair and intelligence made her an obvious choice for Bletchley – but even there, amid the 'apparent anarchy' of this twilight zone between military and civil service – there were certain conventions and barriers that proved stubborn. One she ran across immediately: this being some several decades before the law was adjusted, it was a given that women would automatically be paid less than men. Clarke was warned before she began her codebreaking career that the initial pay would be terrible.

The career path was rather labyrinthine too. 'In my first week, they put an extra table in for me in the room occupied by Turing, Kendrick and Twinn,' she wrote. 'According to [Jack] Good, I rose from the ranks of the girls in the big room; but this was obviously because of my degree.'[3] In other words, Good had assumed that she had started out among the clerical card-index debutantes and the typists. Clarke noted that there was one other female cryptanalyst she knew of at the time, working with Dilly Knox in the department known as 'The Cottage'. But she herself had been allocated to Hut 8 and very swiftly, she found herself taking positions of responsibility on night shifts, monitoring the clicking, ticking machinery – a junior version of the Bombe machine known as 'the Baby' – for any signs that cribs had worked. Clarke was swift to grasp Alan Turing's thoughts and methods; it was in the course of such abstruse discussions that their relationship began.

Famously, Alan Turing and Joan Clarke got engaged to be married; just as famously, it was Turing who broke off the engagement. Though they contrived to remain good friends, there are suggestions that Clarke was more hurt by this rejection than she ever cared to let on.

And against this backdrop and the wild, terrible tension of the Battle of the Atlantic, as Clarke was fighting to break U-Boat Shark codes, the civil service rigidity about her career continued with a note of exasperating comedy. She was promoted, but to the position of a linguist. She later noted the pleasure she took in filling out the form for the position. In the box set aside for foreign languages spoken, Clarke wrote rather defiantly: 'None'. At one stage, the then deputy director Edward Travis took her to one side and confided that further progress might only come if she joined the Women's Royal Navy. Clarke later noted wryly that there was a general suggestion that the pay of women might be improved if they 'had qualifications which were not relevant', including that of trained hairdresser.[4]

Balancing these day-to-day frustrations was the knowledge of being at the heart of Britain's war effort. The German navy's Admiral Dönitz was almost unique in having suspicions that his U-Boats' codes were being broken; he had nothing quite definite to pin this fear down, just some intuition that, occasionally, British shipping and submarines were not where they should have been expected to be. To this end – unlike any other branch of the German military – he had taken the already formidable Enigma and added an extra rotor to the machine, thus instantly generating millions more potential encoding possibilities. The nine months or so in 1942 when Hut 8 – Clarke and Turing and Twinn and Hugh Alexander – were knocked out of action by this addition were the tensest of Bletchley's war, the pressure for them to solve this now apparently insoluble problem bearing down on them from Churchill and the entire Whitehall establishment.

This was clearly Clarke's world; one in which a woman could achieve much without either being patronised by male colleagues or indeed sabotaged and tripped up by less competent male operatives. She recalled agreeing with a colleague that the code work – particularly on Turing's Banburismus method – was 'often so enthralling that the analyst due to go home at the end of the shift would be unwilling to hand over the workings'.[5] The colleague had been too polite to mention that Clarke 'had been a particular culprit, being in a billet within cycling distance instead of having to catch official transport'.[6]

At the end of the war, domesticity was not the only option: Clarke could very have returned to her mathematical studies at Cambridge. Indeed, her wealth of unusual experience might have propelled her into a distinguished academic career. Clarke was modest about her achievements in Hut 8. But the government knew just how crucial her efforts had been: she was made a Member of the Order of the British Empire, receiving her award at Buckingham Palace in 1947.

Clarke was to maintain afterwards that it was the experience of having worked alongside a mind such as Turing's that made her decide not to return to Cambridge. But this again sounds like modesty: for surely a love of mathematics as a philosophical pursuit was far more likely to flourish at university rather than within the confines of a Whitehall department. Instead, it is fair to speculate that life for Clarke as a codebreaker had been intensely rewarding in terms of excitement as well as the intellectual thrill of besting the enemy; and that she had no wish to see that excitement end.

And so it was that she had joined her old Hut 8 colleague Hugh Alexander, in the new concrete premises at the end of Lime Grove, Eastcote. And pleasingly, after the heartbreak of her relationship with Alan Turing, Clarke fell into a new, rather more fulfilled romantic relationship there. A new recruit to the Eastcote operation was a former military intelligence operative called Jock Murray. He was now retired from the army, and came to work as a civilian cryptanalyst. And so, amid a new kind of geopolitical tension, and the construction of a codebreaking operation that not merely tried to see into the heart of the enemy but also acted as a line of defence, the love between Clarke and Murray grew. They were to marry not too long afterwards; and aside from a brief interregnum, when Jock fell ill and had to retire from GCHQ for a while, they remained wedded to each other and to their codebreaking careers.

They had a rather charming hinterland too, Mr and Mrs Murray: a shared passion for coin collecting. They focused on historic Scottish coins, Joan settling on the 15th century as her chosen period of expertise. She not only made herself a brilliant numismatist, but her in-depth research also made her an authority on the literature and culture of 15th-century Scotland as well; certainly enough to be able to write and present a monograph to the Coin Collectors Society. Her friend Lord Stewartby wrote warmly of her nimble ability in mastering these and other areas of coin study. And not one of their fellows in the society had any idea of Mr and Mrs Murray's day jobs. After a brief spell in Scotland while Jock Murray recuperated from his illness, the couple then moved to Cheltenham where, by this stage, the new GCHQ was based. Jock stayed there until 1971, and Joan until the date of her retirement in 1977. This means that – discounting that brief spell away – Joan Clarke had been a cryptanalyst for over 35 years. So we might downplay the influence of Alan Turing a little, and stress rather Joan Clarke's inspirational work in the practical defensive applications of her mathematical ability; and what must also have been the excitement of being one of the very few British women who knew the nation's most closely guarded secrets.

What Clarke had in common with figures such as Hugh Foss, Nigel de Grey and Hugh Alexander was a steel-trap intellect – deadly serious, always firing at full intensity – with a certain humorous understated dryness. The mad passion for coin collecting was the creative equivalent of Hugh Foss's made-up Highland reels and Nigel de Grey's fascination for amateur dramatics: in one sense, a mechanism for escaping the pressure of the work but in another, an odd almost metaphorical reflection of it. Just as Foss's mathematical precision in formulating new dance steps had an element of fierce logic, so too did Clarke's decyphering of the meaning of ancient coins.

The most roaringly obvious metaphor for the work at Eastcote and at Bletchley Park was chess; and chess was the parallel career of senior codebreaker Hugh Alexander. The game had been in his blood since he was very young – he won the British Boys championship in 1926 aged 17 – and even before he had been reeled in for Bletchley duties in 1940, he was already an international champion as well as a published author on the subject. Naturally, his time in Hut 8 – assuming the leadership of it in 1942 after Turing had been moved aside to work on other projects – meant that Alexander had rather less time to think about, still less play chess. After the war, his first career move had been to take up a position with the John Lewis Partnership. But like so many of his colleagues, having been at the very centre of such a monumental achievement proved to have an addictive quality; and in 1946, Alexander was back, now at Eastcote, and heading up the fresh challenges to cryptanalysis.

The work was all-absorbing; but so too was Alexander's love for chess. The metaphor for cryptology – thinking ahead of the opponent, trying to decypher his strategy – took on greater resonance with the presence at international competitions of Soviet chess masters. It was in these contests that the new geopolitical blocs faced one another in intellectual duels; games that were a source of intense national pride, prestige and honour. In 1946 and 1947, Alexander played at two such contests in Hastings (precursors of a rather more spectacular chess coup against the Soviets in the winter of 1953, of which more later). Colleagues said of him that had it not been for his cryptanalytical work, there was every possibility that Alexander might have become a world chess champion. Indeed, it was a Soviet chess champion who paid him the warmest of compliments.

Mikhail Botvinnik said of his opponent: 'with his urge for overcoming and taming opposition, with his enthusiasm for uncompromising struggle, Alexander pioneered the way for British players to modern, complicated and daring chess'.[7]

Hugh Alexander also wrote a great deal about the game, in books and through a column in *The Spectator* magazine. Funnily enough, in discoursing about the principles of the game, and about its serious emotional, as well as intellectual, charge, Alexander might easily have been describing his Cold War opponents in his day job. 'My experience, both of myself and other chess-players, is that it is very difficult to lose at chess with good grace,' he wrote in one essay. 'This is because chess being entirely a game of skill you cannot soothe your wounded vanity by thinking that the cards were against you, that you find grass so slow after hard courts, that the sun was in your eyes when you missed the catch – there are no extraneous influences on which your defeat can be blamed; you are the sole cause of your own downfall – without a mistake on your own part, you cannot lose.'[8]

It is very easy to imagine him delivering the following sentiment to colleagues who were finding it impossible to jemmy their way into a cypher system: 'Try to remember that everyone loses many times and that by examining why you lost and where you played foolishly you will learn more than in any other way.'[9]

Oddly enough, one chess expert who knew rather more about Hugh Alexander's secret career than most was Harry Golombek. In 1945, Golombek took up the job of full-time chess correspondent for *The Times*, following competitions in which Alexander took part. But he had also had the opportunity to play Alexander at Bletchley Park, for he had been there as well. Indeed, when Alexander had taken on the responsibility of Hut 8 leadership, Golombek had found the chance for some games of chess with Alexander's colleague Alan Turing. And as with the game, so with the Park: champions deliberately sought out and recruited; the codes approached with the same lithe mental agility – and considered abstractedness – as the most knotted chess moves.

As a chess player, Alexander's advice to others was: never let up on the aggression. What lay before them was not simply a mental conundrum. It was a duel, and the opponent had to be fought, hard. 'Play for direct attack on the king,' he wrote. '. . . When you are a stronger player and have had more experience you can begin position play, which is very much more difficult, and you will then find that the combinative powers developed by an attacking style will be of the greatest service to you . . . you will be following the example of all the leading masters of this or any other period . . . All the world masters . . . whatever their ultimate style, started as brilliant attacking players.'[10]

Nor was there much patience for the idea of gentlemanly scruples. Any weakness in the opponent should be ruthlessly exploited – even if the weakest players complain 'that such tactics are unsporting'. It is easy to see the jump across to acquired code-books and cypher keys, or mistakenly twice-used one-time pads. Alexander's aggression on the chess board was not without humour; it was after all a game. But from this starting point of conflict came some more abiding principles. 'One of the dangers – even for very gifted players – of going over too early to the more positional styles of play is that you get afraid to attack and try to win with a complete avoidance of risk,' he wrote. 'I cannot emphasize too strongly that this is an aim that it is impossible to achieve and that a habit of cowardice is as fatal in chess as in everything else.'[11]

He also analysed the toll that the game could exact on even its most brilliant players. 'Tournament chess is a very great strain,' he wrote in the 1970s, a little after he finally retired from GCHQ (resisting all pleas for him to stay on). 'To some extent the professional's technique eases it – in so many situations he knows at once the type of plan to adopt . . . [but] it is hard work mentally, nervously and physically to overcome such opposition.'[12] Once again, it is easy to envisage the corollary: the cypher analyst, working deep into the silent night, looping and stretching his or her mind round the fractal chaos of coded messages, under immense pressure to burrow deep into the labyrinth in order to outwit the opposing side. 'Intensive preparation – study of one's opponents,' he continued, ' . . . is important; one must be physically fit or one will tire and blunder . . . However, there are compensations. Chess is a creative activity and there is the same satisfaction in playing a fine game as an artist or scientist gets from his work.' Alexander's next thought was freighted with unspoken irony. 'Moreover,' he wrote, 'unlike an artist, the chess player who plays fine chess gets instant recognition.'[13] No such recognition for the artists of Eastcote.

But in this passage, also written in the 1970s, with all those years of experience in Soviet opponents and Soviet cyphers, Alexander wrote of the chess world: 'Underlying the inevitable personal feuds and jealousies, there is a feeling of community in the chess world that cuts across barriers of nationality, age and class; one only has to attend an Olympiad to feel this – the often sordid disputes and incidents that mar these are nevertheless something "in the family".' World interest in the game was rising at that point; and this was in no small part down to the impact of Soviet players such as Boris Spassky. Was there any chance, with the rise of technology, that the contest would finally be played out? No, said Alexander. The game is 'still not fully explored' and 'will continue to fascinate and infuriate its players for many years to come'.[14]

Alexander also displayed a flourish of admiration for the way that the Soviets had, over the last few decades, developed their ideas on the way that the game should be played. 'With the victory of Botvinnik in the 1948 World Championship pentangular tournament,' he wrote, 'the period of Soviet dominance of world chess began, not to be broken until 1972 when [Bobby] Fischer wrested the championship from Russian hands. In addition to its playing success, the Soviet school has made substantial contributions to the theory of the game.'

Unlike their Russian predecessors back at the beginning of the century, said Alexander, the Soviet school took new psychological and tactical approaches. 'One could afford . . . to accept weaknesses if one got sufficient tactical chances,' he observed of their technique. The Soviet school 'has resulted in a great revitalisation of the game, play being now more varied and interesting than ever before'.[15]

It was impossible that there was not a deeper, wrier note in these remarks, for even upon retirement, Alexander was still being coaxed back into the equally ancient game of cryptology, not merely by his hugely admiring colleagues at GCHQ, but also by a substantial number of fans across the Atlantic in what was by then the National Security Agency.

Curiously enough, despite the awesome intellect that allowed him to take on the world's most serious chess players, and also the world's most serious cryptologists, Hugh Alexander was apparently not at all attuned to the new age of electro-mechanical dazzle. 'He regarded even driving a car as being technically beyond his reach,' as one former Bletchley colleague, Hugh Denham, remarked warmly in a tribute paper circulated within the National Security Agency. Alexander also 'never learnt to program'. But, added Denham, 'he understood clearly enough what computers can do for cryptanalysis and was the loudest propagandist at GCHQ for huge increases in our computer power.'[16]

Indeed, the new institution was to see the return in 1948 of one of Alexander's old chess-playing comrades: Irving John (Jack) Good, who had, since the war, been at Manchester University with Professor Max Newman working on developments in computer science. Although his precise role at Eastcote (and then Cheltenham) is still yet to be disclosed, it is not too difficult to speculate on the sort of areas Good might have specialised in.

Even though Hugh Alexander had tried returning to the John Lewis Partnership in 1945, it was not just the lack of excitement when compared to the clandestine thrill of cryptology: it was also having to work in an office where one was expected to wear black coat and striped trousers, like a bank manager of the time. Hugh Alexander was cut from rather more dashing cloth. And the essential point about him and colleagues such as Joan Clarke and Hugh Foss is that all of them would have presented faintly incongruous figures in the excessively drab and conformist cultural landscape of 1940s Britain. None of them would have been especially easy to place anywhere without their immediately standing out and perhaps also going against the institutional grain.

It has often been said of Bletchley Park that it required a certain kind of brain – not just in terms of IQ but also a certain personality and approach – to be a happy and successful codebreaker. The same must certainly be true of the institution that came afterwards. Unlike Bletchley though, these men and women did not have to prove themselves from scratch; they were building upon triumph, and in that sense commanded respect from America. But their Russian opponents were also building on a different sort of success; that of infiltration. And as well as the espionage disasters involving American atomic secrets, and the undermining of Britain's secret services, there was a shattering blow to come in terms of cryptology too. As never before, the men and women at Eastcote were going to need all their quirky good humour and energy.

Chapter Fifteen
Don't Even Breathe

This wide empty world of dusty pink soil and pale green grassland, quiet save for riffling winds and the sharp cries of wheeling birds, had hardly been touched by the 20th century; impossibly distant horizons rising in dark hills looked exactly as they had done to those merchants of silk and spice travelling in caravans from China to the Mediterranean in centuries past. Yet one day in the summer of 1949, an outrage was committed on the silent land; a roar deeper than hearing, a flash brighter than could be seen, the wide open sky now occluded by a fast-unfurling cloud of darkness.

The mystification that day among the British and Americans when Western spy planes detected nuclear activity from Kazakhstan in the east of the Soviet Union was profound. Before the oracle of Venona had started to reveal the trafficking of atomic secrets, the predictions of the intelligence agencies had been that Stalin would, inevitably, obtain his own bomb; but not for several more years yet. How, the authorities asked, had the Soviets been able to develop their own weapon – code-named First Lightning – so fast? Nor could the Western powers have known that this Soviet weapon had been built on the back of slave labour from the prison camps; uranium and other materials mined in barbaric circumstances, with many workers dying from radiation sickness. The detection of the test was also accompanied by instant geopolitical unease: now that the Soviet leader had the bomb, what would stop him using it to achieve further territorial ambitions?

The truth of the matter was that it took the codebreakers slightly too long to unveil the treachery of the atomic scientist Klaus Fuchs. The postscript to his story seems somehow even more extraordinary than his original treachery. As we have seen, Fuchs had turned up in the ongoing Venona decrypts (under the codenames 'Charles' and 'Rest'); there had been encrypted signals sent from the US to Moscow, detailing atomic secrets – information that had been supplied by Fuchs. Yet he was still above suspicion. By the time that mushroom cloud rose over the cold sands of Kazakhstan, Dr Fuchs was installed in a position of some responsibility at Harwell, Britain's top-secret nuclear research facility in Oxfordshire. It was only now that there were enough matches from decrypts to confirm that he was the man. In 1950, after the tip-off from the codebreakers, he was investigated by MI5, then arrested and put on trial. He was sentenced to 14 years in prison.

Incidentally, it is interesting to compare that sentence to the one handed down to British double agent George Blake in 1966 – of 42 years. There is absolutely no question that Fuchs's actions had the greater resonance, consequences that reverberated over four decades. Eventually, upon release, Fuchs emigrated from his adopted country to East Germany, where he remained until his death. The limitations for the intelligence services involved what we might call 'real time': the atomic traitor was uncovered, but only with a significant time-lag. By the time the Pandora's Box of Venona had been opened, the secrets were already across the Iron Curtain. Although the fact of Fuchs's employment at the heart of Britain's nuclear establishment does make one wonder what else he might have passed across had he not been caught.

The codebreakers and the listeners could intercept the signals; but anticipating where these signals might come from was quite another matter. A further fascinating afterword to the Klaus Fuchs atomic treachery story came decades later in the late 1990s when an apparently nremarkable old lady living in the south London area of Bexleyheath was revealed to have also passed great numbers of atomic secrets to the Soviets and the NKVD. Melita Norwood had grown up on the south coast; she and her family moved to London in the mid-1930s and by that time, she had seen much of the poverty and the hunger wrought by the Depression. She joined the Communist Party in 1936. In today's climate – where the listeners in Cheltenham carefully monitor those who pose security risks – it seems perfectly unthinkable that such a person would pass the vetting that would be required for working in a firm that would supply crucial data for the atomic programme.

Even before the outbreak of the Second World War, the British Non-Ferrous Metals Research Association was not quite as dry as its name suggested. Melita Norwood joined the firm in 1932; it covered all elements of metallurgy research. This included armaments as well as industry – aspects of which would be hugely useful to the desperately modernising Soviet Union. Not long after the war began, the firm struck a regular partnership with the similarly innocuous sounding Tube Alloys. In other words, it was helping with the atomic bomb research. In 1937, Norwood had volunteered her services to the Communists as a spy: she was given the codename 'Hola'. Very quickly, she was spying in the most traditional way: waiting until the office was clear, then opening her boss's safe, removing all the documents, photographing them with a special camera provided by her Soviet handler, then handing over the negatives.

It started with work that had straightforward military applications: metal research for guns and tanks. When she began photographing sensitive documents to do with research into the properties of uranium, she was handing over gold dust to her Soviet controller. In a curious way, her story as much as Fuchs's illustrates the impossible challenge for signals intelligence: the spies who by and large don't send any signals. Extraordinarily, Norwood finally came to be security vetted in 1945 (a shade too late): she passed the vetting with ease, despite her colourful political affiliations. The result was that she carried on working at the Non-Ferrous Metals firm, and continued, well into the 1940s, 1950s and 1960s, to pass a range of material to her Soviet handlers. On her retirement in the early 1970s, the Soviets even arranged for her to receive a modest pension from Moscow. She remained utterly in the shadows until the 1990s, when a defecting Soviet agent handed over boxes of archive material from the KGB and the exploits of 'Hola' were laid bare.

'I did not want money,' the grandmother told reporters. 'It was not that side I was interested in. I wanted Russia to be on an equal footing with the West. I never considered myself to be a spy, but it is for others to judge.'[1] There were calls to prosecute her; but really, with the Cold War itself now history, what would have been the point?

In a sense, these stories – if only they had been known – would have underscored Commander Edward Travis's anxiety to expand his signals intelligence operation back to the scale seen during the war. The Soviet Union, through guile and extensive infiltration, was gaining both power and influence. The detonation of its own atomic bomb in the wastes of Kazakhstan was the signal that the Cold War was now not only very much more serious, but also that the Soviet Union's new global reach would seriously imperil Western interests everywhere from the sands of Syria to the green jungles of what was then Indo-China. Agents such as Fuchs and Norwood had evaded the attentions of MI5; but by devoting more time and manpower to careful monitoring and decrypting of as much Soviet traffic as possible, here was a chance to divine Soviet intentions, and instantly.

Yet treachery brought another hammer-blow, both to Americans and British, but more particularly to the codebreakers. This time the agent was in America. A Russian-born émigré to the US, William Weisband had served as part of an army codebreaking unit in the desert in 1942. So proficient was he with cypher work that come 1944, he was posted back to Virginia, and Arlington Hall. Here he worked on Soviet traffic. According to Richard Aldrich, he had friendly discussions with resident codebreaking genius Meredith Gardner. This was a catastrophe. Weisband had been a fully-fledged Soviet agent since 1934.

And here before him – even though the team assigned to the work was very tight and secure – was the sheer weight and volume of the Venona project. These one-time-pad messages were unveiling Russian spies by the dozen: code names revealed, activities disclosed. Weisband went in to work every day acutely aware that his own identity and his own codename 'Zhora' would also be somewhere in that mass of secret communications. According to Aldrich, Gardner actually recalled at one point Weisband scanning a list of names that the Venona decrypts had most recently thrown up. It is fascinating to imagine how this popular, charming, chuckling figure maintained his outward geniality while every moment of every day knowing that his treachery was about to be exposed. Certainly his nerve-gnawing anxiety was finally conveyed to his Soviet controllers, and thence to Moscow: 'For one year,' ran an NKVD report, summing up Weisband's intelligence, 'a large amount of very valuable documentary material concerning the work of the Americans on deciphering Soviet cyphers, intercepting and analysing open-radio correspondence of Soviet Institutions was reached . . . On the basis of Weisband material, our state security organs carried out a number of defensive measures, resulting in the reduced efficiency of the American deciphering service. This has led to a considerable current reduction in the amount of deciphering and analysis by the Americans.'[2]

What had happened was this: in October 1948, partly as a result of the funk caused by the idea of Venona, the Soviets carried out a gigantic, far-reaching overhaul of every one of their encrypted operations. Not just rather more careful use of one-time pads, but much worse. For the first time, messages between various arms of the Soviet army, navy, air-force, even the police – all of which had provided huge amounts of material to British interceptors – were thoroughly encrypted. Even the most trivial message – which before the operators would simply transmit as was – was now converted into a vortex of code. Added to this was the implosion of the so-called 'Poets' codes that the British and Americans had been reading ever since their forays through shattered, defeated Germany, picking up fresh codebreaking tips along the way. All Soviet systems were changed, overnight, on 29 October 1948.

It was akin to the shattering blow dealt to Bletchley's Hut 8 in 1942. The timing in the case of the Soviets was also frightful: even before they had exploded that first atomic bomb, there was rising paranoia in the West about what Stalin might be planning not just for Europe, but other regions. There were some who – in their neurosis – argued that it was time to allow Germany to re-arm, in order to defend the Rhine against a Red Army that would not stop marching until it reached the North Sea.

On Forest Moor in Yorkshire, as the shrewd winds scoured the rough grass and the firs, the radio operators continued to pick up all Soviet traffic; but there was nothing that could be plucked from the encoded chaos. In Germany itself, along the jumpy border that now separated two wholly alien blocs, radio operators could no longer listen in on chatty exchanges with their opposite numbers; instead, all had become impenetrable.

Yet there was one rather innovative figure who had, that same year, taken a slightly less orthodox approach to intercepting messages, and listening in on discussions. Indeed, the principle on which his idea rested would provide, over the next few years, some of the more divertingly bizarre and sometimes blackly comical stories of signals intelligence, and its growing dominance in the spy game. The man's name was Peter Lunn, and he was based in the Austrian capital of Vienna.

Even by the standards of the time, Lunn had lived quite a life. He was an Old Etonian champion skier, who had pioneered ski racing and had written books on the subject. His grandfather had founded a travel agency that today is perhaps better known in its modern merged form as Lunn Poly. The outbreak of war saw him pulled into the orbit of MI6, and stationed in Malta (a source of distress to him owing to a total lack of any possibility of skiing). Then came the aftermath of war. Lunn was dispatched as station chief to the city of Vienna which, like Berlin, had been split by the victors into different sectors. Of course, there are now a number of ready-made images conjured by the 1949 Carol Reed thriller *The Third Man*; a sinister city of shadows and silhouettes. Curiously, just one year before that, Lunn's Vienna was holding out possibilities of espionage that were very much more bizarre.

The Western Allies, from 1945 onwards, had not only been trying to stabilise the conquered Austria and its abject, freezing and hungry population; they had also been trying to root out Nazis. Austria's 1938 Anschluss with Germany meant that it, too, would essentially have to be completely re-invented as a nation. Austria suffered hideous repercussions for its role in the war: much as in Berlin, the invading Red Army had embarked upon a campaign of rape, with many thousands of Viennese women attacked. In the traumatised weeks and months of peace, this was the crime that the city lived with silently.

In strategic terms, the Soviets, while also concerned with warding off anarchy, had ideas of their own: the first, ensuring that local elections went well for Communist candidates; and also appropriating oil and materials for infrastructure for transportation back to the Soviet Union. Politically, the city of Vienna had always leaned towards socialism; it was out in the small Alpine towns and villages in the Austrian countryside that the People's Party – conservative and deeply Catholic – held sway. But the Austrians had to be terrifically careful. Their country bordered on Czechoslovakia, Hungary and Yugoslavia, all client states of Stalin. Even though the Western Allies shared their occupancy of Austria with the Soviets, that crackling tension, the sense that Austria too could be swallowed whole by the Kremlin, was uncomfortably pervasive. Indeed, in 1948, the visionary US Director of Policy Planning George Kennan had started mapping out contingencies for what should happen if the Red Army attempted a total takeover. What would Allied troops on the ground be able to do about a concerted surge from the Red Army?

So what had started out as a wariness between the two neighbouring blocs soon froze into something more hostile. The tensions rose against a backdrop not only of grand city ruins – once proud recital halls and opera houses shattered, fragmented, exquisite architecture flattened and erased – but of thinly dressed Viennese citizens subsisting on tiny rations of bread, peas and root vegetables. In the year after the war, the average intake for a Viennese citizen was 800 calories a day; by contrast, today, even people on the most radical diets are taking in double that. On top of this was a chronic shortage of heating. There were many who would set out on foot to leave the city boundaries, walk into the nearby forests, chop wood, and then walk all the way back to their homes in the city, piles of fuel tied to their backs. Added to this was a thriving black market; Graham Greene's chilling Harry Lime was the fictional emblem of a much more widespread phenomenon.

By 1948, the Soviet grip on lower Austria had tightened, but the Austrians were chafing under Stalinist methods and ideology; the occupying forces were costing them, not only in terms of appropriation, but also in terms of being unable to kick-start new trade and industry. Vienna itself had recovered a little of its old Habsburg sophistication: that year saw the concert halls boast distinguished visiting artists such as Yehudi Menuhin and Leonard Bernstein. But at the heart of Vienna was something rather darker, as Alexander Kendrick, a correspondent for the US journal *New Republic* put it in the summer of 1948: 'Vienna is less an international capital, in the old sense of the phrase, than an advance base for propaganda, espionage and intrigue. Intelligence agents, detectives and informers for all four occupying powers; displaced persons of a dozen nationalities; black marketeers; spivs, prostitutes, money-changers and night-club-bar girls form a large demi-monde . . . By the time minor incidents filter through successive layers of intrigue, they become events of international importance.'[3]

And amid those tensions – including occasional outbreaks of drunken violence between American and Russian soldiers, fighting over women – the British espionage contingent, Peter Lunn among them, was setting to work on an ambitious idea that would come to brilliant, clandestine, fruition a few months later in 1950. The basic idea was simplicity itself: tunnelling. Lunn came to realise that various Soviet telephone cables actually ran under streets in the British- and French-controlled zones of the city. The technology of phone-tapping had been pursued enthusiastically by British pioneers decades beforehand – pretty much as soon as the first undersea telephone cables had been laid. The British government had made quiet arrangements with specialised engineers to avail itself of what was effectively a world-spanning telephone-monitoring campaign. The work itself was farmed out to the 'Y' Service and the results were collated back in England. In this case, Peter Lunn first of all wanted to be sure that it was possible to carry out secret surveillance and that the mechanics could be installed in rather more awkward conditions, and kept properly hidden. Peter Taylor, one of Dr Tommy Flowers's colleagues from the Dollis Hill Post Office Research station was summoned to Vienna.

Along with Eastcote, and various sub-branches of MI6, the Dollis Hill station had continued, after the war, to pursue all sorts of Cold War research activity: means not only by which to eavesdrop, but also to ensure that the British protected themselves from hostile listeners. Taylor looked at the possibilities of the Soviet telephone line that ran from the embassy and eventually all the way out to a Soviet airfield just outside the city. He concluded that it would indeed be possible to listen in from here.

Intriguingly, Peter Lunn felt it better not to inform the Foreign Office of what he was doing; he had little doubt – and he was right – that he would have been told to desist instantly, for fear of causing a diplomatic calamity at a time when relations were already quite fraught enough. But he did have allies within the Joint Intelligence Committee who had very quietly given their (unofficial) approval. On top of this, Britain's ambassador in the city, Harold Caccia, was kept informed, and his approval was wholehearted. He later said that he could not have lived with himself if the Soviets had invaded; this was his covert contribution. His fears of Soviet intentions were hardly ideological abstractions: the close, cobbled back-streets of Vienna were swarming with hostile Soviet agents. Every single part of the city was under constant surveillance. So how exactly could Peter Lunn establish a nest of secret listeners – first through tunnelling, then setting them up with an underground base from which to listen in to all communications – without enemy agents spotting unusual activity?

Again, somehow without letting the Foreign Office know, Lunn enlisted a small number of Royal Engineers. According to security expert Gordon Corera, there were appalling moments of tension before the army party with the specialised recording equipment even arrived. Lunn and his colleagues waited for them at the designated railway station; but there was no sign of them. It turned out that the men – and the top-secret equipment – had mistakenly disembarked at another Vienna station deep within the Russian zone of the city. If they were caught, there would be little doubt what the equipment was for. The men rang through to the British office and the duty officer kept it explosively short and to the point: 'Don't move, don't look at anyone, don't talk to anyone. In the meantime don't even breathe and we will be out within half an hour.'[4]

The men and their equipment were safely retrieved. Peter Lunn had found cover for his planned tunnel: it would be located beneath a jeweller's shop. The Royal Engineers who constructed the tunnel, just a few feet beneath the surface of the street (Harry Lime, pursued through the sewers, would perhaps have run parallel to it at some point), were not only working under conditions of gravest secrecy; those involved were shortly afterwards sent for new duties in the Far East. Then came the special teams of interceptors. Like those at Beaumanor, or Forest Moor, or Batty's Belvedere in Hong Kong, they were generally very young. In shifts, they would sit in a cavern beneath the jeweller's shop, and listened in to what would soon become a very rich bounty of intelligence.

In that humid tunnel, lit with yellowing light-bulbs, the young men picked up calls and communications not merely between Vienna-based Soviets, but conversations stretching out throughout the Balkans and the Soviet Union; there was much about troop movements and dispositions. Incidentally, as Gordon Corera points out, one of these young secret listeners was Rodric Braithwaite; although distrusted by his senior officer because of his taste for left-leaning journal *The New Statesman*, Braithwaite was a rather brilliant recruit, and later went on to enjoy an incredibly fruitful career, including (the quiet irony) a spell as British ambassador in Moscow, and chairmanship of the Joint Intelligence Committee.

In a curious way, all this lurking about in secret tunnels was symbolic of a conflict that had in part been started by another Moscow ambassador: George Kennan who, a couple of years before, had written that anonymous article, swiftly dubbed 'The Long Telegram', which had detailed Soviet aggression and paranoia and which had advocated a policy of containment. He followed this up with a lengthy analytical essay, also published anonymously in the journal *Foreign Affairs* under the byline 'X' (diplomats were not expected to give voice to such views). By 1948, this need for containment seemed perfectly illustrated in Vienna. To the Western Allies – and in particular, to the more hawkish military commanders among them – it looked as though the Russians were set on dominating as much as they possibly could; that Communism was a cult, or even a form of plague, that could conceivably infect any nation. By 1948, America was already viewing itself as a form of world policeman: wherever it looked as though Communism might take root, the Americans had to counter it, fully armed if need be. This policy, advocated by President Truman, came to be known as 'The Truman Doctrine', and had solidified during the Greek Civil War. In that instance the Western Allies had given backing to those who opposed the Communists. Now, any country in the world that appeared to be turning red would have to be 'contained'. And in Vienna, where Soviets and American soldiers sometimes walked the same streets, hair-trigger tension and mutual incomprehension was woven into the fabric of the city.

But this kind of international mutual aggression came swiftly to be regretted by Kennan. It did not have to be like this. While he continued to abominate Stalin, he also came to be a fierce critic of increasing American militarism. Kennan hated the idea of some kind of security state. Unwittingly, he had led the intellectual charge towards a wholly bipolar world, with both Americans and Soviets now seeking to impose themselves on far-distant lands, both believing that the other was set on total conquest. The struggle in Vienna was a sneak preview; as the Cold War frost sharpened over the years, the death-lock struggle between superpowers was to extend to every continent.

The British security services needed no encouragement; it might have been MI6 on this occasion which was gaining intelligence from tapped cables, but the operatives at Eastcote, side by side with their US colleagues, were wholly committed. (Strangely enough, some of the language that is used today by intelligence officers in Cheltenham carries an echo of that original Government Code and Cypher School ethos: escorting the author and journalist Ben McIntyre on a special guided tour of these otherwise extraordinarily secret premises recently, some figures explained to him that the work of GCHQ was about protecting Britain from 'baddies'. The core of the establishment – ever since it was Room 40 in the Admiralty during the First World War – has been love for country, heightened by the knowledge that the country is under constant threat from irredeemably wicked enemies.)

So much material was generated by means of Peter Lunn's Vienna tunnel that back in London, an entirely separate Y Service station was established within an office at Carlton Gardens, just off Pall Mall. From here, reams of transcripts were analysed extensively by a dedicated intelligence team. Interestingly, this intelligence stream seemed to fall outside the remit of Eastcote and Edward Travis's team (although, strictly speaking, all signals intelligence should have been referred back to them). Instead, there seems to have been a shade of MI6 competitiveness, together with a flourish of triumphalism. Although this was early days for the nascent, independent GCHQ, it did present a challenge to its original parent, the Secret Intelligence Service. First, the codebreakers had enjoyed a near-impeccable war, and their handling of the new, neurotic climate had also been deft. But by the late 1940s, MI6 was not in so happy a position.

It was not just the (admittedly vast) issue of the Cambridge Spies: the service itself, with its insouciant clubland approach, may have been looking dangerously and anachronistically class-bound, particularly during the years of Attlee's government. If it had been dazzlingly and demonstrably effective over the past few years, then perhaps that scent of aristocratic languor and decadence might not have mattered so much. But now the codebreakers appeared to be pointing to a new technocratic era with rather more impressive results.

There will always be inter-departmental scuffles and fights; indeed, the James Bond film *Spectre* focuses in part upon an attempted takeover of 007's traditionalist department by the cyber-security branch – which is of course the modern-day equivalent of Eastcote or GCHQ. And Peter Lunn's brilliant Vienna tunnel was a much-need coup for MI6 prior to the all-time low of the revelation of deep-level penetration by the Soviets. The Vienna tunnel remained operational for several years, until two unfortunate events saw it come to an end. First, the Soviets simply upgraded and moved their cables. Second, there was an unexpected outbreak of subsidence, which saw a Vienna bus get jammed in a pothole and then subsequently sink into the cavern beneath.

But it was to inspire another tunnel in another divided city; and a few years later, when the even more ambitious Berlin tunnel had been excavated, MI6, rather like that Vienna bus, was to sink deep into a frightful cavern of its own making. Nonetheless, the principle had proved effective, and it was also a pointer for the technicians at Eastcote and at

Dollis Hill. Dr Tommy Flowers had not only inaugurated the age of the computer, but was also a wizard at developing the engineering possibilities of electronics. Tapping a cable was one thing; how long would it be before there could be devices capable of listening in to conversations some distance off? And would bugging devices soon be able to be miniaturised practically to the point of invisibility? Such questions were shortly to acquire a greater urgency.

Chapter Sixteen

Invasion of the Ferrets

Ever since the Victorian pioneers of military ballooning took to the skies over the deserts of Sudan in the 19th century, establishing a god-like all-seeing omniscience over rebels below, the dream of being able to observe and hear every move the enemy made, every conversation about battle plans, had been refreshed by new technological developments. During the Second World War, the arts of aviation and photography were melded into a spectacular secret enterprise that revolutionised reconnaissance missions: now it was possible not only to capture aerial views of enemy installations, but also to photograph them in such a way as to render three-dimensional images, from which so much more could be gleaned. From the point of view of Bletchley Park, the aural equivalent of this was the Y Service, faithfully and brilliantly eavesdropping on all enemy chatter, from the Luftwaffe pilots in the air to the commanders in the scorpion-infested deserts.

And now the innovations at Hanslope Park and the research laboratory at Dollis Hill were beginning to offer even more ambitious possibilities for GCHQ, which was placing itself very much at the forefront of this jet-age espionage. For Commander Travis and his cypher-breaking team at Eastcote, the mastery of signals intelligence was soon to be matched by a growing proficiency in what came to be termed electronic intelligence. It was here that the codebreakers really began to prefigure the wildest creations of Ian Fleming's boffin Q.

The dignified real-life version of Q was the brilliant government scientist Dr RV Jones; he was the wizard who divined in the early stages of the Second World War that German bombers were being guided to their targets by specially transmitted radio-wave 'beams' that intersected over the position where the bombs were to be dropped. Dr Jones invented a way to 'bend' these beams; he might not have been able to stop the onslaught of the Blitz but, nonetheless, a great many potential Luftwaffe targets were missed. And importantly, Dr Jones's deep study of this kind of guidance technology was helpful when it came to the bombing raids made by the British. Alongside this was a fast-growing ability to 'read' radar – that is, to monitor the enemy's radar and divine intentions from the nature of the waves. When the war began, radar was still so new as to be regarded by some as a form of black magic; very swiftly, though, planes fitted with radios and antennae came to be essential in fast-moving espionage operations.

Picking up radar signals by flying directly over enemy territory, these planes could relay huge amounts of information back to analysts on the ground concerning enemy positions and plans. What had been rather clunky and primitive technology had, by the end of the war, become sleek and lethally effective. Such spy planes were flown over the vast jungles of Burma, sucking up intelligence on otherwise utterly hidden units.

Added to this, it seems that British advances in this field – so vaulting, so fast – were a source of enormous envy to senior figures in the American air force, who were astounded by their ingenuity. They were not slow to appropriate the principles but even so, in those immediate post-war years, British creativity was held up as the leading example. The spy-planes used for electronic intelligence reconnaissance flights were referred to colloquially as 'ferrets'. One of the chief areas of ferret activity in the late 1940s was over East Germany. In 1948, the Joint Intelligence Committee had let Commander Travis and all at Eastcote know that their number-one priority in gathering information had to focus very strongly on Central and Eastern Europe. So began a series of quite daring cat-and-mouse missions, eluding the attentions of Soviet fighter planes; the ferrets were fitted with the very latest technology that Dr RV Jones and his fellow scientists could devise.

The Joint Intelligence Committee had very specific targets for intelligence, as a memo from the time reveals. 'Development in the Soviet Union of atomic, biological and chemical methods of warfare' was, naturally enough, at the top of the list. Added to this was the development of 'scientific principles and interventions leading to new weapons, equipment or methods of warfare'. But war is not just about weapons or the mobilisation of troops. The committee was also desperate to know about 'Soviet economic successes or reverses (such as the drought of 1946) likely to have an effect on foreign policy' plus, pressingly, 'significant internal political developments in the Soviet Union (especially question of succession to Stalin)'.[1]

This memo, from 1948, also demonstrated that the codebreakers of Eastcote and their Whitehall masters were even more alert to Stalin's influence across the world than their American friends. The committee specifically wanted the cryptanalysts to find out all they could about 'Soviet intentions in Germany and Austria' and 'Soviet relations with Jews in Palestine (particularly the extent of Soviet and satellite assistance of emigration)'. They sought information about any Russian manoeuvres in the Arctic; and (although they were later accused of looking in the wrong direction) also investigated any 'Soviet intentions in China and Korea'.[2]

It was not all about the Soviet Union. The codebreakers also had a remit to investigate the Chinese, and the possible outcomes of the struggle between nationalist Chiang Kai-shek and the insurgent Mao Zedong. Despite the crucial listening station in Hong Kong, China and many other countries in the Far East were in danger of becoming a blind spot. In the case of Korea, it was because there was simply not that much traffic to intercept and analyse.

Nor was it all about a fear of Communism. The codebreakers were asked to carefully monitor 'clandestine right-wing French and Italian movements'. By the late 1940s, Communism in Western Europe was waning as a political and parliamentary force; but a rising young generation was venting its anger in more than one form of extremism. GCHQ was also asked to penetrate 'Zionist movements' and their 'intelligence services'.[3] The chiefs of security in Whitehall must have yearned for Bletchley Park's almost panopticon view of so many theatres of war; but these were years of instability and unpredictability.

Despite the vast scale of what was being asked of them, the codebreakers very quickly understood that these kind of operations should really stay within their departmental orbit, rather than that of the War Office (as the Ministry of Defence was called until many years after the war ended) or indeed any of the other services. Not that the aerial 'ferret' trawls over hostile territory in the east of Europe resulted in codes that needed breaking; but rather like radio traffic analysis, this was another means of almost providing a real-time commentary on enemy activities and troop dispositions.

The 'ferrets' concerned were Lancaster and Lincoln aeroplanes, specially refitted. The codebreakers began making serious use of them in the late 1940s; taking off from the British-occupied zone in West Germany, the pilots and the crew undertook many risky missions, ever conscious of the serious jeopardy posed by Russian fighters. They flew missions along the borders of regions such as Latvia and Lithuania, over the Baltic, and then further afield to the Black Sea, not straying into Soviet airspace but getting as close as imaginably possible. Some planes, taking off from the Middle East, were circling as far afield as Iran. Richard Aldrich noted that as the technology improved, these planes became flying intelligence fortresses. They were jammed with electronic surveillance equipment that was sometimes amusingly at odds with the now-antiquated planes carrying them.

For these aviation adventures, the codebreakers had teamed up with the Royal Air Force, which had of course been greatly slimmed down in the aftermath of the war. Pilots were taught about the importance of the work the listeners were doing, and about the vital importance of secrecy. And once a sweep had been made along the borders of East Germany, or Poland, or any of the other target regions, what would then happen to the raw data?

A specially dedicated RAF base was found for the gathering of all electronic intelligence: Watton in Norfolk. Here was gathered an extraordinary motley collection of outmoded Second World War planes which were all now used by the boffins not merely for grabbing information, but also for purposes of jamming Soviet radio-waves. It was a game that both sides were playing; the Russians were catching up quickly and with some proficiency. While old Halifax planes lurked in the skies of the Eastern European borderlands, Russian planes spiky with antennae were executing similar manoeuvres over Western Europe (and also over American bases scattered in other continents). Naturally, the Americans were swift to join the listeners in the skies: various US aircraft patrolled regions such as the Arctic, remaining alert for any pulses of radar that would signal clandestine enemy activity on the ground below.

There was some photography too; even though the need to stay out of Soviet airspace meant that the chance to capture images of military installations was limited, there were nonetheless shots that were of great help to the analysts back at base. This combination of intelligence gathering – the monitoring of radar pulses, the photography of bases, the recording of conversations on the ground below – was assembled as a sort of jigsaw of data. None of this was done for its own sake. That widespread sense in the late 1940s that conflict was once more going to flare meant that the patrols – already tense – carried the responsibility of reporting whether the Soviet enemy was just about to launch an attack. For their part, the Soviets, afflicted by the grinding paranoia of Stalin, would have been looking at the West with similar jumpy mistrust. The need for total accuracy on both sides was paramount. Any misinterpretation of movements along the Soviet border could have led to a continent, already on its knees, being forced into another bout of unthinkable carnage.

The hazards for the crews of these 'ferret' flights were occasionally unexpected. Signaller Frank Slee was commended for his bravery and quick thinking when 'radio counter-measures' equipment that he was working with in mid-flight overheated and burst into flames. Then there were the attendant technical difficulties of the work. Signaller William Lowther was warmly praised by his superiors for his notable powers of concentration as an on-board wireless operator, reading signals and direction-finding with pinpoint precision under circumstances of great stress and tension.

The man in charge of ensuring that the RAF's brave and brilliant collection of intelligence was directed towards Eastcote, rather than the sister security agencies, was Lieutenant Colonel Marr-Johnson, who had a series of meetings with senior RAF commanders. There was another eager customer: Lieutenant Colonel Marr-Johnson's friends in America. All the data gathered by the ferrets was to be shared with the United States; another sign of the closeness of the relationship.

This was of course just a few years before satellites. Now we all take for granted the idea that on our phones and computers, we can zoom in on pretty much anywhere on earth. After the end of the war, codebreakers and intelligence gatherers looked at maps of the Soviet Union and understood that they knew next to nothing; beyond the Iron Curtain was simply a haze. Michael L Peterson of the American National Security Agency later wrote of this information vacuum, and how intensely nerve-wracking it was.

'Maybe you had to be there in the late 1940s and early 1950s to appreciate the degree of the nation's concern over the threat posed by the Soviet Union . . .' he wrote. 'Maybe you had to be around also to appreciate the enormous gap in our knowledge of Soviet military and industrial capabilities hidden behind the Iron Curtain . . . Today if you look at an intelligence map of the former Soviet Union, you probably couldn't see the geographical features for all the annotations. Covering the depictions of winding rivers, modest mountain ranges, great deserts, and miles and miles of tundra would be circles and squares and diamonds and arrows pointing to boxes of information everywhere.

'. . . That annotated information map didn't just happen. The information took years to acquire and validate . . . In 1945, the Soviet Union might as well have been on Mars.' Peterson quoted from a 1947 USAF document outlining the peril that the crews of these reconnaissance flights faced. 'This mission is considered a most hazardous one both from the natural peril and capture standpoints,' it stated. 'All flight personnel are volunteers and are fully apprised of possible consequences should the plane be forced to land in foreign territory. The crew is warned that in the event of detention repatriation will be attempted but will probably be unsuccessful.

For purposes of cover, the project is described as a weather mission. Equipment for complete demolition of the plane and its equipment has been provided.'[4]

As Peterson went on to say, in fact many missions ended rather more violently, with the crews shot down and killed. The principle of ferrets also caused outbreaks of diplomatic fury. The Soviet ambassador in Washington vented his rage in 1947 after two US ferret missions had been detected over Soviet interests in Big Diomede island, near the Arctic Circle. It was also from the frozen far north that American crews made ferret forays into the vast Russian wastes of Siberia.

The US Navy – which had contributed so heavily towards the codebreaking efforts throughout the war against Japan – was also flying its own ferret missions from aircraft carriers. Amusingly, it was not only the British who had occasion to extemporise. Having decided to take part in ferret flights, the US Navy then realised that it did not have quite enough equipment for the planes to carry. A lot of machinery had been sold as surplus just after the war. The answer? Two US naval technicians were sent out on a shopping expedition. 'Wearing civilian clothes and carrying large quantities of cash,' went one naval report, 'the two chiefs rooted through war surplus stores in New York City. They purchased all the intercept receivers, direction finders, pulse analysers, and other electronic reconnaissance equipment they could locate.'[5]

(Incidentally, Michael L Peterson was himself another example of the special spying relationship; before he later became a writer, he was transferred over to England to be a 'cryptologic staff officer' at the Forest Moor station in the 1970s.)

Another ingenious British–American collaboration involved the fathomless oceans: first, the Americans carried out experiments with submarines in the Bering Straits. The idea was that from deep beneath the waves, they could monitor the transmissions of Soviet naval bases. Two submarines were then chosen to undertake more detailed, full-time patrols. They were, according to Professor Richard Aldrich, sailed to Britain in order to be fitted out in Portsmouth. There were new instruments that could be used to detect any missile activity. At the rear of the submarines were specially fitted aerials. The *Cochino* was one of these submarines, and it set off on a maiden mission to patrol the Barents Sea and to listen out for any traces of Soviet missile use.

But tragedy and horror struck. Not through enemy action, but because of a vast storm that caused a hull breach. This in turn started a terrible chemical fire. And in the desperate efforts to extinguish it, one man died and others were hideously burned. The peculiarly nightmarish quality of serving on a submarine – in moments of serious jeopardy like that – can only have been heightened by the doubly horrible need for the craft to remain completely undetected by the Soviets, for fear that its technological secrets could be harvested. A companion submarine, the *Tusk*, came to the aid of the stricken vessel. Now surfaced, and smashed by roaring mountainous waves, the horror intensified as six prospective rescuers from *Tusk* who were trying to reach *Cochino* were swept overboard and lost; and yet somehow the wounded crew of *Cochino* were transferred, via unsteady plank, to the functioning ship, and then taken back to base for treatment.

No matter how bad the auguries from this initial mission were, these sorts of spy submarine missions were to proliferate greatly; as with all else, the Soviets were very swift to catch up with the Americans' efforts. Such vessels were extremely effective, capturing evidence of missile testing and details of naval manoeuvres. Some years later on, they would also become involved in terrifying duels, Soviet craft attempting to ram British and American submarines.

In 1949, the terms of the Cold War were, in a sense, made official by the foundation of NATO (North Atlantic Treaty Organisation), the formal alliance between Western Europe and the United States. Britain's foreign secretary Ernest Bevin – who had been so anxious for the United Kingdom to acquire its own nuclear capability – was sharply realistic about those who put their faith in more pacific organisations. 'It seems vital to me', he declared on one occasion, 'not to deceive the peoples of the world by leading them to believe that we are creating a United Nations Organisation which is going to protect them from future wars, in which we share our secrets, while we know, in fact, that nothing of the kind is happening.'

Article 5 of the NATO treaty was the opposite of compromise: an armed attack against any one of the member states would be considered an attack against them all, and the response would be gauged accordingly.

This was one branch of America's efforts to rebuild a continent with which it could trade; the other was the money that started filtering through via the Marshall Plan. It remains to some of a certain age a rather sore point that while the British were forced into miserable winters of scrimping in order to repay their wartime debts to America, the people of West Germany were boosted by the easier terms on which they were granted a vast injection of cash that led to an economic golden age for the mighty German manufacturing base. But whatever its own interests – the soaring post-war American economy needed Western Europe to regain its feet – the fact remained that this kind of reconstruction was absolutely vital to ensure that the embers of Nazism were fully extinguished. (Indeed, there are still dark suggestions that those embers were more stubborn than most realised; the TV producer who brought the Adolf Eichmann trial to television in 1961, for instance, recalled going to nightclubs in West Germany in the 1950s where old Nazi phrases were still being used by the clientele.)

And as NATO coalesced, so too did the plans of the US military: another reason Bevin was so determined that Britain should have its own nuclear capability, rather than be shackled to the US. Curtis LeMay, head of US Strategic Air Command, set out a plan for war against the Soviet Union; the firepower that would be required to bring Stalin to his knees. His calculations ran thus: it would take 133 nuclear bombs dropped on 70 Russian cities. Three million civilians were expected to be killed instantly; another four million would be grievously injured. There was a nauseating sense of momentum about such thinking, a gathering idea that the United States might be wise to make a pre-emptive strike before Stalin's forces got the chance to inflict the same radiated horror upon America's cities. This, after all, was the nation where Senator Joseph McCarthy's enthusiasm for permanent, rolling witch-hunts against Communists was catching on throughout all sorts of institutions and communities; a nation where a travelling exhibition of American constitutional documents – on board

'The Freedom Train' – required entire towns to come out and worship these sacred texts of American exceptionalism when they arrived at the railroad station.

The curious irony is that the idea of pre-emptive attack was actually forestalled by the growth of the US military-industrial complex, and by the vast financial investments pumped into the quest to perfect bigger, better nuclear bombs: rather than irradiate the whole of Russia (and by extension, inevitably, vast swathes of Europe) could not America's scientists simply outpace the Soviets and develop super-bombs so nightmarishly terrible in their potential that the Kremlin would be utterly cowed? And so the weapons race – particularly towards the goal of the hydrogen bomb – began.

And NATO (formed of France, Britain, Belgium, the Netherlands, Luxembourg, Canada, the United States, Iceland, Italy, Portugal and Denmark) was not just about the Soviet menace either. It was also a means of helping to ensure that Germany, or at least the western half of it, would remain stable. For while the Americans were fretting about Stalin, the French were still rather more acutely anxious about the possibility of their neighbours becoming aggressive once more. While France and Britain were among the first signatories of the NATO treaty, the West Germans were kept out of it: for the time being, they still could not be trusted militarily. For the others, the signing of the treaty saw more waves of American money – this time being spent on military establishments and hardware – shoring up the line between the West and the Soviet bloc. Even as Britain continued with strict rationing, American bases of all varieties sprouted around the British landscape. From the point of view of the codebreakers, this was to include the striking listening establishment at the far tip of Cornwall.

The year 1949 also saw the Allies allowing West Germany to govern itself, ending the post-war period of occupation. British and American military bases would remain on West German soil, but the country itself would finally be going to the polls to elect its first post-war chancellor. That man was Konrad Adenauer. The government that he headed up was – thanks both to American aid and also a certain native work ethic on the part of the West Germans – almost preposterously successful, and indeed he stayed as chancellor for the next 17 years. Adenauer's government was not based in Berlin, but Bonn. There was some suggestion that even if his country had not been split, Adenauer actually had little time for the regions of the east – the sundering suited him perfectly well. Indeed, it also suited a number of politicians in other countries. Some, like the British prime minister-to-be Harold Macmillan, took the view that for reunification of Germany to remain far off was very much for the best: it would stop the Germans ever being tempted into resuming old territorial ambitions.

Since the Berlin Blockade of 1948, tensions in that city, deep within the Soviet zone of occupation, had been heightening. But this was still some time before the vast concrete structure of the Berlin Wall went up. Here, West and East continued to co-exist – just – without any flare-ups of violence. (In the years before the Wall's construction in 1961, it is estimated that some three million East Germans crossed over to the Western sector, and from there defected to Western Europe; many of these were doctors, lawyers and other trained professionals. Conversely, a rather small number of artists, writers and intellectuals made the journey to East Berlin, preferring to live in what they regarded as more ideologically pure austerity.)

This was the world that was being transmitted back to Eastcote and analysed. The men and women of GCHQ, charged with monitoring all incarnations of Communism, were now charting the Eastern bloc's response to the super-charging of the West German economy, with all the temptations that prosperity presented for so many citizens of the East. George C Marshall had wanted the Russians to participate – and benefit from – the American money that was pumping in to the continent. Stalin, though, had refused. And now the landscape was beginning to assume its new shape: while West Germany disconcertingly sprang to rebuilt life in next to no time, a grey pall of poverty continued to hang over Poland, Czechoslovakia and others. There are two types of warfare: military and economic. As the West pulled sharply away from the Soviet bloc, so the pressure on the Kremlin started to rise. People living under Stalinist rule began to understand what it was that they were being denied.

Those citizens of Czechoslovakia, of Hungary, of Romania, were now required to live according to Stalin's blueprint. In agriculture, for instance, any last traces of a peasant class were swept away; the collectivisation of private land began, and the poorer agricultural labourers were swept up into five-year plans. Meanwhile, there was also extensive industrialisation; under the ruler of steel (the meaning of Stalin's adopted name), this was very much to be an age of steel. But, as Tony Judt has observed, even though the populations of Western Europe largely ignored what was happening in the East, there were vast numbers of people in the Eastern countries who had looked west towards cities like Vienna in search of culture and art. The culture of Soviet Russia was in many ways an alien imposition. This is not the sort of intelligence that is generally picked up by cryptanalysis; but the Eastcote codebreakers would nonetheless have been deeply aware of the rich life of cities such as Prague and Bucharest, and they must have wondered what sort of a story this new and sudden – even sullen – silence told.

But GCHQ's curiosity had its budgetary limits too. Even if the organisation was once more expanding, to absorb those with the cultural as well as mathematical expertise to analyse the cryptology of its targeted nations, the financial arrangements dealt with by Commander Travis, Captain Hastings and Nigel de Grey at Eastcote were a matter of great delicacy and care.

Even the most everyday costs of GCHQ costs were a matter for haggling and scrimping. One memo, from Harold Fletcher (an old Bletchley hand) to the Foreign Office ran: 'We shall find it necessary to send out each week a certain amount of laundry in the shape of roller towels. In the past, the cost of such laundry has been borne by "Special Funds" but as you know, these no longer exist. We have approached the Ministry of Works on this matter in the hope that they would accept liability, but they have informed us that this is a departmental commitment. I shall be grateful, therefore, if you will let me know whether the Foreign Office will be prepared to meet the accounts, which we estimate will be in the neighbourhood of £2 each week.'[6]

As much as their American counterparts in Arlington Hall may have protested that their work was being underfunded, it seems very unlikely that they would have been reduced to roller-towel bathos.

Moreover, there are moments now in recently released papers that afford a fascinating – if not faintly comical – glimpse into a pre-technological world of security arrangements. One such memo concerned the containers in which hyper-sensitive material would be conveyed to the necessary superiors in Whitehall, without the possibility of espionage. 'The blue despatch boxes at present being used for delivery of our material to you are to be withdrawn, and will be replaced by boxes with a different type of lock,' wrote the unnamed 'Head of 3 Department' in 1949. 'The new key is enclosed herewith; on receipt of your acknowledgement, the new boxes will be brought into use. Would you return your old key to us in a new box and send back any of our old boxes which may still be in your possession.'

'The new boxes', the memo concluded, 'can be easily recognised by the name "GCHQ" stamped on the lid.' There is something highly evocative too about the furniture of the letter, from the address given as 'Room 3/2911, Lime Grove, Eastcote, Ruislip', to the telephone number in case of queries: 'PINNER 7500, Ext. 43.'[7]

The very business of keys raised other security issues, this time the subject of an internal memo. 'It is important that, in order to avoid the compromise of GCHQ, keys and the consequent danger to confidential documents, the following directions should be carefully followed . . . The person to whom a key is issued is personally responsible for looking after it and ensuring that it can never be lost or copied . . . If in abnormal circumstances it is essential that a key should be taken away from the office, it should be carried securely attached to the holder's person. To take an impression of a key on plasticine or soap is the work of a few moments only. The opportunity for this must never be afforded by leaving keys lying about eg on the dressing table.'[8]

The dressing table! What wonderfully demure enemy agents they must have been worried about. Key etiquette required that in order to request a key, one had to make representations to the Establishment Officer in Room 3 at Eastcote; if the key was to be passed to another, then the transaction had to go through this office, and the key in question would remain the full responsibility of the previous holder until this exchange was properly acknowledged.

There was another very serious point. 'GCHQ keys may not be taken out of the United Kingdom,' the memo continued. 'On any occasion on which the holder of the key proceeds abroad, the key should be returned to GCHQ for safe custody unless it is needed by a successor.' And what about those keys that had been taken around Britain to one or more of Eastcote's listening out-stations? They 'should be returned by Registered Post in sealed envelopes'.[9] Again, there is now something unutterably charming about spies having complete trust in the Royal Mail to deliver top-secret keys without fear of theft.

Some secret business could only ever be conducted face to face, and in the early weeks of 1949, Sir Edward Travis, accompanied by his assistant Commander Clive Loehnis, set off on a globe-circling tour to meet up with Australian signals intelligence superiors, and also their counterparts in the United States. A memo to a British diplomat outlined – in the era just before jet travel – what an undertaking this would be. After Australia, the memo ran, they 'are returning to the UK via the USA . . . they will leave Honolulu on Saturday 26th March on flight number BP444 due at San Francisco on March 27th . . . They will need dollars and hotel accommodation for three nights. They will be travelling to Philadelphia on Weds 30th March by the UP (Union Pacific) overland train route . . . it would be kind if you could book them onward drawing room accommodation on this train.'[10]

Despite the considerable setback of the Soviet encryption changes, Travis's codebreaking department had found its confident stride; quite independently of MI6, he and his lieutenants were quietly ensuring that they were covering as much of the earth as they could. The blank spaces on the vast intelligence maps were slowly but steadily being filled in: GCHQ's bank of knowledge of military and scientific developments was growing. Certainly, the saga of the Cambridge Spies was due to cause huge trauma to other corners of Britain's security operation, but the codebreakers – voyaging across the Atlantic and journeying across Europe – seemed quite secure about their own personnel, and about the aims of their organisation.

They were, as ever, ahead of their time. The White House and the leaders of the Western European nations saw – in the aftermath of the Berlin Blockade and the Soviet coup in Czechoslovakia– the advantage in becoming closer militarily. In the earliest days of NATO, a supreme headquarters was set up in a pleasant suburb of Paris near Versailles. The first Supreme Allied Commander Europe was General Dwight Eisenhower.

This development could hardly go unanswered by the Soviet Union; soon afterwards, it gathered together the Baltic and Eastern European states under its thrall into the Warsaw Pact, a military pact to counter NATO. But during this period, the spread of Communism was hardly confined to the east of Europe. The cryptanalysts were struggling – with limited resources and personnel specialising in the Far East – to hear and analyse some of the curious noises which were now coming from the other side of the world.

Chapter Seventeen

Dominoes

High above the blue rippling waters of Hong Kong, the humid breeze whispering through the hills, the secret listeners in Batty's Belvedere (as the out-station was called) had been chronicling a fresh war. After the surrender of Japan, civil war had broken out in China between the nationalist forces, led by Chiang Kai-shek, and the Communists, led by Mao Zedong. Signals intelligence (or 'sigint') – if good – is occasionally a means of gazing straight into the hearts of leaders. The sigint in this region was not good; efforts were made, but with the West so closely focused on every twitch in Eastern Europe, there were other regions where even the greatest expertise could not make that much headway.

The conflict in China was complicated by the weight of more powerful countries pressing in on it. The Soviet Union was occupying the lands of Manchuria, to the north; the Americans, under President Truman, were giving their overt backing to Chiang Kai-shek's forces – they did not want to see the Communists grabbing this region. The British were in a position to closely observe; curiously, this was to be one of those points where they and the Americans fell out rather sharply.

Mao Zedong prevailed in 1949: the People's Republic of China was founded. The Americans simply refused to acknowledge Mao's ascension. Stalin wanted the kind of relationship whereby Mao adhered closely to Soviet thinking and desires. The British were – by contrast – a little subtler (or more serpentine, whichever way one might look at it) in their dealings with this new regime. Partly this was to do with trade between China and the United Kingdom, which was strong; and partly, perhaps, because of the unlovely history shared between the two nations. In this new post-colonial age, the British wanted to put diplomatic relations with previously oppressed and exploited peoples on a more elegant and civilised footing.

There was also the matter of the British colony of Hong Kong. This eruption of Communism – with the threat of expansionism that accompanied it – suddenly made Hong Kong – a tiny area surrounded by ideological foes – acutely vulnerable. So it was that foreign secretary Ernest Bevin informed the Americans that the government intended to give proper recognition to this new Chinese government. His argument to secretary of state Dean Acheson was this would be a way of making sure that China did not swaddle itself completely in Russia's embrace. Acheson was extremely doubtful that it would achieve any such thing.

And when Britain did publicly announce its recognition of Mao, it turned out that Acheson was right: the People's Republic of China was magisterially dismissive of Britain's overtures. Ambassadors and diplomats were broadly ignored. Mao Zedong, initially, apparently only had time for the Russians. Again, while this was partly ideology, it is difficult not also to imagine that a driven moderniser like Mao (so driven, indeed, that his modernisations were to lead to famines that claimed the lives of some 30 million people) would have studied the history of Britain's opium trading with China in the 19th century very closely. The humiliations heaped upon China by the British at the height of Victoria's reign still resonate now; Mao must have felt that weight of history even more acutely.

The idea of the British having any long-term influence in the region became even more fantastical the following year: with the encouragement of Mao, the neighbouring territory of North Korea (a Communist regime run by Kim Il-Sung) launched an attack against the (American-backed) south of the country. It would prove to have astoundingly bloody consequences, for Koreans, Chinese, American and British troops alike.

The lightning assault across the region demarcated by the 38th parallel had been utterly unforeseen. There had been no prior intelligence: no indications of unusual troop movements, no brilliant cypher-breaks of crucial messages between military leaders. Neither the Americans nor the British, for all their extensive listening facilities, had picked up any warning. In fairness to Commander Travis and GCHQ, they could not be expected to gaze into a crystal ball over every last square mile on earth. And given that the Joint Intelligence Committee had directed the cryptanalysts to focus on the Soviet Union, it was clearly taking some time to build up an equal level of expertise in the Far East.

That said, the British and the Americans had not been completely oblivious to the dangers inherent in the region. In 1948, a CIA report observed that: 'Eventual armed conflict between the North and South Korean governments appears probable . . . in the light of such recent events as Soviet withdrawal from North Korea, intensified improvements of North Korean roads leading south, People's Army troop movements to areas nearer the 38th parallel, and from Manchuria to North Korea, and combined manoeuvres.'[1] Yet equally, this was not the only area in the world on a potential razor's edge. And there were still substantial US forces in Tokyo, occupying Japan after its apocalyptic defeat; the military there was dismissive of any North Korean threat, not least because they knew how heavily armed the South Koreans were. If anything, the Communists in the north appeared rather more vulnerable than the regime in the south.

Added to this, the messages given out by America had been rather easier for the Chinese and North Koreans to read: Dean Acheson had announced in 1950 that Korea lay outside America's 'ring of interests'. Kim Il-Sung saw an opportunity to seize the entire country; according to former Joint Intelligence Committee grandee Sir Percy Cradock, he received gentle though reserved encouragement from Stalin, along the lines that if the adventure backfired, Russia would immediately step back, and Kim Il-Sung would have to rely on China for help.

According to Sir Percy Cradock, the British in 1949 knew that their American allies had better intelligence on Korea; and indeed a small team from the Joint Intelligence Committee, on a visit to Washington DC that year, had asked to be included in on what they knew. But the Americans refused: a punishment for the British recognising Mao Zedong's government. In the years to come, there would be further outbreaks of American petulance in the face of what they regarded as British stubbornness; fractures in an otherwise remarkably easy-going intelligence relationship. In this instance, no-one benefited, as the intelligence had either not been heeded or lacked urgency. North Korea launched its attack and the US and British were each as surprised as the other.

This moment in 1950 was – for some American military – the point at which they were braced for the worst. Russia now had the capability to destroy whole cities in sun-bright blasts; the question according to some was whether North Korea's headlong attack over the 38th parallel was a means of diverting attention away from some larger plot? A Stalinist plot for Russia to lunge deep into Western Europe?

The notion that Communism could be a form of contagion – the 'domino theory' of one country after another falling – was still a little distance off (President Eisenhower cited 'the domino effect' in a speech in 1954 when talking of the convulsions in Indo-China). In 1950, President Truman and those around him in the Oval Office had now formulated a view that Stalin was effectively in control of every Communist state on earth; that nothing could be done by North Korea without his bidding. There were many in the military, too, who were convinced that Stalin was the great overlord, planning each move with scientific precision.

In the meantime, the British interceptors of GCHQ had been reporting back to the Joint Intelligence Committee, and the JIC issued this rather more measured judgement: 'We believe North Korean aggression was originally launched not with the primary object of diverting American attention from Europe, or as a prelude to provocative action against our weak spots of the European or Middle East periphery, but as a limited operation within the ambit of an intensified drive to expel western influence from the whole of the Far East and South East Asia.'[2]

Yet the fever was spreading elsewhere. In the week of the invasion, a fervidly anti-Communist 'Congress For Cultural Freedom' was being held in West Berlin, within slingshot distance of the East Germans. The event was financed by the CIA. This 'Congress' put out a statement. 'Indifference or neutrality in the face of such a challenge amounts to a betrayal of mankind and the abdication of the free mind,' it ran. And at the same time secretary of state Dean Acheson outlined the entire purpose of US opposition to the Soviet Union. 'All the problems of the United States are related to the problem of preserving its existence as the kind of country which we know and love.'

And as a part of the effort to preserve that way of life, troops were committed to Korea. This, however, was not strictly war at this stage; the troops were sent with the blessing of the relatively newly formed United Nations. And the UN was then able to call upon troops from other countries to help too. It was important to all parties that this should not be seen as a baldly ideological stand-off between the US and the USSR. Yet what ensued was a hideous conflict that in some ways more resembled the primitive charnel-house squalor of the First World War than a struggle taking place in the nuclear age.

Fast-evolving technology was only so much use; the intelligence services of both Britain and America lacked sufficient agents on the ground in Beijing and Pyongyang to provide 'humint', or human intelligence. The American codebreakers of Arlington Hall, however, were on the case. 'By far the most important and effective sources of operational intelligence . . . were decrypts of enemy wireless transmissions by the vast signals operation established outside Washington for the purpose,' wrote Sir Max Hastings. 'But the available quantity of "sigint" was restricted by the enemy's shortage of sophisticated communications equipment.'[3]

Nonetheless, intelligence was harvested, the operatives at Arlington Hall taking care to master the Korean language much in the way that over in Bedford, near Bletchley, a masterclass in Japanese for codebreakers had turned out so many apt linguists. Meanwhile, the British were said to have had some expertise with Chinese cyphers, which involved a somehow breakable form of one-time pad. For the Royal Air Force, swooping missions over Communist lines at least gave ideas of where and when bombing runs might be targeted; and in more traditional terms, it was found to be possible to listen in and intercept communications on Korean and Chinese telephone lines.

In the very early stages, America's General Douglas MacArthur scored a remarkable military coup by getting his forces, via amphibious landings, deep behind the North Korean lines. But they were not just facing Kim Il-Sung's army: Mao's People's Liberation Army were moving in, in their millions. Opening victories gave way to painful and bloody stalemates. It was during this conflict that the term 'brainwashing' came to be used: Western prisoners of war were said to have been subjected to relentless, months-long conditioning to do with the superiority of Communism over capitalism. The idea of hypnotised soldiers later found its popular cultural moment in the thriller *The Manchurian Candidate*. Since that time, there has been some revisionism about exactly how effective these ideological mind assaults were: some of the prisoners, it has been suggested, only gave way in order to try and make life a little quieter; their world views, upon release, appeared not to have been modified so greatly.

A rather more concrete result of the conflict, however, was a sharpening of the focus of the American cryptology efforts; Arlington Hall did not enjoy the centralised power of the codebreakers of Eastcote. Prior to 1950, there had been increasing amounts of confusion in the US military about the various different codebreaking branches – naval, military, air force – and an attempt at rationalisation combined with some severe cost-cutting. Out of the three old departments now came the Armed Forces Security Agency. The explosion of violence in Korea reversed the staffing freeze; hundreds more civilians – as well as service personnel – were recruited into the secret realm. The Pentagon's anxiety that Korea might just be the long fuse leading to a much bigger, more terrible war at last made it see that it was important to invest in intelligence.

The difficulties were still vast; ever since all the Soviet encryption systems had been changed – and thus closed off to codebreakers in American and Britain – there had been large patches of intelligence dark matter, voids in intelligence which could not be filled with inspired guesswork. One of those patches of dark matter was communications between Stalin and Korea. The Armed Forces Security Agency quickly started to make up for this shortfall: having started out with only a handful of Korean and Chinese specialists, they soon recruited hundreds. On the ground over in Korea, signals experts had formidable local difficulties to deal with, including rough mountainous terrain – not only bad for interception, but also awkward in terms of transporting equipment. But the air forces were on hand; the brave crews of the planes making intelligence-gathering ferret flights swooped over enemy Korean territory, vacuuming up secrets and relaying them back, while staying ever alert for the presence of any Soviet fighters in the air.

For the codebreakers, another hurdle – negotiated it seems with some style – was not merely the Korean language (a few cryptologists were Korean themselves, the rest either were taught the language, or indeed taught themselves). It was the unfamiliarity of all the military terms used in that language. For instance, one of Bletchley Park's great achievements throughout the war had been its card file index: a roomful of cards, the result of painstaking logging of every single German term for every single moving part of a weapon or vehicle, every term for every aspect of military operations or manoeuvres. This card index had grown over the space of several years; here, the codebreakers were having to start from scratch.

Happily, by this stage the codebreakers had found a few levers into Chinese communications; and so it was that they were able to follow the deployment of troops, and messages passed between foreign minister Zhou Enlai and various diplomats. The bank of knowledge expanded fast.

In other words, despite having faced code blackouts, underfunding and disorganisation, the US and UK codebreakers still managed in time of crisis to produce useable, valuable intelligence. This did not save the US cryptologists from facing caustic criticism over their stuttering start back in Washington DC, though, and the Korean War was in many ways to have repercussions on American and British codebreakers that can still be felt today.

One of the lessons the Americans learned was that they would benefit from following the example set by the British: ever more centralised code-breaking, as opposed to competing departments in different military wings working without co-ordination, overlapping and missing other elements. And this centralising move led to the dissolution of the AFSA in favour of the even more compact and rigidly controlled National Security Agency, which came into being in 1952 and is still very much with us today.

Budgets improved; and more money brought not only extra recruits – brilliant logicians and linguists – but also more of the spectacular technology still in development. America was making lofty leaps forward in the new science of computing, while Britain was not doing so badly considering the sparse money available. But more than this: the codebreakers – British and American – understood after being tested in the crisis of the Korean War – that theirs was a discipline that had to be self-contained. The intelligence produced by these brilliant brains could not be allowed to become the subject of inter-departmental wrestling matches. In America, the National Security Agency swiftly became as monolithic a feature on the intelligence landscape as the equally fresh CIA and the Federal Bureau of Investigation. In Britain, the codebreakers of Eastcote were able to keep themselves ever more at arm's length from MI5 and MI6. They sent the fruits of their efforts instead to the Whitehall grandees of the Joint Intelligence Committee who co-ordinated and filtered intelligence from all departments.

Another parallel between the American and British operations was the sheer number of National Security Agency personnel who had had their formative codebreaking experiences during the war. Geopolitics and high diplomacy aside, this was also why – on the personal level – there was so much mutual respect and friendship between the two agencies across the Atlantic. There was a shared warmth, as well as professional, pride. And long afterwards, the US codebreakers continued to sing the praises of British operatives like Brigadier John Tiltman, using him and Hugh Foss and others as shining examples in lectures to younger codebreakers being inducted into the mysteries of this dark world.

The Korean War did not end – as many feared it would – with mushroom clouds. Instead, there was a rather more wearily familiar outcome. For the Koreans, both of the south and north, the conflict was devastating, resulting in somewhere in the region of a million deaths. The same was true of the Chinese army. American mortality came in at 37,000. The death rate of British personnel was not quite so heavy, but still numbered into many thousands. Many of the British soldiers in Korea were there as part of their National Service: teenagers conscripted into the forces with no choice in the matter.

Brian Hough, from Manchester, was aged 18 when he and his fellow soldiers set sail for Korea. The sights that greeted him at Busam, he said, were 'from medieval times'. He knew nothing of Korea or indeed much about this part of the world; nothing of its history, or culture. The nature of the war came as the greatest shock. 'It was trench warfare,' he said. 'We laid in the trenches and dug holes in the sides of the mountains every now and then and that's where we lived. They were rat-infested. I think I was more afeared of them than I was of the Chinese.'[4]

This did not feel like a jet-age war. The young soldiers were forced to exist in sub-zero conditions, and when the enemy came, eyes were taken out with mortar blasts, and bullets caved in skulls. There was filth and squalor and blood.

Then, many young soldiers returned to Britain to find that no-one wanted to hear a word about their experiences. The country was still absorbing the World War; and the weariness was deep. This in part is why the Korean War scarcely figures in modern history: a blip, a fight in a far-away place, best forgotten. One such soldier was the future actor Maurice Micklewhite (later Sir Michael Caine). He recalled in his biography his ship sailing into Pusan harbour and the 'stench' of the place that could be registered 'three miles out'. He and his fellow Royal Fusiliers were sent up to the 38th parallel, living in dugouts composed of mud and bamboo. They came under nightmarish bombardment from the opposing Chinese forces. 'It was a strange time, something just outside the bounds of reality,' he said.[5] As well as the physical danger, the constant 24-hour noise meant that sleep became more and more impossible; and even if fatigue was reaching its height, he recalled, there was also the crawling physical disgust of knowing that huge rats would be running over your prone body.

From a wider perspective this fighting – and all the other countless skirmishes throughout those three years – were in part the result of all sides misinterpreting each other's intentions disastrously; a theme that was the become a recurring leitmotif of the Cold War being fought out in proxy around the world.

Yet as American and British intelligence agencies made further efforts to fathom this confused landscape, there were greater signs of the codebreakers and interceptors drawing even closer together. A memo sent out in the US in 1951 addressed what seemed the very pressing question of Hong Kong: just how secure were those British operatives in Batty's Belvedere? Just as uncountable hordes of the People's Liberation Army were pouring into the mountains and plains of Korea, what was to stop them annexing this particularly vulnerable corner of British imperial rule? And what would be the plan if they did?

'In the event of emergency withdrawal from present location,' the memo read, 'US is committed to providing relocation of British Hong Kong COMINT unit on US or US-controlled territory. This is in part quid pro quo arrangement in return for accommodation of our units on British or British-controlled territory plus others now in Europe . . .'[6]

This was now more than a simple comparing of codebreaking notes. 'US now receives full intercept output of Hong Kong Unit which is important and does not duplicate US effort,' the memo continued. But the spy chiefs were not wholly happy: as the start of the Korean War had demonstrated so very sharply, there were dark gaps in intelligence results from that part of the world. 'Present combined US/UK intercept facilities in the Far East are far short of requirements,' the memo continued. 'Considered full advantage to be taken of British unit.'[7] And should disaster have befallen the unit – akin to the 1942 fall of Singapore, when the codebreakers had to scramble to escape, leaving not a clue or a trace of their work behind – then the US idea was to transplant the entire operation to US-controlled Japan.

The Americans were aware that the British, like themselves, had been developing some rather neat technological advances; and soon after, the Eastcote codebreakers were told by their superiors that GCHQ would now be regarded as being fully in charge of electronic intelligence, as well as the more straightforward communications intelligence. As ever, a committee was formed: the Technical Radio Intercept Committee. It was about the future of sharing knowledge; the British were not to keep any electronic intelligence from their American friends.

'GCHQ is entering the non-communications listening field,' ran the memo from 1951. It was referring to the growth in computing, upon which the following chapter will focus. 'They [the codebreakers] will be responsible for transmissions of information from the field to London . . . new ground units, manned by RAF or Army personnel, will report through GCHQ to the Technical Radio Intercept Committee.' But their reports would have to go further. 'Exchange of raw intercept information is not satisfactory,' continued the memo. 'US Navy [is] feeding logs to Royal Navy and getting only collated reports in return . . . [the] exchange of raw intercept information must be kept to top secret channels . . . Commander Loehnis and Mr Smith will attempt to see that TRIC passes raw intercept information to US Force and US Navy personnel in London.' An element of pleading came in. 'If US Navy does not start getting raw data,' the memo continued, 'they will stop giving raw data.' It added that 'Commander Loehnis [has] requested information on procedure to follow for obtaining intercept equipment in the US.'[8]

The balance of power in the hermetic world of decryption changed remorselessly, and fast. The British navy and air force were still of immeasurable use for the collection of intelligence, just as those colonial listening stations were strategically vital. The Americans were now in a position to give orders. But Britain still had lightning bolts of ungovernable genius; and those US scientists who had been working throughout the war on prototype computing technology would – by 1950 – observe with some admiration the vast leaps made by UK boffins who were still among their connections. The world of computers and codebreaking was a small one.

Chapter Eighteen

The Cat's Cradle

There is something measurelessly evocative about these images now: the dark rooms filled with wardrobe-height machinery, upon which can be seen hundreds upon hundreds of electronic valves, dials and switches. Even so, the photographs cannot quite summon the low hum of electricity, or the smell of oil and of warm diodes, or the uncomfortable heat on summer days as the machinery grew hot through constant use. Nor, through these images of men (sometimes women) examining circuitry or meters, can they convey either the thrill or indeed the serial frustrations involved in the development of the new science of computing.

The photographs taken in late-1950s America – the Harvard Mark One project, the ENIAC project – have a well-funded sleekness, a richly proportioned straightness of line. The pictures taken in 1950s England have a more winning untidiness. The work that was being done immediately after the war at the National Physical Laboratories in Teddington, at Cambridge and at the University of Manchester, had been spawned directly from the Colossus machines. The codebreakers had seen the extraordinary potential and now Attlee's government – although in practical terms utterly broke – was terrifically keen that Britain should exploit it.

As we have seen, while Alan Turing initially found himself working at the National Physical Laboratory, fellow codebreaker Maurice Wilkes landed in Cambridge and Turing's one-time mentor and also fellow Bletchley Park veteran Professor Max Newman went off to head up the mathematics department at the University of Manchester. Their lives would all intertwine, and with those of their former colleagues now codebreaking at Eastcote.

Turing now is revered as the father of computing: the visionary who, in the 1930s, had postulated the idea of a machine that could think; the mathematician who also fully engaged with the philosophical implications of the idea. There were some who found Turing's lash-up approach slightly patience-trying; yet his work at the NPL led to the eventual development of the ACE. The acronym was for Automatic Computing Engine. The abstract proposal for this machine was put before the authorities in 1946, but at a rather awkward time in terms of funding; finances were tight and although Turing was given two young assistants, much was needed in terms of technical equipment. Having said that, Turing never lost his flair for improvisation: returning to his laboratory one day, he came across a length of discarded drainpipe; enlisting a couple of others to help carry it, he then used bits of this to help further his construction efforts.

Turing still had his security clearance too, and he remained in touch with Hugh Alexander at Eastcote, who was constructing new cryptanalytical approaches in response to a fast changing world. Quite unlike any other of the services, GCHQ was by its nature all about eccentric monomania and lateral enthusiasms. But this occasionally meant that figures such as Turing could be ungovernable. At the NPL in Teddington, the patience of the principal Charles Darwin with Turing's computing experimentation was stretched beyond endurance – there were other projects equally demanding of time and money. Turing at first declared that he was going to take a sabbatical and return to Cambridge, while staying on half pay at the NPL. But then, as the sabbatical began, Turing – to the vexation of Darwin – quietly accepted an invitation from his Bletchley colleague and friend Professor Max Newman to take up a position at Manchester University.

In an age when the term 'Northern Powerhouse' is witlessly deployed by public relations officers, it is instructive to think of the pioneering work that was taking place 70-odd years ago within the soot-smirched gothic buildings of Manchester University.

Naturally, while figures such as Turing had a passion for pursuing a vision of thinking machines as an end in itself, there were many in Whitehall who focused on the rather more practical applications; not just scientific, but military too. For all those who saw the poetry in storing data in a cathode ray tube – the data actually being visible as dots of light that would dance – there were many others who were thinking defensively. How could they not? Both America and Russia had tacitly agreed to their roles as opposing superpowers, both locked in what they saw as struggles for survival. A key component of the Cold War would be about technological triumph. Later, this would move to Outer Space, as well; in the 1940s and early 1950s, computing was the mark of scientific superiority.

Thanks to the war, there were those who moved with genuine ease between the scientific and intelligence communities on both sides of the Atlantic. Turing was one, having been sent over to the US in 1943. Another was the Bletchley organisational genius Gordon Welchman who, as we have seen, decided to emigrate to the United States full-time with his family in 1948, to pursue computing and electronics in the private realm. Another figure – who was to prove absolutely key to GCHQ at Eastcote and Cheltenham, as well as then progressing to being a hugely respected academic in America – was Irving J Good, or Jack Good as he was known to all his friends.

Good had been something of a prodigy. Born in Hackney in London's East End in 1916, a childhood bout of diphtheria led to his confinement to bed, and also one of those bedazzling moments of intellectual revelation: in his case, discovery of 'the irrationality of the square root of two'.[1] He went to school at Haberdashers' Askes school in north London, then went up to Jesus College, Cambridge to study mathematics. When war broke out, he was specialising in 'fractional dimensions'; one reason, perhaps, why he was not considered ideal material for the infantry. Instead, the more esoteric world of cryptology beckoned, and with it came many strong, abiding friendships.

The post-war dispersal of many of the codebreakers meant, for Good, the acceptance of an offer from Professor Max Newman to come and teach at the University of Manchester. But while teaching mathematics in theory, Good was also by this stage utterly mesmerised by the new field of computation. So while Alan Turing was fighting for funding down at the National Physical Laboratory, Jack Good was contributing ideas and expertise to the Manchester 'Mark One' computer.

And after three years of this, Good was once more drafted southwards, towards the cryptanalytical corridors of Eastcote. It is simply impossible to imagine that this wonderfully witty codebreaker left all his computational knowledge behind him. The premises of Eastcote had – as mentioned before – housed a great many of Turing's bombe machines throughout the war, all working their way through the different worldwide versions of Enigma. The machinery that replaced them was no less jealously guarded. Jack Good – like everyone else who worked there – was careful to say nothing to anyone.

But the lines of communication between Manchester and Eastcote were as strong as their US equivalent of Arlington Hall with Harvard or indeed Bell Laboratories. Although he kept his secrets, Good did remark jokily in later years that his post-war work might have had very different outcomes had he chosen to reverse his career path. He said that if he had gone back to being a pure mathematician, 'he might have discovered something so important that bad people would have done harmful things with it, whereas his current work at GCHQ was pointless but harmless'.[2]

Incidentally, another measure of Good's fantastic fascination with the uses of computers and the boundaries of mathematics came in 1968 when he gave advice to the film director Stanley Kubrick upon the making of the metaphysical science-fiction epic *2001: A Space Odyssey*. Like Wittgenstein, Bertrand Russell and of course Turing, Jack Good also had an abiding interest in the pursuit of philosophy; the precision of mathematics was considered important in establishing absolute clarity in terms of philosophical ideas.

Good and Turing also enjoyed lively correspondence; Good used to refer to him jocularly as 'the Prof', even though Turing had not quite attained this status. Just before Good took up his new position with GCHQ in 1948, there was still time for rather more abstract pursuits. 'Dear Prof,' wrote Good to Turing in the summer of that year, 'When I was last in Oxford I met a lecturer in physiology who said that he thought the number of neurons in the brain was only about two million. This seems amazingly little to me even allowing [for] the fact that the number of processes from each neuron is something like 40. I wonder if you could tell me the right answer, with or without a reference.'[3] The question was not wholly random, and indeed might be read as a form of code in itself: at this stage, Turing had been doing some research into the structure of the human brain as a means of investigating further the idea of constructing an electronic brain. He had been delving into how the intellect grows from infanthood. It was not enough for a machine simply to obey instructions. It must also, at some points, learn how to make its own decisions. How would such an electronic structure be possible? Good's question might have been by way of a slanted request for progress, from one brilliant mathematician now heading back to the life of codebreaking to another working in a field that all the codebreakers would have to become completely familiar with. In the same letter, Good went on to impart some discreet job news, having heard of Turing's imminent departure from Teddington to Manchester.

'I understand that by next October, we will have swapped towns,' wrote Good. 'Judging by the international situation I think you've had the better of the bargain.'[4] It is a teasing reference; Turing must surely have known where Jack Good was going to work and the kind of Cold War climate that the cryptologists faced. But Good ended on a much lighter note. 'How near were you,' he asked Turing, 'to getting into the Olympics?'[5] It was not a facile question: Turing was a seriously good long-distance runner, with a marathon time that more than qualified him to take part in the 1948 Games which were held in London. Unfortunately, by that time Turing was carrying a leg injury. Previously, he had managed to run marathons in around two hours and 30 minutes: extraordinarily good for a hobbyist.

Ensconced among his fellow cryptanalysts at Eastcote, Jack Good wrote again to Turing. There was more chat about the brain and neurons. But there were other developments he was keen to pass on. 'Dear Prof,' he wrote, '. . . I visited Oxford last weekend. Donald [Michie] showed me a "chess machine" invented by Shaun [Wylie] and himself. [Michie and Wylie were former Bletchley colleagues.] It suffers from the very serious disadvantage that it does not analyse more than one move ahead. I am convinced that such a machine would play a very poor game, however accurately it scored the position with respect to matter and space. In fact, it could easily be beaten by playing "psychologically" ie by taking into account the main weaknesses of the machine . . .

'When in Oxford', Good continued, 'I succeeded in hypnotising Donald . . . Would you agree that a very typical property of the brain is the ability to think in analogies? This means taking only a part of the evidence into account . . . Do you know of any reference to Russian electronic computers?'[7]

That blend of intellectual high spirits and sly fishing for intelligence – were there any rumours in the Manchester scientific community of Soviet advances in this field? – blended in with the now reflexive opaqueness about the work he and the others were doing.

In a curious way, the story of their former colleague Gordon Welchman illustrates the sorts of dilemmas that Turing, Good and, at GCHQ, Hugh Alexander and Joan Clarke faced, as the possibilities of the electronic age widened out. For as the work at Manchester University demonstrated, there was clearly also going to be quite a commercial future for computers. For Welchman, all that lay across the Atlantic in large firms where his particular brand of expertise would be very highly valued; his extraordinary security clearance would see to that. Back in Britain, the opportunities might have seemed more cramped. However, the spirit of innovation was still very much there. When Turing joined Professor Max Newman, work on the 'Mark One' being carried out by FC (Freddie) Williams and Tom Kilburn was at a very advanced stage: memory was no longer held in cathode ray tubes, but in magnetic drums, with the addition of teleprinter read-outs, a less cumbersome way of programming with a single keyboard.

In 1948, the government was not wholly blind to the possibilities either: Sir Henry Tizard, who had been behind so many advances in the war, and was now chief scientific adviser in Whitehall, was mesmerised by the possibilities that he had seen in Manchester. Acknowledging that money was tight, he made it clear that development must be carried out 'speedily'; that Britain should try to 'maintain the lead' that it had taken in this new discipline, even as the Americans were working with utmost concentration on their own projects, and that he personally would give full support when it came to 'supply of material' and 'obtaining necessary priorities'.

There was a certain amount of hard-headed financial realism. A local company called Ferranti was called in to work with the Manchester mathematicians to make the world's first commercially available computer. Turing was one of the team who sought to make this fantastically complex concept into something that middle managers could use.

While Alan Turing was interested in the wider intellectual possibilities – an electronic mind that could play chess, and brilliantly parry the serpentine twists and gambits of the organic mind, or even, as he suggested on one occasion, a machine with television cameras attached that could take an interest in food, sex and sport – Ferranti was thinking of the business applications, such as those early punch-card machines favoured by the John Lewis Partnership. In its early advertising literature, Ferranti explains that a man sitting at a desk can only perform so many calculations a day; the Ferranti computer (or the Manchester Mark One) would be able to perform the same number of calculations in two seconds. The machine would also be able to carry out all wage calculations, and other assorted administrative tasks. But beneath this practicality lay an advance that was, in its own way, as significant as nuclear power.

If Professor Max Newman's brilliant team at Manchester was developing miracles, then what were the Soviets achieving in Moscow? Jack Good would not have been alone in wondering this. The cryptanalysts at Eastcote, drawing in signals from military bases, from cities, from embassies, also needed to be able to eavesdrop on the work of Soviet scientists.

Intriguingly, Alan Turing himself could not resist the curiosity: what if the Manchester computer could one day be used to generate completely random numbers? If so, it would become, in principle, a genuinely unbreakable cypher-generating machine. Turing wrote: 'I have set up on the Manchester computer a small programme using only 1,000 units of storage, whereby the machine supplied with one 16-figure number replies with another within two seconds. I would defy anyone to learn from these supplies sufficient about the programme to be able to predict any replies to untried values.'[8]

'It was during this period', wrote Turing's biographer Andrew Hodges, 'that he found himself being consulted by GCHQ. It would indeed have been remarkable if they had not consulted the person who knew more about cryptology and the potential of electronic computers than did anyone else. And had he not described cryptanalysis as the most "rewarding" field for the application of programming? Few, however, were in a position to perceive this fact, the subject being more secret than ever.'[9]

The friendships and associations and intellectual quests continued. The 1950s brought a new scientific fashion for 'cybernetics' and there were meetings of like minds at what was called The Ratio Club; Turing gave a talk on 'Educating a Digital Computer' which was attended by a highly interested Jack Good.

And the cat's cradle of codebreaking links grew denser. At Manchester, Turing was eventually joined by the young mathematician Peter Hilton who had worked with him in Hut 8. Hilton was recruited to the university from Oxford by Max Newman. There was little sense that Manchester was a provincial come-down from the dreaming spires; rather, there was intellectual excitement combined with the sense of a new kind of country being formed out of the convulsions of war. It was a country prefiguring Harold Wilson's famous phrase 'white heat of technological revolution' some 15 years before he coined it. Turing gathered Hilton into the further developments in the computer department – and both men were linked by the silent secrecy of the proto-computers that they had worked with at Bletchley.

Like Turing, Peter Hilton was gripped not only by the applications of mathematical logic, but also by the underlying philosophy. Bletchley's graduates might have scattered wide, but the bonds they had forged were strong. Hilton, in turn, was good friends with Shaun Wylie, a mathematician reckoned by many of his contemporaries to have been one of the best all-rounders at Bletchley Park: gifted at cryptanalysis, a youngster who made a big impact with his work on Tunny, but who was also a dedicated fan of amateur dramatics (a little like Nigel de Grey and Frank Birch) and who understood the importance of immersing oneself in pursuits other than codebreaking. After the war, Wylie went to Cambridge where he was made a Fellow of Trinity Hall; he was fondly remembered as a brilliant teacher by students – but he could not stay away from the pursuit of cryptology for long. Eventually, in the late 1950s, Wylie relented and re-joined GCHQ, now as their chief mathematician. Along the way, he and Peter Hilton co-authored a book on aspects of topology. The discipline of codebreaking was, for all of these people and many others, an aptitude that made them constantly in demand. The secrets of Bletchley could never be unlearned; and these gifted people had a talent that was now needed in a war that could conceivably stretch out without end.

In the Manchester mathematics community, the proximity to the manufacturers Ferranti was intriguing for another reason. It represented a further cat's cradle intersection of incredibly sensitive work – not merely on computers, but also on military technology, such as the development of automated guided missiles. All of which was perfectly natural; the government, and foreign secretary Ernest Bevin in particular, were anxious that Britain should be able to stand alone in terms of defence. It was around this time, too, that – elsewhere – Britain's first atomic weaponry was ready for testing. This was about independence: a proud nation that should not have to look across the Atlantic for its nuclear protection.

Alan Turing, his young colleagues recognised, was both an unearthly genius and a rather slovenly engineer. This was not laziness on his part; he was forever attempting to construct lash-ups himself, both in the laboratory and also at his house in Wilmslow. In domestic terms, he always resisted the idea of getting workmen in; if a new path had to be laid, then he wanted to be the one to lay it. He just couldn't do it very well. And so, too, with the delicate mechanics of these vast new computing machines. The young men and women around him were rather startled to find, one day in the early 1950s, that Turing had been made a Fellow of the Royal Society. One colleague confessed that he had never really seen him as Royal Society material.

Turing also inhabited the twilight life of Manchester. At Bletchley, he had been relatively open about his sexuality with colleagues. Yet homosexuality was still very much illegal – Turing mistakenly believed that a government commission was looking into the possibility of decriminalising sexual acts between men – and the atmosphere was growing steadily less tolerant. Manchester had some streets in which gay men, who had come to understand the code, could meet up: furtive, watchful encounters in darkened, smoggy alleys, as steam engines screamed on viaducts above. Turing – so hesitant and curiously unable to engage in other circumstances – knew these codes well. In time, he came fatefully to meet the eye of a young man called Arnold Murray. This was the start of the affair that would lead to the tragically early end of Turing's life.

A little time before this, the codebreakers at Eastcote had made a serious effort to employ Turing's services full-time once more. Thanks to his continued friendship with Hugh Alexander, Turing was readily available to consult, and his advice was always considered extremely valuable. So valuable in fact that Alexander offered Turing a salary of £5,000 a year to come back to work on cryptanalysis at Eastcote full-time. To put it in perspective, that sum would now be roughly equivalent to £100,000: a substantial amount for a cash-strapped department to offer for an invisible civil service position.

We might extrapolate a little further than this, it would not only be the British who would be benefiting from Turing's codebreaking genius: his admirers in America would also have been very pleased to have such a mind back in this enclosed community. Certainly, the level of the financial offer was most unusual at a time when every other economic transaction in Britain was gaunt with austerity.

Yet the climate was changing. The earthquake of paranoia produced not only by the Venona decrypt revelations, but also by a wider, almost unconscious national sense of an enemy within, would go on to make men like Turing outcasts. In other ways too, the world was becoming daily less forgiving and more fearful. As the Americans developed their first hydrogen bomb – a weapon so nightmarishly powerful that even Winston Churchill shuddered at it – the game of espionage became ever more deadly serious. And against this, the codebreakers would also find themselves facing the complete disintegration of British power in the Middle East. In many ways, this period was to be a stern test of whether the Eastcote operatives could match up at all to the intense pressures and expectations weighing upon them.

Chapter Nineteen
'Berserk with Fanatical Nationalism'

The term 'black gold' had particular resonance and urgency for Britain at the start of the 1950s: the struggles in Malaya meant that the government was ever more dependent on the money gained from other natural resources. The abundant oil that had gushed from the ground of Iran had already enriched the British Treasury to a quite startling degree, and on terms that were extraordinarily unfavourable to the Iranians. This was no colony, nor even a dependency; Britain had no sovereign rights over the country that had been one of the cradles of civilisation. But for some decades, the British had the oil contracts and it had the extraction technology, and the majority of the people in Iran were left little the wiser about how they had failed to benefit.

The close of the war also brought the end of a sense that the British had been behaving fairly. And the clandestine manoeuvrings of both Britain and the United States – the US saw just how great this Iranian prize would be for the booming American economy – were slippery.

There are few people around today who would make the claim that Britain and America's manipulation of Iranian sovereignty was solely about making sure that it did not fall into the hands of a rapacious Soviet Union. However, there were new American powers at play, particularly the freshly formed Central Intelligence Agency. By contrast with those flint-faced operatives, the men and women of GCHQ were not in the business of toppling governments or causing regime change. But in the early 1950s, they were having to work hard to accurately read the fast-shifting geopolitics of both Iran and Egypt.

The Eastcote codebreakers had managed to hold on to a few small covert stations in the north of Iran, in order to collect up as much Soviet traffic as possible. This was bountiful territory for them: from these vantage points, they could monitor activity around the Caspian in Soviet territories such as Uzbekistan and Kazakhstan – the sites not only of nuclear testing but also of vast labour camps to which dissidents and political prisoners had been deported.

On top of this, these were unstable times throughout the entire region. In the early 1950s, the old listening station in Egypt at Heliopolis just outside Cairo, was – despite the increasing noise of Egyptian nationalism – still at the centre of the Middle Eastern surveillance effort. But not for long: in the course of the conflict to follow, all these bases become very insecure.

As Christopher de Bellaigue has written, British businessmen had been making inroads into Iran from the late 19th century; they were allowed in because the then Shah was facing huge economic difficulties. First, the British did a deal for the growth and export of tobacco; then came vast infrastructure projects. Roads, dams and railways were built, and all with what might be termed British inward investment, which naturally always meant that British business exerted a monopoly and a stranglehold on Iranian finances.

One might incidentally wonder, in an age when Britain is itself relying on Chinese investment in future domestic nuclear energy, whether such business should be automatically seen as exploitative; in the case of Iran, however, the habit of monopoly soon came to mirror a certain frame of mind, colonialist in flavour if not in practice. As it was, the cosy 19th-century arrangements had been broken up after furious protests from Russians in the north of the country; this was another round of the Great Game between Russia and Britain, played a little further west than Afghanistan, but the principles were the same. As much as Iran had to listen to British money, it also had to be mindful of the desires of its mighty Russian neighbour. This was why, in 1946, after Second World War alliance had crumbled away, codebreakers like Alan Stripp were up in the north of Iran, helping other agents to make sure that the country did not fall into the grip of the Soviets.

Back at the start of the 20th century, there had been plenty of intellectuals within Iran who saw perfectly well in what direction the country was being steered, and who shrewdly made protests to ayatollahs to try and rein in the power of the Shah and of the British. But the First World War rendered them all powerless; in the struggle against the Ottoman Empire, Britain and Russia carved up Iran between them.

Then, in the aftermath of the First World War, as the Ottomans dissolved, the British foreign secretary Lord Curzon swiftly drew up the Anglo-Persian Agreement which would in effect have handed Iranian sovereignty to Britain. Again, the rationale given was that if the United Kingdom had not stepped in, Lenin's Red Army would have stormed the country. At the time, Curzon said of the Iranians: 'These people have got to be taught at whatever cost to them that they cannot get on without us. I don't at all mind their noses being rubbed in the dust.'

He didn't mind; but they very much did. The urban nationalists and the Iranian parliament were in tumult and the agreement was forgotten. But in the fog of recrimination, very few spotted what was going on behind the scenes at the Anglo-Persian Oil Company. The younger Winston Churchill had bought huge numbers of government shares in the concern; and worked the contracts so that 84 per cent of the company's profits went straight to Britain without so much as seeing the interior of an Iranian bank. By 1947, the concern had been renamed the Anglo-Iranian Oil Company. And the Treasury in Whitehall was earning somewhere in the region of £15 million annually on the company's profits; Iran got half of that.

Brought up in this febrile atmosphere of intellectual revolt and British contempt was a bright young man called Mohammed Mossadegh, who would turn out to be an absolutely pivotal figure. Indeed, relations between Britain and Iran today are still feeling the aftershock of the events in the early 1950s that he was instrumental in sparking.

Mossadegh was a thoroughgoing anti-colonial nationalist. Why, he asked, should nations like Britain have the power to suck, vampire-like, on Iran's terrific natural wealth? After the war, his following grew to the extent that he came to wield serious political weight; and in 1951, the Shah was forced, by public insistence, to stand aside and appoint Mossadegh as prime minister. Mossadegh was unusual in commanding a following among secular and deeply religious figures alike. He united the hard-line socialists and the profound conservatives. He was felt by some to be another Gandhi. He addressed the United Nations in New York, and told the Assembly: 'Hundreds of millions of Asian people, after centuries of colonial exploitation, have now gained their independence and freedom.'

And one of Mossadegh's first acts in 1951 was to nationalise the Anglo-Iranian Oil Company. Britain had been warned at the United Nations that in the future, the profits of oil were to be shared, not sequestered. Britain was not quite ready to see it that way. One factor that may have hardened its stance a little was the recent fall of the Labour Attlee government, and the return of Winston Churchill and the Conservatives to 10 Downing Street. Whereas Clement Attlee had been, in his heart, a devout internationalist anti-colonialist, there were many elements in the Tory party who quite genuinely felt – as Curzon had put it all those years ago – that Iran needed Britain more than Britain needed her.

So there was a stout refusal to share oil profits: the British were the ones taking the oil out of the ground, so therefore their efforts should replenish the Treasury. 'Oil can be the pillar of Persian revenue only while it can be brought, against many difficulties, to the world's markets,' declared *The Times* in 1951. 'The Persian state cannot supply the technical skill, initiative and commercial knowledge upon which the place of Persian oil in the international ramifications of the industry depends.' No Iranians had been allowed in senior positions at the Anglo-Iranian Oil Company; it was run by de facto colonial figures. Oddly enough, even some of the left-leaning UK newspapers like *The Observer* agreed that Britain had a perfect right to continue profiting from the oil wells. Mossadegh was portrayed as a 'Frankenstein' figure and even – in more excitable corners of the British and American press – compared to Adolf Hitler. This was some five years before Egypt's Nasser attracted a similarly hysterical response, Mossadegh was being demonised as a dangerous enemy. His followers, and all those who favoured nationalism, were seen as fanatics.

Mossadegh's tragedy was that he chose this heroic moment of defiance at a point in history when there was another, deadlier, game afoot. Several years after George Kennan's advocacy of the idea of containment of the Soviet Union, the Cold War had plunged below freezing, with both superpowers now settling into the narrative positions that they had effectively created for themselves. Washington DC was in the grip of a morbid mass anxiety about the contagion of Communism. If it had reached so far into American institutions, what would happen in countries apparently less developed and sophisticated? And more: what could be done to thwart the Soviets in their maniacal appetite for world conquest? One very straightforward strategy was to deprive them of the vast quantities of fuel needed to expand their armies further.

And this was how the abundant oil fields of Iran came to be seen through the eyes of American hawks: a potentially vast and lethal prize for Stalin to grab and exploit.

According to Christopher de Bellaigue, there were those in Whitehall and MI6 only too eager to fall in with this paranoid scenario, to ensure that the steady flow of funds to Britain's revenues were not interrupted. In America, the new Eisenhower administration, together with a ruthlessly enthusiastic CIA, plotted to have Mohammed Mossadegh overthrown and replaced by Shah Reza Pahlavi. De Bellaigue contends that MI6 – which itself had suffered a gruelling period following the debacle of the Cambridge Spies – was all too eager to help. This might be too cynical a reading, and the British agents may have been every bit as concerned about the spread of Communism as their American counterparts.

The coup went ahead: Mossadegh was overthrown, the Shah was installed – and immediately, the American press began singing extravagant hymns of praise to this fresh new ruler who was opening up a golden new era of trade and understanding between Iran and the West. Quietly, the CIA channelled millions of dollars into the country, to shore up the chief political and military figures around the young shah. *The New York Times* understood it all as a morality tale about the dangers of nationalism, and the need to check those little Hitlers who developed these dreams. 'Under-developed countries with rich resources now have an object lesson in the heavy cost that must be paid by one of their number which goes berserk with fanatical nationalism,' proclaimed an editorial. It might be grimly added at this point that the British government must have taken this sentiment very firmly on board; how else – when they were to characterise Nasser in Egypt in similar terms in 1956 – did they imagine that they would win the support of the Americans in their own adventure?

The repercussions of those events in 1953 are still felt today. The Shah, with his torturing secret police, was himself overthrown in 1979 and replaced with an extremist theocracy that only now shows, at the time of writing, any signs of starting to thaw. But in the 1950s, Mossadegh's overthrow secured not only the oil, but other advantages, too. It would still be possible from there to monitor Soviet activity quite some distance into the Urals. In the years to come, the listening stations in Iran would grow in value as surveillance technology sharpened. But there was always a sense, or undercurrent, of insecurity about such outposts. The threat of Islamic insurgency was never far beneath the surface. In the meantime, the oil continued to flow; and after the interventions of America and Britain, more of the funds began to seep into Iran, helping the Shah shore up his reign. It has been pointed out that if only Mossadegh had agreed to some form of compromise over the oil, he too might have seen the British government relent.

But from the point of view of GCHQ, the region had to be covered with terrific care: there was no question that the Soviets – sharing borders with Iran as they did – nursed fierce territorial ambitions in this area. For if they could have secured Iran, it would not only have meant access to unlimited oil, but also access to a naval base on the Persian Gulf, which in turn would give the Soviets a route to Turkey and India. Such an idea was acutely worrying to codebreakers and security chiefs alike; it could so easily have been one of the trigger points for an unstoppable war. Incidentally, the interventions from the West may still cause anger within Iran, but it is perfectly possible and respectable to argue that the alternative was that the country fell into Soviet hands, which would have had a ripple effect of destabilising the Middle East as well as the Indian subcontinent.

Elsewhere, by the early 1950s, the codebreakers and secret listeners were in regretful retreat. In Egypt, where the codebreaking station at Heliopolis still employed a significant number of civilians, the pressure was not from religious grievance so much as raw nationalism; even several years before the 1956 Suez debacle, it was becoming impossible to maintain an intelligence base there, still less any other kind of military establishment. The loss of Heliopolis was felt on two levels: first, as a strategic base, capturing a wide range of signals and encryptions, it had been doing brilliant work ever since the war. The second, for many operators, would have been the withdrawal from what, for many, had been a rather elegant existence, certainly when compared to the smog-bound nature of life back in London.

Cairo in that pre-Nasser period was still the domain of King Farouk, and for the expatriates, still very much a milieu of elegant restaurants and sophisticated nightclubs, in an entirely different dimension to the life being led by ordinary Egyptians. The writer and academic Edward Said – though born a Palestinian – was sent to school in Cairo in that period; although Egypt had won its independence from British influence in 1935, the school and its teachers appeared to have only an abstract idea of what this might actually mean. Victoria College was, he wrote, 'a school in effect created to educate those ruling-class Arabs and Levantines who were going to take over after the British left. My contemporaries and classmates included King Hussein of Jordan, several Jordanian, Egyptian, Syrian and Saudi boys who were to become ministers, prime ministers and leading businessmen . . .

'. . . Although taught to believe and think like an English schoolboy,' added Said, 'I was also trained to understand that I was an alien, a Non-European Other, educated by my betters to know my station and not to aspire to being British.'[1]

That age was ending. Senior figures in the Egyptian military – who were still brooding after being defeated in the Arab–Israeli war of 1948 – looked with disgust at the bloated, self-indulgent and wholly ineffectual

King Farouk; at the luxury of his court and at the corruption to be found close to him throughout Cairo. They looked at the British, treating the land and the people as if they were somehow their own, and at the British forces, which by that time were largely confined to the Canal Zone. And they plotted.

The coup came on 23 July 1952 at midnight; King Farouk and his friends were apparently enjoying a late-night picnic of caviar and champagne in the city of Alexandria. A team of 200 officers and around 3,000 troops took control of Cairo's broadcasting station; they also took command of the city's tanks. There were soldiers in Alexandria too, but Farouk did not think of commanding them to defend him. He said that he wanted no bloodshed. Given recent history in that region, the story of Farouk's fate is quite remarkable for its absence of violence; the new leader General Naguib (soon himself to be turfed aside in favour of Colonel Nasser) allowed the king and his family to take to the royal yacht, together with some belongings and crates of champagne. Farouk and his family made first for the island of Capri, and thence to the millionaires' retreat of Monaco. Farouk was eventually killed not by a bullet, but by the culmination of a lifetime of excess: he collapsed in a smart restaurant while entertaining a blonde in the small hours.

But his removal – and the installation of an entirely new, fiercely nationalist regime in Egypt – meant that for the British, withdrawal was inevitably going to lack the grace that they had somehow managed in India. What was certain was that the intensely secure operation at Heliopolis would have to be moved. And so it was that codebreakers were transferred instead to Cyprus.

It was not the most comfortable fit: the military installation there had already taken in the listening outpost from Sarafand in Palestine; the gradual removal of Britain's footholds in this region of the Mediterranean was a source of some disquiet both there and in Whitehall. For the Americans, however, there is some suggestion that the military and nationalist supporters in Egypt had been given some covert support by the CIA; for once again, the prime objective was ensuring that no Communists could get any kind of foothold. For Britain to lose the old

Combined Bureau base was most unfortunate; but no Americans would have looked on at her struggle to keep a colonial grip on Egypt with any kind of sympathy. Once again, the old country was tasting humiliation, the maddening nature of which would culminate in the crisis of 1956 – prime minister Eden comparing Nasser's nationalisation of the Suez Canal to Nazism, followed by a harrowing and abortive military attempt to grab it back, and then the cold refusal of America to give Eden and Downing Street any kind of backing.

That was all to come. One immediate difficulty for the codebreakers was that their new and ever expanding improvised base at Cyprus was far from being serene. The island had been under the control of the British since the 19th century; it formally became a British colony in 1925. In the late 1940s, as the Communists had sought to get a foothold in the Aegean, the military bases there had become utterly indispensable, not least because of the centrality of intelligence gathering. By the 1950s, the closeness of British and American intelligence once again came to the fore as the Americans set up their own surveillance and transmission site on the island. Even before they had done so, there appeared to be an assumption that the work done on the island was a venture that both would have an equal share in. Neither power could afford to lose their position there; but as with the rest of the British Empire, change was rushing in as unstoppably as a storm. It had to be managed with consummate care. The chief difficulty was that, as well as a largely Greek population, there was a significant minority of Turkish Cypriots. By the late 1940s, nationalist feeling among the majority population was beginning to smoulder; the people wanted to be formally conjoined with Greece. The presence of the British was ever more fiercely resented. And the tall aerials installed by GCHQ were both a symbol of British control and also a temptingly juicy target for local insurgent hotheads.

The British bases had to remain inviolate; intelligence gathering was not their only role. From here, the wireless interceptors would also analyse radio traffic, determining from where signals were being sent. In other words, they formed part of a great early-warning system, constantly watching for outbreaks of Soviet aggression in the regions around Turkey and Greece. On a daily basis, in the late 1940s and early 1950s, quantities of raw intelligence were being sent back to GCHQ Eastcote. Additionally, the intercept experts went about jamming Soviet stations and signals. This, together with the added presence of the RAF, was why Cyprus was indispensable, no matter how fervently its people wanted complete independence.

Through the eyes of those young men conscripted for National Service, either working as wireless interceptors or otherwise, Cyprus itself was unthinkably colourful and beguiling; not just because of the wonderful fresh food (an age before kebabs were co-opted by the British to serve as a synonym for drunken nights out), but also because of the tokens of older faiths than the Church of England. Bob Montgomery, who was a 'cypher mechanic' with the Royal Signals, remembered being mesmerised by the icons of the Greek Orthodox churches, and also the local custom of offerings made to saints in the form of pieces of bright white cloth left hanging on small trees. Montgomery himself, while on leave, adventurously took a trip up into the mountains to visit a Greek Orthodox monastery – the air suffused with rich perfumes and the monks themselves the soul of generosity, offering to supplement his meagre army sandwiches with some of their own food and drink.

It was his open, enquiring mind that clearly led Montgomery to be selected for an extremely secure job that he was mindful he could not discuss – very early on in his National Service training at Catterick in Yorkshire, he signed the Official Secrets Act. There had been, he recalled, some 'selection process' which he had barely been aware of. The next thing he knew, he was immersed in highly technical electronic training; not decyphering, so much, but rather setting up all the machinery and transmitters and keeping the more classified electronics running smoothly. He also kept an eye on volumes and direction of traffic, anything that might serve as an indicator of trouble. On his travels through Cyprus, Montgomery appreciated the sight of women working in brick kilns, and his chances for swims in indigo harbour waters. But as an alert, intelligent young man, he also noted the local political tensions.

What the Cypriots wanted was 'Enosis': not so much independence as the full embrace of their Hellenic heritage, joining with Greece and sharing its statehood. Some of this was religiously motivated; those same Orthodox monks who had shown such kindness to Bob Montgomery were deep conservatives who revered the Greek saints and prelates through the ages. Elsewhere, those who worked the land, those who fished the seas and those who worked in the towns, wrote Tom Nairn, 'found the fully fledged hypnotic dream of Greek nationalism already there, beckoning them. It was inevitable that they should answer that call to the heirs of Byzantium rather than attempt to cultivate a patriotism of their own.'[2]

This was not all dreamy romanticism; there was also a significant Communist movement, AKEL, at work on Cyprus too. As a result, the British bases were guarded with the greatest of care. 'Cypher mechanics' like Bob Montgomery had to take care too; his superiors needed to check the local situation carefully before they let him and his friends go off exploring the local culture, and not all the Cypriots they met would have been as willing to greet them warmly.

After the retreat from Egypt, as the numbers of cryptologists and other cypher staff increased, so too did the security on the island. Back in London, there were officials at the Foreign Office who had an idea for smothering – at least a little – the growing calls for union with Greece, and the rising temperature of potential violence. They looked at the minority Turkish population of the island and decided – as one diplomat termed it – that this was a card to play. The mainland of Turkey was a mere 40 miles (65 kilometres) across the sea; the Greek mainland some 400 (650). Very quietly, the British made representations to the Turkish government about the well-being of the Cypriot Turks and about their future. Some way down the line, there was even the outside possibility mooted of partition; of an island divided, with the British maintaining their bases in what would now be Turkish territory.

Events are never so easily guided, and cynicism frequently backfires. Efforts to turn Greek against Turk were, in the years to come, to have the most violent and tragic repercussions. In the 1950s, as with Egypt, the Americans looked on with a mix of distaste and horror at some British tactics; as if the Americans were somehow any less ruthless in seeking to arrange the results that they wanted. As it happened, it was the Americans who were propping up the mainland Greek government financially; and the security of the Cyprus bases – through some turbulent decades to come – remained. Indeed, in November 2015, those military bases were once more in the news, with Britain offering RAF facilities to France to help with its assaults on Daesh, or Islamic State. In cypher terms, there are corners of Cyprus that also remain very firmly in the business of intelligence.

By 1953, GCHQ had established and developed a rather brilliant empire of intelligence, and had made itself invaluable to the government. Partly as a result of technological change, and partly as a result of the quicksilver minds of Travis, Nigel de Grey and Hugh Alexander, who constructed a codebreaking structure that worked piercingly fast, signals intelligence was quickly becoming more prominent that human intelligence. One male or female secret agent on the ground could only ever hope to learn so much by means of infiltration or subterfuge. On the other hand, someone with the power to listen in to the quietest, most private conversations, someone who could look at the chilly chaos of binary digital codes, and summon the hidden meanings, could change the terms of the invisible war being fought on all continents.

On top of this, by 1953, confidence in Britain's human intelligence had been comprehensively shattered by the revelation of treachery at the very heart of the establishment. By contrast, the newest intelligence service was facing its greatest challenges, while looking to expand its own territory.

Chapter Twenty

The Loss of a National Asset

The British establishment – this use of the term was coined by political journalist Henry Fairlie in 1955 – looked and sounded in the early 1950s much the same as it had done long before the war. From the olive-green corridors of Whitehall departments to the high ceilings of the richly furnished club rooms in which politicians, senior civil servants, judges and members of the House of Lords would mingle, that quiet, unspoken, profound assurance seemed immovable. And yet there had been profound changes in society. Clement Attlee's socially crusading government had found huge support and help from what now looks like a seriously radicalised middle class. Not even the return to power of Winston Churchill in the early 1950s could turn back this social tide. The Ealing Film producer Michael Balcon, reflecting years later on this period, proclaimed that it was men and women such as himself who had been thinking the truly revolutionary thoughts on improving British society. The country now had a health service that was free to all; an epic house-building programme; and a creative cultural zest, as displayed to the world at the 1951 Festival of Britain. By 1952, with the death of George VI, and the accession to the throne of his young daughter, there was almost a sense of slick modernity that came with the idea of Britons being the 'New Elizabethans'.

In a curious way, the codebreakers at Eastcote – preparing for their move to bigger, more spacious premises down west – were a symbol of this bright, modern post-war society. In contrast to their sister service MI6 – still very much flavoured by the ethos of public schools and Pall Mall clubs – the men and women of GCHQ were of different provenance. Arthur Bonsall – a formidably brilliant presence who had made such an impact with his work on Luftwaffe codes – was born in Middlesbrough and educated at Bishop's Stortford College. His distinguished career at GCHQ would later see him reaching the top of the organisation. Equally un-grand was the immensely popular figure of Wing Commander Eric Jones. In 1952, this former textile merchant was to take over the entire organisation.

The old director Edward Travis had for some time been suffering from lumbago; the pain from his lower back – although this was obviously never stated – could not have been helped by the fantastic stress of his job. In the years that he had built up this new service, the common purpose of war had given way to something many times more complex. On top of this, the main objective – that of getting a reliable, regular hook into Soviet and Communist codes – had proved elusive. Whatever form the department took – from the First World War's Room 40, to the Government Code and Cypher School, to GCHQ – this was a responsibility that could not be borne for a huge amount of time.

There were those from other departments, other services, other corridors of power, who clearly felt that the stockily built Eric Jones was a little below the salt; comment was made on his apparent ponderous manner, which could also appear pompous to some. Yet the truth was that he was a man who weighed his words extremely carefully. As befitted a cryptanalyst who was sensitive to the tiniest subtleties of different languages and different translations, he always saw it as a matter of vital principle that people should express themselves as clearly and truthfully as possible. Upon ascending to the directorship of GCHQ, he ensured that all cryptanalysts were issued with what he saw as an absolutely key reference text: Fowler's *Modern English Usage*.

In this reverence for language, Jones was in a way quite similar to Alan Turing, in the sense that there was a fascination for the symbolism of words (or in Turing's case numbers) and an acknowledgement that getting these symbols to fit reality precisely was one of the great philosophical struggles. It was Jones's perceived straight dealing that made him such a huge hit with the American codebreakers; indeed, while he was director of GCHQ, they tried to poach him for a senior job over there, involving the US Air Force. Jones modestly declined.

His leisure hours were also determinedly un-aristocratic. By contrast with, for instance, the young Radio Security Service operator Hugh Trevor-Roper, who spent his spare hours near Bletchley Park riding with the Whaddon Hunt, Jones was a man who favoured golf. He was also a very keen skier. Most importantly, he was a calm and trusted figure who seemed to inspire affectionate loyalty. He was presiding over a department (still called the London Signals Intelligence Centre in some quarters) that was steadily expanding. Jumps in radio technology, as well as computing evolution, were greatly widening the possibilities open to the cryptanalysts.

There was certainly no longer enough room for them to operate amid the avenues and villas of Eastcote. For the last few years, the codebreakers had been casting about for a potential new base. Moscow's acquisition of the atomic bomb was one pressing reason why they should consider somewhere far from London, which would of course be the prime target in any outbreak of nuclear war. (In one of those exquisite historical coincidences, just one mile away from Eastcote, there was to be a hugely unlikely nuclear spy drama with the arrest of a couple called Peter and Helen Kroger in impeccably bourgeois Ruislip. The Krogers, American citizens, had moved to London, and he had set himself up as an antiquarian bookseller on Charing Cross Road. Helen Kroger, meantime, was far from an average 1950s housewife: neighbours recalled her loud, confident manner, even the piercing whistle she could give with two fingers. But here, nestled in the staidest of all London avenues, the Krogers were in fact at the centre of a Soviet spy-ring. Communist agents who had been spying on British naval establishments were reporting to them. The Krogers in turn were reporting their intelligence to Moscow via radio transmitter. As well as having its own historical curiosity, the story also now begs the question of what would have happened if they had moved in five years earlier; the sensitive antennae of the establishment hidden away just a matter of yards down the road would surely have identified it instantly.)

A suitable site for the new GCHQ had been identified in the late 1940s: a genteel spa town set in some rather beautiful Gloucestershire countryside. The legend is that intelligence operative Claude Daubney was the first man to point to Cheltenham as a possibility quite simply because of its racecourse; he was fanatical about his race meetings. True or not, it swiftly came to be seen as a fine option. It was some distance from London, but had a good regular train service. The town itself, though not enormous, would be large enough to house what was an ever-growing staff (unlike, say, at Bletchley Park, where codebreakers and debutantes were crammed into billets with very confused families of railway workers and brickmakers from the local town).

The only initial obstacle was the comically pervasive one of bureaucracy and a slightly truculent workforce. Even before any such move had been officially settled on, some typists in the administrative section were most unhappy about the prospect of leaving London. 'Thank you for your letter . . . with regard to established typists who may not wish to transfer to Cheltenham,' ran one interdepartmental memo to the War (or Defence) Ministry. 'I have made a note of Miss MacAvoy and Miss McBride as being the people we can get in touch with should established typists wish for a transfer.' Equally, there was a top-secret letter from the Foreign Office, eager not to let incredibly dependable and discreet administrative staff go. 'We have been asked by the Ministry of Civil Aviation whether you have any established typists who, rather than transfer to Cheltenham, are thinking of resigning and looking for other jobs.'[1]

Rather like the dissolution of Bletchley Park, the business of transferring the nation's secret communications headquarters could hardly be achieved overnight. As well as relocating the staff and finding them appropriate housing, the work they did was naturally a 24-hour operation all week round; at this point in the Cold War, there was not a corner of the globe that the cryptologists could afford to take their eyes off. There was also the matter of clandestine equipment – several generations of codebreaking and code-generating machinery – to be moved without a living soul noticing. It is worth remembering that from the point of view of the general public and the press, the organisation simply did not exist.

Down in Cheltenham, they were not building from scratch, although such an intensely sensitive and secure operation would obviously need some highly specialised and very well-defended premises. In fact, back in 1939 as war had broken out, the government had thought about the precautionary move of relocating parts of the War Office to Gloucestershire; fields at Benhall Farm and Oakley Farm just outside Cheltenham were quietly purchased.

Then, in the early years of the war came the first of some utilitarian blocks, and indeed the initial transfer of War Office staff from London. Gradually the site grew, and further buildings were added. It acquired a military presence; the Gloucestershire regiment was billeted there, as indeed were army wireless mechanic trainees. In terms of civil servants, there were roughly 2,000 working at the site. As the war progressed, and after America joined, Cheltenham played host to a US department called Services of Supply. With the Americans also came a very large number of telephone landlines. This was one of the factors that made the site so interesting to GCHQ ten years later. For naturally it was not just the early proto-computers that lay at the heart of the work: it needed a large quantity of telephone and teleprinter connections, too. Not all regions possessed these. Even if the brilliant Tommy Flowers of the GPO was working hard to bring the country up to date, there were some regions (as with superfast broadband today) that were lagging behind.

Cheltenham was not the only medium-sized town that the codebreakers were looking at. Oxford was briefly considered; and Cambridge was given some serious thought (not least, doubtless, because of the possibilities of recruitment from colleges and an osmotic flow of professors). Shrewsbury, the pretty town in Shropshire, was an early candidate. Manchester was another idea (again, it is easy to speculate that the work at that city's university being carried out by Max Newman and Alan Turing on the new generation of computers was a strong factor in its consideration). Harrogate was another possibility given serious thought (and again, the proximity of the nearby Forest Moor aerial array, with its daily harvest of Soviet communications traffic, must have been some inducement).

But Cheltenham simply had the better links to London. Once it had been (more or less) agreed upon in complete secrecy by Commander Travis and senior figures in the War Office and in the Treasury, they started to let the staff know that the move was coming. Amusingly, among the key people who did not know of any such decision were the councillors of Cheltenham Town Hall; they were startled when they eventually learnt, near the turn of the decade, that it was their area that had been chosen for the influx of 2,000 new professionals (described simply as working for the Foreign Office).

As it happened, the news was welcome. Cheltenham – with its beautiful Victorian and Regency architecture, its wide gracious avenues and its proximity to the rich beauty of the Cotswolds – had somehow to maintain its gentility. The surrounding area had, for decades, seen a great deal of light industry, and there was a lot of agriculturally-based manufacturing. By the end of the war, though, firms were closing up and moving away. On top of this, the council was anxious to replenish and renew the town's housing stock; like everywhere else in Britain in the late 1940s, the pressure on housing was uncomfortably intense. The idea that the town could be a home to 2,000 well-paid middle-class civil servants was terrific; but first, there would have to be a mighty construction programme.

There is always something pleasing about the British propensity for bureaucratic niceties throughout periods in which it seems the entire world is having a nervous breakdown. Given that one of the reasons for moving out of London at all was to put the codebreakers beyond the range of Soviet nuclear weaponry; and given that from Malaya to Korea, the appetite for war seemed not to have been slaked in the last few years of bloodshed, one might have assumed that there would be an air of urgency about pulling off an incredibly complex moving exercise. There was apparently none. As soon as Cheltenham Council had recovered from its surprise, and expressed its enthusiasm, there were others in Whitehall who suddenly wondered if the department might not be moved rather more economically elsewhere. Doubly amusingly, among the last people to have heard about any such prospective relocation was the foreign secretary Ernest Bevin.

Also crucial to the project was that the actual buildings to house the cryptologists were either already owned by the government (as the Benhall Farm buildings were) or freshly built; the danger of a commercially owned building being compromised with enemy spying equipment was too great. These were the very earliest days of electronic surveillance but already it was possible to get functioning bugs into walls and ceilings. The site had to be utterly clean.

As the move began in 1952, one of the institution's most consulted veterans was entering a period of huge personal crisis. Up in the wet and soot of Manchester, Alan Turing's relationship with the young Arnold Murray was developing and becoming more complex and jagged. They talked, they met for meals, they slept together at Turing's house in Wilmslow. Murray was from a working-class background; Turing inhabited a world he had never even glimpsed before. It was a world of ideas and of extraordinarily fascinating technology. Murray was captivated when Turing told him of the work that was taking place on fashioning electronic brains. Regardless of his lack of schooling, Murray was apparently open to discussing computers, psychology and the mechanics of the mind. Nonetheless, he and Turing operated in parallel dimensions.

At the time, Turing had begun a sideline in broadcasting, accepting invitations to give talks and take part in panel discussions on BBC Radio. Before the advent of mass television viewing, this in itself was a brush with celebrity. There was the possibility of Turing becoming a household name. He was also being sought out right the way across the scientific community for conferences on computing and artificial intelligence. He did not appear to sense the peril that a continued relationship with Arnold Murray could bring. According to Turing's biographer Andrew Hodges, the one subject that should have been brought up at the very start of their association was money. Thin-faced Murray was poor; as their assignations became more regular, Turing was prepared to pull out his wallet and give him cash. But Murray angrily rejected an initial offer: direct payment would make him a rent boy.

However, one morning after Murray had stayed over, Turing discovered money missing from his wallet. Possibly now he smelled the danger; can he have realised that whatever he did now, it was too late? He wrote to Murray, explaining straightforwardly that their association was at an end. But not long afterwards, Murray presented himself at Turing's front door, indignant and angry. He demanded to know why he had been dismissed so curtly; and he flatly denied having taken any money from Turing's wallet.

But at the same time, he asked Turing if he might have a loan of £3 because he had bought a new suit on credit, or hire purchase as it was called then, and he needed to repay an instalment of debt. Turing gave the young man £3; but a few days later, he received a letter from Murray asking for another £7. Turing, rather than simply handing money over, demanded to know the name and the address of Murray's tailor, so that he could check that there really was such an arrangement. This demand resulted in Arnold Murray once more presenting himself on Turing's doorstep in a fury of hurt indignation: why did Turing not trust him? The result of this was that Turing eventually relented and wrote out a cheque for £7.

Hodges suggests that one of Turing's impulses upon first meeting Murray was to lift him out of the painfully circumscribed life he was living, to feed him ideas, knowledge. And Murray had initially seemed very open to the sorts of discussions he would never have had a chance of getting anywhere else. Did he have any kind of affection for Turing? Or was he simply a deprived young man who had seen an opportunity? Possibly both cases were true.

Events took a chillier turn when Turing returned home one day to find that his house had been burgled. There seemed to be minimal reasoning behind the items that were taken, among which were some shirts, fish knives and an open bottle of sherry. Turing reported the robbery to the police, who came around and dusted for fingerprints. There was an itching suspicion at the back of Turing's mind; perhaps anyone else might have left it at that, heedful of the peril ahead, but there was an impatient directness about Turing. He wrote to Arnold Murray, demanding the repayment of that £7. On top of this, he asked that Murray should not call round at his house any more. Why did Turing imagine that Murray would accede to this? If innocent, the implied accusation would have been stingingly hurtful. If guilty, the young man would be scrambling to find a way to cover himself.

And so Murray ignored Turing and once more arrived at his front door. In the bitter argument that ensued, he apparently threatened to go to the police and tell them 'everything', meaning his illegal relationship with Turing. Turing was, according to Hodges, perfectly unmoved by this suggestion of blackmail and invited the young man to 'do his worst'.[2] At this Murray calmed down and somehow the atmosphere became amiable enough for Turing to offer him a drink. And it was during the course of the ensuing discussion – Turing telling Murray about the burglary – that the fateful wheels started moving. Artlessly, Murray told Turing that even though he was surprised the robbery had taken place, he nonetheless knew who had done it: an acquaintance of his called Harry. The two of them, old friends, had apparently met up and after hearing about Murray's connection with the great scientist, Harry had announced his plan to carry out a burglary.

Armed with this intelligence, Turing did a curious thing. He went back to the police, reported his suspicion of this new suspect, and invented a story about how he had come to hold this suspicion. Would it not have made more sense simply to leave the police to get on with their own investigation? Turing also leaned on Arnold to try to get some of those stolen items back. But the act of going to the police a second time was certain to make Turing himself an object of some suspicion: how would a university academic in a middle-class household, complete with housekeeper, possibly have any kinds of connections that would lead him to burglars and petty criminals?

Curiously, it was around this time that the entire atmosphere concerning sexual orientation had changed; throughout the war, there was no secret about Turing's homosexuality. He had propositioned his colleague Peter Twinn (who gently turned him down); in America, he had sought out sexual encounters without blinking. It was hardly as if the authorities were unaware, and even though such acts were strictly speaking illegal (on both sides of the Atlantic), there had never been any sense that anyone was interested in seeing Alan Turing prosecuted.

But then had come the post-war hurricane of Venona; the horrifying revelations of treachery so deep within the establishment. And with this came the repercussive paranoia: the sense of invisible enemies within. In part, homosexuality represented a blackmail risk, agents and operatives lured into stupid encounters with Soviet agents who could then leverage their moments of weakness. But there might also have been something more going on, a sense that homosexuality was in itself as subversive as Communism. A feeling that it was a kind of sexual treachery. Certainly, the new ferocity with which gay men were pursued by police and by the wider media could not be explained in wholly rational terms. We see this in the cases of Lord Montagu of Beaulieu, journalist Peter Wildeblood and the actor John Gielgud, all arrested and prosecuted in that strange, febrile period, when Sunday newspapers labelled homosexual practices as evil.

Part of the tragedy of Alan Turing was his sheer incomprehension that the state could regard his sexuality as a crime. When the detectives returned to his home to question him further – and to ask exactly how it was that his informant knew so much of underworld activity – Turing responded quickly and openly to their suspicious questions about the nature of his relationship with Murray. He went further and told the detectives – who seemed at least impressed, not only his by honesty, but also by what they saw as his bravery – that he thought that there was some Parliamentary commission looking into the legalisation of such acts. In this, Turing was wrong but also ahead of his time: the Wolfenden Report, which recommended the decriminalisation of homosexuality, was published in 1957, and it was not until 1967 that it was finally permitted in law. For Turing, though, a nightmare lay ahead.

No entrapment had been necessary (unlike in so many other cases); the Wilmslow detectives had their man. Turing and Murray were both charged with gross indecency. Despite his role in the burglary, and the cold extortion of money from Turing, there were a few who might have felt a pang of sympathy for the otherwise chilly Murray. He lost his job at the printing firm instantly. However, as Andrew Hodges relates, Murray was to be conditionally discharged; and although the unwelcome and hostile attention of neighbours made it impossible for him to stay in Manchester, he pitched up in London's more Bohemian quarters, learned the guitar and fell in with a set of beatniks and poets.

For Turing, the outlook was bleaker. First he had to tell his mother and his brother of his orientation since, unlike his working peers, they had had no idea. After his arrest and his bail, he continued working and attending scientific conferences, and his colleagues were broadly sympathetic, telling him that it was unlikely that any sentence would be particularly severe.

But when the trial and the sentence came in April 1952, it turned out to be savage. It was not the two years in prison generally recommended in such cases; instead, the punishment was more futuristic and frighteningly untested: 'organo-therapy'. In essence, Turing was required to submit to a course of oestrogen injections, the idea of which was a form of chemical castration. The course was to last for a year.

There was that, plus the unpublicised loss of his security clearance. It is difficult to imagine just how much of a psychological blow that must have been to him. The horrific and humiliating side effects of the 'therapy' – Turing became bloated and developed breasts – was one thing. The idea of being shut out, in perpetuity, from the most important secret work in the land must have been worse.

It has to be said that he had not been forsaken by his colleagues. Quite the reverse. Turing asked not only Max Newman but also Hugh Alexander to testify to his character throughout the trial. Either might easily have found a way of declining to do so. Neither did. Max Newman stoutly defended Turing; when asked if he would have such a man in his own home, he replied that as a matter of fact, he frequently did. Hugh Alexander went even further. Bearing in mind that no-one in that court-room, including the judge, would have had the slightest idea about Bletchley Park or GCHQ, Alexander – without going into any specifics – simply described Turing as a 'national asset'. It was also made clear to the judge that Turing had been appointed an OBE; again, no explanation was given for it, but the honour was implicitly for war work.

The chemical treatment was crude; the side effects distressing. But

Turing got on with his work, and there was no sense of being shunned by colleagues and peers in the realms of mathematics and computing. Yet he had been shut out of quite another world. There was a further consequence: as a result of his new criminal record, he would no longer be permitted to enter the United States. Any possibility that he might, like so many other former Bletchley friends, find some means of continuing that Atlantic-crossing cryptological relationship were stamped upon for good.

It is also possible to imagine the frustration that Hugh Alexander felt about the entire case. Turing was an asset in many senses. He was not, though, the only asset that the cryptanalysts would lose in 1952. Turing, before his trial, had also written to his very old friend – and sometime fiancée – Joan Clarke, who was still with GCHQ at Eastcote. He explained in that letter that the 'homosexual tendencies' that he had confessed to at the termination of their romance were rather more pronounced and indeed active than he had perhaps suggested to her. As always, Joan was forbearing. And any pain that she might have still felt as a result of their break-up ten years beforehand would most certainly have been erased by the development of a new relationship, this time with a fellow Eastcote cryptanalyst: Lieutenant Colonel J (Jock) Murray, a 42-year-old officer with extensive experience of India and also of the Baltic region.

Lieutenant Colonel Murray had not been at Bletchley Park; his had been a straightforward military career that had taken him from Ahmednagar to Rawalpindi, and also to Estonia where, in the 1930s, he had become an expert interpreter skilled in Russian. In India, he had served with the Bombay Grenadiers. Murray's move into Military Intelligence came after his own lively and curious intellect had been noticed. Throughout the war, he continued to serve largely in India and throughout the Far East. When it all ended, he was transferred to work with the War Office. He retired from the military in 1948, aged 38; but such a mind was too valuable to be allowed to drift into civilian life. He was approached to join the cryptologists in Eastcote in 1948 and his work was greatly appreciated.

It was in those monotonous blocks that he first met Joan Clarke. As rare pictures of Joan with her Eastcote colleagues show, here is a striking woman surrounded by male peers, dark-haired, confident, the round spectacles denoting her studiousness, the wide smile suggesting a happy nature. Aside from the few American women who also worked there in the 1940s, GCHQ was an overwhelmingly male institution. Joan Clarke, who knew how much she was capable of achieving, looks very safe within her skin in all these smiling images. This was the woman with whom Jock Murray was soon to find such a strong connection.

The year 1952 was pivotal for them both. First, it was then that they got married. This was an era, as mentioned, in which newly married women were expected to drop their jobs instantly. There was little in the way of argument about it; it was simply one of those social norms so embedded as to be relatively unquestioned. It might perhaps had been different for the newly married Mrs Joan Murray – her abilities, after all, were rated very highly among her male superiors – were it not for the fact that her new husband was suffering ill-health. It turned out that Murray would have to be the one who would have to withdraw from GCHQ: he simply could not continue working in such a pressurised environment while his health was so poor. So both Jock and Joan stepped down in 1952, moving to a small Scottish village called Crail, on the east coast between Edinburgh and Dundee.

How does one fill the vacuum left by such crucial and fascinating work? Murray had long had a fascination for antique coins; he was an expert numismatist. Joan was beguiled by this and swiftly took up the pursuit herself. Murray had become mesmerised via the history of medals in India; it was a small step to the parallel study of ancient coinage, and the complex meanings encoded within the images and lettering. He and Joan also threw themselves into deep study of the history of Scotland. They would spend hours together in the archives of the small local town hall, examining records that stretched back as far as the 16th century. Again, there are aspects of history that are analogous to codebreaking: the ability to work with fragments of intelligence from scattered items of documentation, and the skill at interrogating these texts in order to create a simulacrum of the world.

Given both the secrecy and the privacy surrounding cryptological staff, little is known of the exact nature of Murray's illness. But it is known that it caused him to be hospitalised, that he required several major operations, and that it caused him some discomfort and pain for a number of years. But those who knew him testified to his constant cheerful good nature throughout that period, as well as his inexhaustible appetite for his esoteric studies. Equally, it is tempting to imagine that this is not quite the sort of life that Mrs Murray had intended for herself: a London-born Cambridge-educated codebreaking expert, now away up in what was then a rather remote part of the country. But it is equally clear that she threw herself into this life with real conviction and good humour.

This was not the end of their codebreaking careers; very far from it. Gradually, with painful slowness, Lieutenant Colonel Murray's health improved (the keen winds of the Fife coastline might have helped somewhat), and it was clear in the years that elapsed that the couples' former colleagues at GCHQ were consistently issuing invitations for them to return. The Cold War was not losing any of its intensity. Such expertise was needed.

And so it was that a few years later, in 1962 – not long before the outbreak of the Cuban Missile Crisis, the nuclear stand-off between the US and the Soviets that brought the planet dramatically close to a lethal exchange of atomic warheads – that Jock and Joan Murray returned to a grateful GCHQ. The assets were back in place. Pleasingly, they did not entirely leave their old Crail lives behind: when they moved down to Cheltenham to be within cycling distance of work, they also brought with them that passion for rare coin collecting. And so it was that the Cheltenham Numismatists Association suddenly found itself with two fresh experts, seemingly from out of the blue, bringing a whole new life to the society.

Given the deliberate facelessness of the organisation, one of the striking elements of the early years of GCHQ was the warmth that it had for so many of its personnel. Part of this was the ever increasing depth of secrecy: the codebreakers knew that they were in a very select company. But it was also to do with the vast and unfathomable stress of the work; the need to decrypt, translate, analyse messages from hostile regions with absolute pinpoint accuracy, and at lightning speed, for fear that at any moment the enemy might be making a strike. Working with that ever present threat thick in the air seemed to encourage an outward air of amused insouciance in the codebreakers. There could never be any question of their profound seriousness; indeed, the intensity of this life had a sort of addictive quality that made those who had been ordained to it very loath to give it up. But this meant that, in order to compensate, their off-duty personas could be as light as helium. It also meant that they were qualified to take on extra-mural challenges with a sort of tap-dancing elegance, which others would have baulked at. Though he worked very far into the shadows, senior cryptologist Hugh Alexander was about to step out into the glare of the limelight in order to deliver a heavily coded message to the Communist world about the intellectual firepower that Great Britain could still summon.

But before he did that, there was an operation unfolding on the borders between East and West in Europe that not only demonstrated the innovative brilliance of Dr Tommy Flowers and his General Post Office team – but also the continuing hazard of treachery within the nation's secret realms.

Chapter Twenty-One

The Tunnel and the Traitor

The darkness that had settled over much of Europe was not easily penetrated from a distance; the nature of Soviet control was more insidious and destabilising than obvious displays of violence. The tanks would only come later. Unlike the Nazis, who had loudly coerced a wider public into communal hatreds – of Jews, disabled people, gypsies – the Communists operated by means of stealthy infiltration, and their targets were frequently unaware that they were about to fall victim. In East Germany, throughout the late 1940s, the disappearances of local politicians and journalists had begun as isolated cases, then gradually became hundreds, then thousands: men were found guilty of subverting Communist rule, and deported to labour camps in the permafrost wastes of Russia's deep interior. There was no right of appeal, and very often no way back. These camps – freezing, insanitary, with starvation rations and guards for whom the power to administer beatings was a bonus – were lethal; it was for many, in essence, a slow death sentence.

In countries such as Hungary, Romania, Czechoslovakia, Soviet officials targeted not only opposition politicians, but also citizens who ran civic groups: not just unions, but also organisations such as the YMCA, the Scouts, the equivalents of the Women's Institute. For Stalin to have complete control over a country, his agents had to be in charge of every level of the community. Youth clubs were particularly key. In the late 1940s, for instance, many young people in Budapest had developed a fondness for listening to American swing; the new Communist overseers of these clubs smashed their records.

This was the world that the codebreakers were listening to; a world where, incredibly, show trials were once again being conducted. They had been used in Russia in the 1930s by the super-paranoid Stalin to wipe out an entire generation of military officers and apparatchiks that he suddenly distrusted violently. Now these nightmarish pantomimes had begun anew in order to deal with defiant Hungarian politicians who dared to continue to oppose Soviet demands on their territory. There was hardly any pretence that the trials were legitimate. The point of them was a naked display of raw power, the power of life and death.

At Eastcote, there had been absolutely no doubt in the minds of the senior codebreakers of the true nature of Stalin's leadership; there had been no question that his regime would thaw or change. For them, it was clear that the sharpening Cold War was an inevitability. As much as the gathering of coded communications enabled them to see into the heart of those nations behind the Iron Curtain, the patches of silence told their own story.

Where were the voices of the sophisticated, cultured young people of countries like Hungary and Czechoslovakia? The Soviets smothered them, treating them like stubborn pre-electrical-age rural peasants, because that was all that the Soviets had experience of. Indeed, the only part of the Soviet bloc where such control was weaker was in Poland; there were pockets of the country with quite spectacularly ungovernable pre-electricity rural peasants, who answered to the grander and more metaphysically unassailable authority of the Catholic Church. Not even Stalin wanted to take on the Pope.

But the traffic of transmission worked both ways, and at around this time, in London, a close cousin to GCHQ – a special department that broadcast radio programmes directly into Eastern Europe – was being run by a lively mind called Sir John Rennie, who was later to head up MI6.

Rennie had been a diplomat in Poland in the late 1940s and early 1950s and had seen quite clearly how people there had to live with a constant sense of threat hanging over them. This was coupled with universal privations: scarce goods in shops, sparse quantities of certain foodstuffs. When he came back, he was to take over a brainchild of the former foreign secretary Ernest Bevin: this was the 'Information Research Department'. The idea was very simply to broadcast propaganda – the truth about the failures and the multiple evils of Stalinist rule – to listeners from Warsaw to Bucharest. These radio programmes were the spy version of pirate radio: put out by secret transmitters, tuned into by young iconoclasts. It was a very serious business; even if anyone had cynical doubts about the suddenly rapacious nature of America's military-industrial complex, this could hardly match Russia's chilling and murderous treatment of those who even mildly disagreed. In this, Rennie shared the same point of view as GCHQ: there was a moral dimension here, not merely an icy calculation of geopolitical strategy.

Conversely, there were many young people in Britain at that time – as the nation was preparing for the bright, colourful coronation of its new young queen – who would have regarded such broadcasts from the heart of the British establishment as hopelessly reactionary, and held that there was virtue to be found in the more austere, less material Eastern bloc. Without direct knowledge of the millions of lives, the quantity of blood that Stalin had so casually shed, and without much of a sense of the boulder that pressed down on younger generations in Soviet bloc countries, these idealistic members of the Communist Party of Great Britain – otherwise simply known as The Party – could only see Russia and Communist Europe as striving towards a noble ideal, the creation of a serious, equal society, a dimension away from the raucous, greedy, ruthless capitalism of America. These young people would have honked with scorn at Sir John Rennie's productions. A few years later, in the brilliantly horrible 1959 Boulting Brothers film satire *I'm All Right Jack*, union leader Fred Kite (played by Peter Sellers) grows moist-eyed as he compares the vulgar, gaudy consumerism of 1950s Britain to the purer life of the working classes in Russia. 'All them cornfields,' he sighs, 'and ballet in the evening.'

In West Germany, the playwright Bertolt Brecht went a little further:

he made the unusual journey across to the other side to live in East Berlin. For him and other Germans, Konrad Adenauer's government, fattened with vast quantities of Marshall Aid American money, was not yet free of the shadow of the Reich; for all the 'de-Nazifying' programmes that had taken place, there seemed now to be a more generalised silence, a determined reluctance even to think about the recent past. For figures such as Brecht, East Berlin had a contrasting purity. So what if the shops were empty, and the debating chambers were free of dissenting voices?

The parallel worlds encompassed in Berlin were sharpening in their contrasts. As mentioned, even without that colossal sum of US cash, the economy of the Federal Republic under Adenauer would still have leapt ahead; and as it was, by 1953, West Germany and its people were enjoying comfort that would have seemed unimaginable just eight years beforehand. East Berlin – the landscape still pocked with so many grey and dusty bomb-sites – was a more morose proposition. Before the looming concrete symbol of the Berlin Wall, there were tightly guarded checkpoints, and barbed wire. Citizens of the East who wished to pass across could still just about do so.

After his terrific intelligence successes in Vienna, Peter Lunn was transferred in 1953 to Berlin. Lunn's tunnel, the construction beneath the Vienna streets that had enabled a close circle of young secret listeners to intercept a wild array of Soviet intelligence, was an idea that was even better suited to Berlin. Unlike the last time, when the buccaneering Lunn had chosen to keep the operation from the higher reaches of the Foreign Office, for fear of their closing it down out of diplomatic panic, there were now a (small) number of well-placed senior enthusiasts willing to give it the go-ahead; not only in the Foreign Office and War Office but also across the Atlantic.

And again, though Lunn was attached to MI6, this ambitious operation – to burrow beneath the divided city, and to physically modify Soviet telephone lines – was handled by an extraordinarily secret branch of GCHQ's Y service. In other words, it was not even known about by all the MI6 agents who were operating in the streets above. It was, however – tragic-comically – known to one particular British operative whose

subsequent betrayal was to blow up infuriatingly in the faces of the
Western Allies. But in 1953, the Allies thought they had done everything
imaginable to keep what was termed Operation Gold utterly clandestine.
The Americans, too, kept a very close guard on the numbers of people
who had any kind of knowledge about what was going on. As with so
many other codebreaking and interception operations, this was to be an
Anglo-American affair with complete trust between the two powers.

This was an even more intricate construction job than the one beneath
Vienna, but the Americans had access to a property which was particularly
close to a cluster of East German diplomatic telephone lines. The target for
the interceptors was mouth-watering. Across these lines would be carried
calls to and from Moscow, plus to all the other significant Eastern European
capitals. It would be like listening to the heartbeat of Soviet Russia: the
orders, the plans, the directives, the intelligence on military manoeuvres.

Constructing a tunnel underneath alien territory without being detected
was one thing; building it so that it could house complex interception
technology without the tunnel overheating and crippling vital machinery
was another. Once again, this was a job for the Research Department at
Dollis Hill: a couple of engineers were sent over to fathom not only how
to combat unexpected difficulties like build-ups of condensation, but also
to bring new techniques in tapping phones that would ensure that the
Soviets would never realise what was happening. Phone-tapping itself at
that stage involved metal clamps; but according to security expert Richard
Aldrich, the Dollis Hill wizards also brought an innovative technique that
allowed clamps and cables to be frozen. The zero temperatures would help
ensure that the East Germans never heard any giveaway clicks or ticks
while they were making their calls.

On top of this, agents managed to obtain from East Berlin maps and
plans of key buildings and key telephone lines in their target areas. Peter
Lunn and his team had done the most breathtaking job, for once it was
operational, the Berlin Tunnel began to harvest an astounding amount
of intelligence. There were hundreds of telegraphic and voice circuits
planted on lines deep in the tunnels, and the interceptions gathered were
sent immediately back to London where, in an elegant building next to

Regent's Park, hundreds of staff transcribed the conversations that had been bugged. These conversations were then sent off for analysis. The Americans set up a sort of express bureau in Berlin near the site of the tunnel, so that they could analyse the intelligence in something close to real-time. Yet while there can be no gainsaying the terrific chutzpah and ingenuity of the entire idea, the fact was – both grimly and yet at the same time slightly farcically – the Soviets had known all along.

The reason for this was that one of the chosen British few who knew about the operation was the agent George Blake. A couple of years previously, Blake had been captured in the Korean War; his Communist gaolers subjected him to brainwashing. Rather more than this, it was during this period of imprisonment that he was approached and turned by Soviet intelligence. By 1953, Blake was back in London at MI6 and part of the rarefied circle of people working within Section Y. According to Richard Aldrich, when Blake received detailed plans of the tunnel system to be built, he took a copy, climbed aboard a pre-designated London red double-decker bus, and there he met his Soviet contact, to whom the plans were passed.

However, there was a heartening and grimly amusing twist too; for even though the Russians now knew everything, they had to ensure that the British and Americans did not know that they knew. This meant, in essence, that Soviet intelligence could not issue specific warnings to East German officials; if they had done, the Allies would have realised, and doubtless then tried something even more cunning. All the East German officials were told was that they ought to take general care when in conversation on the telephone. There was an almost comical horror on the part of the Soviets when they realised just how incredibly negligent the East Germans were about such warnings.

And so it was that despite Blake's efforts, in fact the Berlin Tunnel did yield excellent, useable intelligence. There was plenty there for the Regent's Park personnel back in London to translate and analyse. Among the deliberate false leads and trails – this was, after all, a means for the Soviets to burrow into British and American intelligence, by gauging their reactions to carefully seeded false messages – there was a wondrous amount of day-to-day genuine traffic, with a wealth of references that helped the British fill in all sorts of knowledge gaps about Soviet placements and intentions.

Indeed, there came a point when this curious farce had to be ended by the Soviets; and that day came in 1956, when they feigned carrying out repair work beneath the streets and 'accidentally' burrowed through to the Allies' tunnel, with its array of quite dazzling up-to-the-minute Dollis Hill equipment. The Russian engineers were said to have been rather impressed with the technology. And with this *faux* discovery, they also went public. The tunnel hit the newspapers. The story clattered around the world. The circumstances of the betrayal and discovery were of course maddening; and yet on either side, there was some admiration of the sort of ingenuity and nerve that went into the work of eavesdropping on the enemy.

Back in 1953, the landscape had once more shifted: Stalin died in the spring of that year. There began an extended process of wrangling in the Soviet Politburo to determine his successor. The Americans under Eisenhower and the British under prime minister Winston Churchill looked on; did the passing of this titanic figure make war less or more likely? Strikingly, there were figures within the CIA who were advising the White House that Stalin himself had been – in his own way – a stable force, not given to reckless acts, and skilled at steering away from potential points of conflict. Now, in the spring of 1953, the concern was that whoever came next – senior politician Georgi Malenkov was thought by many to have the natural advantage – might be more manic and less able to deal with the colossal pressures that were being exerted all over the world. One factor was predicted to remain exactly the same: there would be no new flicker of warmth in the relationship between the two superpowers. The Cold War was to remain at dangerous freezing level.

The death of the tyrant also caused some within the White House to wonder why it was that the National Security Agency had failed to provide advance intelligence concerning Stalin's terminal illness. Indeed, according to author Matthew M Aid, signals intelligence intercepts in the weeks and days beforehand – detailing Stalin's meetings with Indian and South American dignitaries – suggested that he was functioning as normal. When the news of his death broke, it came not from a decyphered message, but from the international news agencies. Added to this, during this period, the NSA was locked in bitter competition with the relatively recently formed CIA, which had its own little codebreaking department and which had actually poached some codebreakers across from the NSA. History always shows that fractured cryptological operations are never as successful as those properly unified under one umbrella.

This was not the most fruitful period for the codebreakers in Eastcote either; but there was little that could be done against the intractable problem of the Russians changing their codes after having understood their vulnerability. Added to this, it was unreasonable to expect the codebreakers to be end-of-the-pier fortune tellers, seeing clearly into all possible permutations of the future. Within the Kremlin, for instance, there were conversations and whisperings that would never have been transmitted across the airwaves; the only way that they could have been intercepted would have been for a secret listener to be hidden somewhere within the same room. As it happened, the boffins of Dollis Hill were, throughout the 1950s, working on listening devices that could be used some distance away from a target building, to pick up and record whatever was being said from within. But such miracles were hardly universally available.

Nor, as the furious political struggle within Russia in the gaping wake of Stalin's death continued, could the codebreakers have possibly anticipated the uprising to come in what had seemed one of the most compliant of Moscow's stolen states. In the summer of 1953, industrial workers in the Russian sector of Berlin, the very heart of the German Democratic Republic, suddenly staged protests. The initial cause appeared to be the preposterous productivity targets set by Kremlin apparatchiks, and the consistent authoritarianism of the country's ruler Walter Ulbricht. But these violent Berlin demonstrations were to spread from one East German city to another.

The Soviet response to this East German insubordination was a foretaste of how Moscow would deal with all such future disobedience across its Eastern European empire: it sent in Russian tanks and Russian troops. Here was a point at which both Britain and America leaned forward; with the possibility of the contagion of further unrest – and resulting industrial paralysis – would it be wise to help or encourage these young urban workers? It was thought, on balance, that it would be wiser not to; any visible signs of the Western powers working actively to destabilise the East might be – in those frayed, frightened, leaderless times in the Kremlin – the very spur just one ambitious senior Politburo figure would need to declare war.

In any case, the mere fact that the youthful working classes were taking to the streets to protest, not merely about unreasonable work quotas or even living standards, but about the very nature of Communist rule itself, was a fascinating sign of possible inherent weakness in the Eastern bloc. The street demonstrations that had spread all over the German Democratic Republic were also finding faint echoes – in different ways – from Czechoslovakia to Romania. From discontent over factory policy to the continued forced collectivisation of agriculture – which forced many farmers in Eastern Europe off their own property and into alien (and ineffective) new production methods – the warning tokens of dissent could be heard, and indeed picked up, by the listeners in Britain, who assiduously passed intelligence on to the Americans. If there had not been so many Soviet troops on the streets of East Germany, there might have been greater temptation on the part of the West to give the rebellious young some covert assistance. Equally, those rebellious young might very well have finished the job themselves without any outside interference.

But the Soviet response – given that no-one in the Kremlin now had Stalin to look to for fearful guidance – was pragmatic. Across the Eastern bloc, Soviet demands for more produce and more food to be sent to Russia were scaled down; coupled with this was a lessening of the blunt use of police terror against dissidents; and political prisoners already locked up received (in a few cases) pardons, and were able to return to their homes. For if the urban young could not be kept on-side, then the regime would not be remotely sustainable.

The continuing intransigence of Soviet cypher systems meant that the codebreakers and their intelligence cousins would have to develop new means of eavesdropping; ingenious tunnels notwithstanding, there was still much room for technical and scientific innovation. The Dollis Hill research department continued its work (while it also went about devising the aforementioned ERNIE system of selecting numbers of Premium Bond draws). But with Winston Churchill returned to Downing Street, it was also quite clear that it was time to pull together some of the more formidable wartime talents to give a sense of unity to all espionage work. So it was that one of the greatest unsung minds of the time was lured back to Whitehall to cast an eye over what might be done for GCHQ to harvest as much Soviet information as they could.

Reginald Victor Jones was now a Professor; this still (relatively) young 40-something scientist had, after a piercingly brilliant war, been offered a post teaching physics at the University of Aberdeen. None of his young students would have been aware that this angular figure had been behind the triumph of misdirecting Luftwaffe bombers, or sabotaging the aim of the later V-1 rockets. For these triumphs, Jones had been awarded the CBE.

And now he was lured back to London by an admiring Churchill (in fact, during the war, Churchill had frequently been irritated by Jones, as the young man had stubbornly argued with the prime minister over operational matters; but Churchill had come to see that Jones was usually right). Now the professor was to be made Chief of Scientific Intelligence. This would carry across all departments and services: from the War Office, to the armed forces, to the intelligence departments, and particularly to the men and women of GCHQ.

Codes were only a part of it; what could a new generation of ingenious bugging technology achieve? If one were to focus some sort of super-microphone at the embassy of an Eastern European country, how many of the ambassador's conversations and calls might one pick up? Professor Jones also took a shrewd interest in GCHQ's move from Eastcote to Cheltenham, which was gradually underway (speed being rendered impractical by the need to establish incredibly complex, expensive and confidential machinery as well as personnel – they could scarcely have allowed GCHQ a month off to move everyone down from London in one go).

Professor Jones recalled that he had discussed the Cheltenham site with GCHQ operative and racing enthusiast Claude Daubney. He and Jones jokingly discussed the notion of scientifically setting up a means of cracking the bookmakers – just theory of course, nothing practical. By 1953, GCHQ was blossoming in terms of the numbers of fresh personnel and also in new computational expertise. The rise of Communist China, the Korean War, the tectonic uncertainty over the Soviet Union's intentions and aggression in the aftermath of Stalin, all meant that this still relatively new service was given a huge injection of investment.

It is worth remembering how much admiration Churchill had had for the codebreakers of Bletchley Park. The entire business of cyphers had mesmerised him. This was clearly the case now, too. As the new queen came to the throne, the extraordinary level of activity down in this Gloucestershire country town intensified. There was another development that mirrored the war: just as Bletchley Park had seen a dedicated group of brilliant Americans moving into its huts by means of liaison in the later years of the war, so 1953 saw an even closer conjoining of the two nation's cryptanalytical skills. With the earlier Venona decrypts, the joint British-American team had been very small, and attached to that task only. This new melding of experts served a rather wider clientele. The American team would be there in Cheltenham to receive any codes or messages from GCHQ's innumerable listening stations around the world: codes that immediately pertained to US interests. And so from Cheltenham, these Americans in turn could relay the vital intelligence back to the CIA, or to Washington.

Perhaps now such an arrangement might seem a little like the more powerful Americans leaning on their British allies quite heavily for assistance, whether the British liked it or not; but it is important also to recall that the senior figures of GCHQ had been among the architects of that brilliantly successful wartime transatlantic partnership. Commander Loehnis was among the former Bletchley men who, in 1953, had gone to Washington for talks about how this new Cold War relationship might be strengthened. For the politicians and military leaders, there might well have been mutual suspicion and even dislike; but the codebreakers were in another realm: they talked to each other with relaxed good humour and also a keen sense of their skills and abilities. In the years to come, this terrific harmony would come to be tested, quite violently; but in 1953, as the codebreaking institute put down its roots among the straight lines and clinical architecture of 1950s office new-builds, there was a sense of real purpose.

Josh Cooper – the brilliant codebreaking veteran whose career had started with the Government Code and Cypher School in the mid-1920s – had then been among the first to smell the danger of Bolshevism. Now, here he was in Cheltenham, at the age of 52, his multiple eccentricities undimmed (he would suddenly resume conversations that others thought had ended days beforehand), but his towering experience and ingenuity was a beacon to the younger adepts. Although one of his chief talents was for linguistics as opposed to pure mathematics, Cooper had been among those who evangelised the new era of the computer; he had seen the potential some distance off. He was now heading up GCHQ's research department, delving deeply into such matters. This was precisely the sort of unfazed talent that the Americans had such open admiration for: the minds that could seemingly be turned to any sort of discipline, while maintaining a laser focus on the reason that they were turning these dazzling cartwheels. The lives of some of Cooper's contemporary colleagues were, at this crucial point in the 1950s, to take some dizzying turns. But the institution that they had founded was beginning a whole new phase of life.

Chapter Twenty-Two

The Great Game

This new intelligence service had selected a most unlikely setting for its moment of symbolic triumph. On the seafront at Hastings, Sussex, just facing the pier, stood a theatre built in the Spanish colonial style – white, with large windows and an elegant green-tiled roof. In the summer months, hundreds of visitors would visit the White Rock Pavilion for shows starring comedians such as Arthur Askey and the Fols de Rols variety performers. In the frozen January of 1954, with no holidaymakers in sight, the entertainment was a trifle more cerebral. Inside the Pavilion, there was a sort of feverish excitement. This was the annual Hastings Chess Congress, an international tournament that had been held since 1895. This year, the tournament held layers of significance that the general public – chess fans and idle onlookers alike – could never have guessed. The British and the Soviet teams were matching wits and playing hard for victory, watched closely by heavyweight Russian NKVD agents (travelling as observers of the chess team) and British codebreakers alike.

At the table was a renowned young Soviet Grandmaster: David Bronstein. The challenge of matching his labyrinthine intellect was not to be taken lightly. And yet this was exactly what his British opponent Hugh Alexander appeared to be doing. Here was one of GCHQ's greatest and most valuable cryptographic minds – who had spent the last few years deeply immersed in the exquisite complexities of Soviet codes

– sitting just two feet away across the board from this Russian titan, and playing with an extraordinary detached amusement. The outcome of this contest would have terrific resonance. Bronstein was not the only Russian chess genius there by the shore of Hastings; also present was an older Grandmaster, Alexander Tolush, a native of Leningrad (still St Petersburg when he was born). There was a thrill of electricity running through the gaudy surrounds of the White Rock Pavilion, be-suited spectators looking on at duellists hunched over carved pieces.

And as if to prove that the world of codebreakers was almost absurdly tightly-knit, even one of the official onlookers had GCHQ connections. 'The Russians were expected to steal the show,' exclaimed a report in *The Observer* by Edward Crankshaw, the newspaper's correspondent. Crankshaw had, in 1944, been part of the Bletchley Park team of young turks, along with Harry Hinsley and Gordon Welchman, who had been asked to write a confidential paper on the future shape of GCHQ. Something of a literary critic in his earlier life, Crankshaw had also been in military intelligence during the war and posted to Moscow. During that time, he had been part of the tortuous process of conveying intelligence from Bletchley Park code decrypts across to senior Kremlin figures without their guessing that Hugh Alexander and his colleagues had broken all the most important Nazi cyphers.

Now here he was, preparing to rub salt in Soviet wounds. By 1954, Edward Crankshaw was – quite appropriately and pleasingly – regarded as an expert on Russian affairs, and he worked full-time for *The Observer*. He was acutely aware of the real contest being played out before him in the White Rock Pavilion. The sly way he wrote it up was brilliantly calculated to cause Kremlin operatives to boil with rage and frustration:

'It is just twenty years since representatives of the greatest chess-playing country appeared at the Hastings Congress,' Crankshaw's report began.' Any Russian would have been an event. But the two who came are spellbinders . . . For the first week, they did steal the show, not, as it turned out, by wiping the floor with their opponents but by their admirable bearing, and their unfailing and often highly adventurous sportsmanship, which was in keeping with the spirit of this remarkable congress. It was the happiest display of international amity and this aspect of the Russian invasion should not be forgotten in the excitement of seeing an Englishman suddenly come forward to steal the show for himself.'[1]

Strictly speaking, Conel Hugh O'Donel Alexander was Irish; but there was no ambiguity – to the very few who knew – about who he was representing here and why. 'The hero, of course, was Hugh Alexander,' continued Crankshaw, 'the forty-four-year-old Cambridge mathematician and ex-champion of England, young and gay for his years, and an amateur of amateurs. His battle with Bronstein was an epic of genius, nerve and wit – all concealed beneath a surface of unbroken elegance. It will be remembered for ever by those who watched it . . . an achievement of the highest order – on the part of Alexander for obvious reasons, on the part of Bronstein for the smiling gallantry with which he fought on for hour after hour and day after day, steadily losing from the moment that he saw that his own spirited attack had gone astray.'[2]

The undercover Soviet agents looking on within the White Rock Pavilion, did they know precisely who this 'amateur of amateurs' Hugh Alexander was? From the British point of view, there would have been that part-pleasurable frisson of uncertainty. On the one hand, blanket secrecy around Bletchley and GCHQ would have bestowed anonymity; yet after the wide and horrifying betrayals by Burgess, Philby and Maclean of so many within British intelligence, who could be entirely certain what the Soviets knew and did not know? And if these Soviet agents – the KGB was formed that year – did not know, they must have stared at Hugh Alexander and wondered why this apparently effortless chess genius was never seen at matches played in the Eastern bloc. After all, the new era of aeroplane travel put Moscow and Helsinki firmly within practical travelling distance for tournaments – indeed, the same went for most cities behind the Iron Curtain. But even if Alexander had wanted to (and actually, even this most blithely adventurous codebreaker would have balked at the idea), he would never have received permission. He was party to the deepest national secrets; the risks were simply far too great. What if some accident were to befall him? Or something much worse? Hugh Alexander's extensive codebreaking knowledge – particularly the knowledge of how far the Soviet cypher systems had been penetrated – was beyond value and could not be subjected to the hazard of an Eastern European adventure.

The Soviet agents, meanwhile, were in Hastings to keep a very close eye on their own Grandmasters. This was routine with international chess tournaments all the way through to the 1970s: blazing intellects chaperoned by heavy KGB muscle. One might speculate that players such as Bronstein and Tolush had themselves been drawn in to the unfathomable complexities of codebreaking, and that they too had secrets that could never be spoken. In fact, the reason they were watched so closely was to act as a deterrent to defection. Although this was still some years away from the Berlin Wall sundering East and West – with anyone attempting to escape to the West being cut down by gunfire – any earlier attempt to get out of the Soviet system still presented its own dangers.

Crankshaw exulted in the incongruity of the battle taking place before him. 'The basement hall of the White Rock Pavilion did not look like an arena for the display of high-thinking and higher chivalry,' he wrote. 'It looked more like the scene of a village whist drive. At trestle tables, covered with green baize, fifty pairs sat in rows, all organised in sections of ten players. Only the chessboards and the double stop-clocks for each pair indicated that twice fifty intellects were stretched to the limit.

'There was incessant movement, but no loud talking. Wandering between the lines of tables, competitors waiting for their next moves murmured confidences, glanced curiously at other people's games . . .' They and the spectators were focused on Bronstein and Alexander. 'Bronstein was all attractiveness and quiet charm, small, neat, in a double-breasted blue suit and a rather startling tie of flaming red and blue,' continued Crankshaw. 'He has the self-containment of a great musician. Pale, with a forehead that is fine and ample rather than immense, with horn-rimmed spectacles, the gentlest and most diffident manner, a delightful smile and an air of extreme sensibility, he offered for most of the time a spectacle of perfectly controlled relaxation, like a cat on the hearth . . . Only under extreme pressure, as in his duel with Alexander, did he show the slightest sense of strain. Then his features became a little drawn and his mouth a little tight.'[3]

There was more at play here than simple national pride: under Stalin – and the pervasive paranoia that he succeeded in introducing to every level and every moment of Soviet life – there had been a fear of being seen as inferior to the West. Stalin was now dead, but the dread remained. Senior Kremlin figures, none more so than Nikita Khrushchev, who was eventually to take over, were neurotic about how they were perceived by the West; that while the Russians may have had overwhelming troop numbers and weaponry, they were falling behind technologically and strategically. It was vital for the chess players – and by extension the Soviet authorities – to be able to demonstrate that the reverse was true: that Communism was fostering intellects that could out-think any attempted Western encroachment on what they regarded as their territory. The metaphorical game was now being played out on every continent: East and West manoeuvring to get all their lethal pieces in place, from the far east to the soon-to-be-former colonies in Africa.

And as much as Hugh Alexander was steeped in a world so secret that not even many MI5 or MI6 operatives would have guessed his provenance, he must have settled his clear blue gaze on the Soviets who faced him across those chessboards and wondered if they too spent their working lives decoding and analysing the most intimate enemy secrets (if Bronstein and Tolush were cryptologists, there is as yet little indication, but given the disproportionately large numbers of chess players at GCHQ, Alexander would have been mad not to suspect). As much as his opponents were under pressure from their political masters, Alexander would certainly have been acutely conscious of his own obligation to perform dazzlingly, and show the Kremlin in turn that Britain had lost none of its guile and intelligence.

Equally, though, Hugh Alexander also had the most brilliant capacity that any codebreaker could have: the ability to draw back, to shake off the hugest pressure, the most dreadful tension, and to gleefully enjoy the mental assault course before him. This capacity had preserved sanity for many codebreakers. 'Alexander is on wires,' wrote Crankshaw of his contest with Bronstein. 'His whole body moves with his mind. His face lights up with delight at a successful thought. He laughs against himself when a move goes wrong for him. He strides about through the crowd with an air of a man seeing visions – dashing back sometimes to the board to see if his vision was right after all. When it is his turn to move, he positively plunges back to the board, pouncing on it, and then going off into a visible agony of concentration. He has to share every irony, every success, every setback, with his opponent.

'When he and Bronstein were playing in different games,' continued Crankshaw, 'they got on famously together. For both have the same high-spirited attitude to life and chess – though Bronstein is subdued, Alexander ebullient; both the same mathematical genius – though Alexander seems to have the greater intuition, Bronstein the more god-like view of serried regiments of permutations; both, above all, the same sense of humour. The respect of each other for each other is immense.'

There was a parallel: just as physicists swiftly forgot any sense of national differences or ideology when they met, so too there was a brotherhood of chess players. The suggestion of friendship between Alexander and Bronstein, even if it only existed strictly within the confines of this seaside-town variety theatre, is intriguing, for it also shines a light into Alexander's relationship with his own superiors at GCHQ and ultimately within the Foreign Office. The ban on travel behind the Iron Curtain was perfectly natural and understandable; but Alexander's taking several days of leave to play his ideological opponents on the south coast did not appear to cause any flutter. His presence in Hastings, indeed, must surely have been officially sanctioned. Hugh Alexander's colleagues will have relished the multiple levels of intrigue that could be pulled off within the confines of an out-of-season music hall.

(Just three years later, Ian Fleming's Bond thriller *From Russia With Love* was published. Early scenes involve a Soviet chessmaster called Kronsteen – perhaps a little wink at Bronstein? – urgently being called away from the table by undercover KGB men, to immerse himself in the sinister geopolitical chess-piece strategies of his icy superiors. But Kronsteen delays abandoning the game for a few minutes until he can make his triumphant move – an act of disobedience that he explains to his murderously angry SMERSH boss as protecting his espionage cover;

for if he had rushed off, would observers not have thought it odd that a Grandmaster would leave the board for anything? Given that Fleming, in naval intelligence throughout the war, was one of the few to be wholly familiar with the Bletchley codebreaking operation, and the prolific use of chess players, was this passage his unsubtle declaration that he knew all about the Soviet system too?)

And indeed there was an extraordinary double victory for the British at those tables. Hugh Alexander got the better of David Bronstein on that bitter grey January day; incredibly, in the same tournament, he also brought Alexander Tolush crashing down. The defeat of two Soviet Grandmasters was unprecedented. The habitually amused Alexander caught the attention of a press that otherwise did not concern itself too greatly with the esoteric world of chess. His admiring former Bletchley colleague Stuart Milner-Barry (who had moved away from codebreaking into the senior civil service) later wrote of his old friend: 'He defeated Bronstein in their individual encounter in a marathon Queen and Pawn ending which went on for over 100 moves; and slaughtered the other Soviet grandmaster Tolush in no time with the black pieces . . . In spite of his congenital state of untidiness . . . he was a surprisingly well-organised person. If he had not been he could not have kept under control all the things that he did.'[4]

The Hastings tournament had been a ferocious embarrassment for the Soviets; so much so that when one of the Russian team, Alatortsev, came to write it up for the Soviet newspaper *Evening Moscow*, he neglected to mention the results at all, preferring instead to claim that he 'had received many letters from all over Britain wishing . . . success. The senders expressed the hope that the visit of the Soviet chess players would strengthen the friendship between peoples.'[5] Alatortsev also found a moment to observe sourly that the British working poor could only 'gaze in awe' at department store windows and that 'it was always somewhat cold in the hotels' and the chess players 'were always putting shillings in the gas meter'.[6] In other words, amusingly bitter misdirection.

And in the meantime, those in Whitehall who knew of Hugh Alexander's true provenance could afford to feel – at a time of national insecurity – a sense that the old country still had the sharpest minds. Indeed, Alexander went on to juggle his unthinkably stressful codebreaking day-job with chess-related work: as a result of that 1954 triumph, he went on to write columns for *The Sunday Times* and *The Spectator*.

Chess was also key to the emerging generation of computational thinking. Part of Alan Turing's vision of a thinking, conscious machine – thinking that had evolved at Bletchley Park and now at Manchester University – was of a computer that could play the game. Throughout the late 1940s and early 1950s, Turing had been writing philosophically about the very nature of human intelligence itself: how it came to be formed, and the ways in which machine intelligence might differ sharply. He and Shaun Wylie – the mathematician who was soon to return to the codebreaking fold of GCHQ – had corresponded on their early attempts to write programs that would enable computers to play chess. They were able to get as far as the computer 'thinking' one move ahead, which by itself was rather an achievement. But how long would it be before a computer could take on a Grandmaster and win? Alan Turing was interested in the idea of chess being, as it were, a hermetically sealed activity: there was simply the board, the pieces, and the potential moves that could be made. No machine would have to interact with an opponent any further than that. The game itself was not, for him, the important point. The quality of chess that interested him was that it showed how a nimble, lithe, sinuous human mind worked.

Programming a machine to play chess – even in those earliest days – was for Turing a bit of a chore, because in principle, any device could run through pre-programmed possibilities, like his Bletchley Park bombe machines. What he wanted to see was a machine that could take in a chess board and then surprise its opponent. The corollaries between chess and cryptanalysis were also inescapable. Codes, like the chess board, were something that could be approached without having to interact with anything other than the encoded text. At Bletchley, machines – properly programmed – had been able to decypher coded text at speeds no army of humans could dream of. If it were possible to tell a computer to produce wholly random letters and numbers in order to create a new cypher, could a machine on the opposing side counter it effectively? Could a machine deal with random surprises?

Hugh Alexander had, in 1952, contributed a short essay to a book that Turing and others had written about computers playing games (it was not only chess; there was also much speculation on whether a mechanical device could convincingly and successfully play poker). Alexander was keeping a very keen eye on the developments in the computing department at the University of Manchester.

The experience of Bletchley Park had shown Alexander and all those other veteran codebreakers that it was folly to rely completely on technology; Hitler and the Nazis had done so, and unwittingly revealed their most secret thoughts and orders by doing so. The Germans had not understood technological vulnerability. But in Manchester, Alan Turing and his mentor Professor Max Newman had been pushing towards computers that had both practical and philosophical possibilities. There is something about the crystalline purity of the codebreaker's reasoning: closing everything else off into order to focus like a laser on summoning the truth from a chaos of random letters. That purity – that unsullied, unbroken concentration – was the sort of consciousness that could also be the advantage of a thinking machine.

By 1954, Alan Turing was cast out into the wintery wilderness, his relationship with the codebreakers now firmly shut off. After his trial and conviction in 1952, friends and colleagues had certainly gathered around; but with the revocation of his prized security clearance, he was now excluded from the most fascinating problems of cryptology and defence. That curious establishment witch-hunt of homosexuals in the early 1950s was only a part of it; there were also suggestions that in security circles, senior figures in America as well as Britain regarded Alan Turing as worryingly unpredictable. Why did he take those (for the time, rather unusual) holidays in Norway and Greece? In the 1950s, these were destinations far from the usual tourist maps, and too close to the Eastern bloc for those security operatives not to take anxious notice. No-one ever seemed to question Turing's essential loyalty to his own nation, but at the same time he was regarded as disorganised, eccentric and stubborn.

The fear was clearly not that he would defect to the Russians, or deliberately hand them intelligence, but more that Turing was an innocent compared to the more ruthless KGB operatives and he could be duped, blackmailed, or by some other means purely accidentally hand the Soviets some crucial sense of how far Britain's cryptanalytical forces had developed.

To those who worked with Turing in Manchester in the days and weeks before his dreadful death, there seemed little change in his essentially shy, dishevelled temperament. Apart from his stammer and his slightly gauche, eye-contact-avoiding manner, he was popular with neighbours and academic friends, too. He had struck up a friendship with a psychoanalyst called Franz Greenbaum, and Greenbaum's young daughters remembered having talks with Turing about games such as solitaire. On one occasion, Turing joined the Greenbaum family on a day trip to Blackpool. Recalled daughter Barbara: 'We found a fortune-teller's tent and Alan said he'd like to go in so we waited around for him to come back.

'And this sunny, cheerful visage had shrunk into a pale, shaking ... face. Something had happened. We don't know what the fortune-teller had said but he obviously was deeply unhappy.'[7]

Others recall that the reason his death was such a shock was that there had been nothing unusual in his manner or behaviour beforehand. Turing was found dead in bed one morning by his housekeeper; by his side was a half-eaten apple. The apple was found to have been contaminated with cyanide, which had come from the laboratory at the back of his house. The inquest found that, among other symptoms of 'violence', Turing's jaws had been working furiously. The policeman who was summoned to the house reported on the white froth around Turing's mouth. The coroner found that it could only have been suicide: a man of Turing's learning could not have failed to have known what the effect of such contamination would be.

It was also noted at the inquest that there were no unusual worries or pressures bearing on him at that moment in June 1954; indeed, he had just received an invitation from the Royal Society in London, of which he was a Fellow, to attend a special talk. The implication was that a scientist of Turing's standing was still clasped deep within the bosom of the establishment. In the newspaper, no mention was made of his conviction for gross indecency two years beforehand.

The world of the codebreakers remained a close one; and a few days later, in the pages of *The Manchester Guardian*, a hugely affectionate tribute to Turing was contributed by one who signed himself simply 'MHAN' – the initials, in fact, of Professor Max Newman. He wrote: 'Mathematics and science have lost a great original thinker . . . Turing took a particular delight in problems that enabled him to combine mathematical theory with experiments that he could carry out, in whole or in part, with his own hands . . . His comical yet brilliantly set analogies with which he explained his ideas made him a delightful companion.' Newman paid tribute to the dazzling nature of Turing's thinking about computing – stretching the very idea of what a machine actually was and what it could be made to do – and how he had, in his final months, started taking an avid interest in the 'chemical theory of the growth of living things . . . In this work, he found the fullest scope for his mathematical powers; his great flair for machine computing and his power of tearing his way into a subject new to him – in this case, a chemistry of living tissues.'[8]

A charming obituary in *The Times*, on 11 June 1954, also omitted any mention of Turing's conviction. It made a teasing reference, too, to the nature of his work between 1939 and 1945. 'The war interrupted Turing's mathematical career for the six critical years between the ages of 27 and 33,' was all it would say, before giving a punchily condensed summary of Turing's philosophy, the mathematical problems too intractable to be solved by machinery, and the differences and similarities between human and computer brains. 'Few who have known him personally can doubt that, with his deep insight into the principles of mathematics and of natural science, and his brilliant originality, he would, but for these accidents, have made much greater discoveries.'[9]

It was only Turing's mother who did not believe the verdict of suicide. Instead, she thought it had been an accident; in previous years, she had always warned her untidy son about the dangers of dealing with hazardous chemicals and absent-mindedly licking his fingers. She believed that he had taken the apple into his back-room laboratory, and there it had become poisoned with the fatal dust. Another theory has it that this is precisely what Turing had wanted his mother to believe; knowing that she would be destroyed by the idea that he had taken his own life, this alternative seemed kinder. There are of course all sorts of other theories to this day; one or two former Bletchley Park veterans openly wondered why it was, if Turing was so hell-bent on self-destruction, that he had gone out and bought himself some new socks just days beforehand? But that way lies a disorientating hall of mirrors of conspiracy theories. The point was that Britain had first cast out one of its pre-eminent cryptanalytical intellects, and now that intellect was lost forever.

And such minds were needed quite urgently. The intensity of a chess tournament, with all its intellectual grandstanding is one thing; but in 1954, there were increasing numbers of senior figures within the military establishments of both the US and the USSR who believed that nuclear confrontation was inevitable. Deep in the Pacific, near the Marshall Islands at Bikini Atoll, the world had been permitted to witness the latest and most terrible development in apocalyptic weaponry. The first hydrogen bomb, developed by the Americans, was detonated; it was believed to be one thousand times more powerful than the atomic bombs used on Nagasaki and Hiroshima in 1945. Here in the Pacific, an island was quite simply vaporised, and the mushroom cloud that rose poisonously into the sky eventually spread out over 100 miles (160 kilometres). Everywhere beneath was showered with radioactivity. A Japanese fishing boat called *Lucky Dragon* had been within 80 miles (130 kilometres) of the epicentre of the explosion; the crew immediately came down with radiation sickness. The explosion had been larger than the US military and scientific establishment had expected; this was a weapon which changed the philosophy of war.

The prospect of global doomsday had now become nightmarishly easy to imagine. These were weapons that could not only wipe out entire populations but render regions of the earth uninhabitable for generations to come. The hydrogen bomb could only bring one conceivable response from the Soviets, and that was for their scientists to seek to create their own version. At what point must the scientists on either side have advised that the use of such devastating technology could very easily wipe out much of the planet's population? It was in 1954 that American civilians in public buildings and schools began to carry out elaborate drills on taking shelter and building up supplies in the event of such a war breaking out.

In Britain, the move of GCHQ from Eastcote to the former agricultural land on the outskirts of Cheltenham was – in part – a precaution against the day that London had nuclear death rained down upon it; in the event of such a cataclysm, the nation's security and communications would not be compromised. By 1954, the move – which had brought a faintly comical array of bureaucratic headaches and not a little ill-will among Cheltenham business leaders – was almost complete. The distance of some 100 miles (160 kilometres) from London would possibly have brought only limited advantage in the event of an atomic missile attack. But the new premises at Cheltenham offered both day-to-day operational security and tight-knit unity. While a few personnel were to remain at the primitive blocks of Eastcote – GCHQ could not quite be moved out in its entirety – the vast bulk was now being settled into purpose-built accommodation where staff and complex machinery had enough room to attend to ever-expanding duties.

There had been some job-swapping going on: personnel in varying grades who had been reluctant to move from London exchanged their jobs with civil servants from the Ministry of War, among others, who were happy to move out. The outskirts of Cheltenham saw a flowering of government-funded house-building (at the start of a general golden age for government housing provision). All these civil servants needed proper homes; they could not be expected to endure – as the early Eastcote GCHQ codebreakers did – the rather infantilising business of renting pokey digs with landladies. And so, over the space of several years, hundreds of new houses and flats were built on the outskirts of the town, and the general upsurge of economic activity was broadly welcomed within Cheltenham. There were a few dissenting voices, for as GCHQ also began recruiting in the town for new staff of all grades, local businessmen realised that the brightest and the best of their potential workforce was being lured away by the prospect of work that seemed not only more exciting but also more secure.

And the issue of housing seemed initially fraught. For, while all these smart new dwellings, all these closes and cul-de-sacs and avenues, were being built for the 'Foreign Office' (the cover of GCHQ was that it was quite simply a branch of the FO), Cheltenham still had over a thousand people on its council-home waiting list. As in London, the end of the war had brought huge accommodation difficulties for many. In Cheltenham, there was sizzling local resentment that new houses were being handed straight over to outsiders.

Worse yet: some of the completed new houses, on the smart new residential estates, were empty for a long time after the last bricks had been laid; so if there was a delay in people coming down to the town, opponents said, why could the residences not be allocated to local people in need instead, with the 'Foreign Office' staff being catered for closer to their arrival date? It was left to figures such as GCHQ's Edward Hastings to explain to the town council that such an idea – though understandable – was not practical; that a surge in numbers was expected imminently.

The late 1940s and early 1950s had brought many new town communities to Britain; just outside Bletchley Park, for instance, was the fresh modern development of Milton Keynes. Cheltenham involved a slightly more delicate operation to ensure that the most high-security personnel would mesh with ease into what had been a conservative and staid community.

The logistics of the move were exquisitely tortuous too: the incredibly secret cryptanalytical machinery being transferred from Eastcote to the new building at Benhall (at Bletchley, such moves were achieved via army trucks; but the key thing was that the transfer should not draw any sort of attention and look utterly unremarkable. Who knew what agents could be there spying on the route?). There was not one moment, one split second, where Britain could be left without the round-the-clock attention of the listeners and the codebreakers; not one fraction of a moment when the guard was lowered or weakened in any way. But this also meant that in the period between 1952 and 1954, there were some codebreakers who had to face a reverse commute. In a few cases, those with families were either still waiting for suitable Cheltenham housing, or were still making domestic arrangements concerning moving the family. Those people worked at Cheltenham throughout the week and then got on the train at Cheltenham Spa to catch the express back to Paddington.

But the codebreakers – in their impenetrable guise as ordinary Foreign Office civil servants – also brought a brilliant infusion of life to the old country town. It was not long before the GCHQ cricketers were taking on other local teams, and also throwing themselves in to inter-county championships. Naturally, the town's chess society also received the most almighty and unexpected boost. Codebreakers were not merely cerebral; the town's tennis and football clubs received a similar injection of new blood and new life. Like Bletchley Park, many of the new recruits (GCHQ tried to reel in as many people from the surrounding area as they could) were youthful and lively. They brought a love for jazz and literature. The highbrow nature of these attractive newcomers also had an invigorating effect upon the town's cultural efforts (indeed, one glance at today's mighty Cheltenham Book Festival, held every year in October, makes one wonder how much of its growth was down to the literary appetites of the codebreakers on the edge of town).

There was nothing new about geopolitical uncertainty and neurosis; there had never been a moment of history that had not been darkened by the threat of war. But the conditions in the mid-1950s were something entirely new because now, the war would be both total and sickeningly fast. Rather than years spent patiently re-arming – and then further time spent training battalions of soldiers – the new threat was one of bombs that could bring more destruction than even an entire army, and all in a matter of minutes. This was the moment – serendipitously – that GCHQ fully flowered into its new incarnation. The codebreakers were still delving deep into the heart of the enemy's intentions, still unscrambling their most deviously encrypted messages. But now, Sir Eric Jones, with his lieutenants and his fresh GCHQ team of some 2,000 people, were also employing the most fantastic technology to listen to the most obscure corners of the earth, detecting the faintest tremors that could lead to a geopolitical earthquake. The organisation was not staffed with clairvoyants, and they did not use crystal balls; so accusing them in hindsight of having missed some key developments rather overlooks the point that no system on earth can anticipate the intentions of every single regime, every single ruler, every single otherwise anonymous military figure who has been plotting his coup in secrecy.

But from this point, what they could do – as a dedicated and new intelligence service – was provide what they saw as pure, unadulterated, crystal-clean intelligence to Whitehall; there was none of the mess or unpredictability of human intelligence, just the forensic surveillance and analysis provided by brains that occasionally seemed in uncanny synchronisation with their machinery. All those Bletchley Park codebreakers – Joan Clarke, Nigel de Grey, Hugh Foss, Hugh Alexander, Frank Birch, Jack Good and so many others – had now built an institution ready to go further than ever to make sure that even the most fearsome enemy encryptions could be read instantly.

And so it was from that curiously incongruous collection of plain 1950s office buildings in pretty Cheltenham that GCHQ addressed itself to the future. Most of their work in that period is still wrapped up in complete secrecy. But we know what they would have been listening to, and the communications they would have been addressing. For Britain, there were the post-imperial traumas yet to come: the shame of Suez, the ugliness of the retreat from Kenya, the separation from the African colonies. Mixed in with those would be further shocks to the wider intelligence services; the revelation of yet more traitors and double agents. And all this against a lurid panorama of American and Russian hostility, from the Cuban Missile Crisis of 1961 to the near hysteria of the space race. Nigel de Grey and Edward Travis had, in the aftermath of war, been concerned about building an intercept/decryption operation that could be instantly put on red alert at the first signs of the next worldwide conflict. Thanks to them, this reincarnation of Bletchley Park, nestling amid Gloucestershire's green hills, was now poised on red alert permanently; and the coming era of satellite technology was only to add further dimensions to their reach. It is to be hoped that soon, a little more of their historic work will be laid out in the public domain to enrich our understanding of the various levels of the Cold War.

But for the moment, today, the individual codebreakers working so deep in those GCHQ shadows, still firmly rooted in Cheltenham, are the direct and spiritual heirs of those free-wheeling, occasionally madly hilarious masterminds; today's unsung, highly secret achievements are a straightforward tribute to the visions and intellects of those astounding pioneers.

Notes

All documents prefaced by 'National Archives' are held at the United Kingdom National Archives at Kew.

Chapter One

1. National Archives HW3/169
2. National Archives HW14/151
3. Betty Flavell, interviewed for the Bletchley Park Trust: www.bletchleypark.org.uk
4. Neil Webster, quoted in *Cribs for Victory: The Untold Story of Bletchley Park's Secret Room* (Polperro Press, 2011)
5. National Archives HW62/16
6. National Archives HW62/16

Chapter Two

1. Gene Grabeel, featured in National Security Agency archive features – www. nsa.gov/about/cryptologic-heritage
2. National Archives HW8/36
3. Alan Stripp, in an essay contributed to *Codebreakers: The Inside Story of Bletchley Park* (Oxford University Press, 1993)
4. As above
5. As above
6. The poem reproduced in the in-house Beaumanor magazine, *The Woygian* Winter 1948
7. Gwendoline Gibbs – her essays can be found at http://www.bletchleypark.org.uk/resources/filer.rhtm/655471/gibbs+g.pdf
8. As above
9. National Archives HW62/16

Chapter Three

1. National Archives FO366/2221
2. National Archives HW14/164
3. National Archives HW64/68
4. National Archives HW14/164
5. National Archives HW64/68
6. As quoted in *GCHQ – The Uncensored Story of Britain's Most Secret Intelligence Agency* by Richard Aldrich (Harper Collins, 2010)
7. Mass Observation diaries; available for consultation by appointment in file 48/1/A at Sussex University or the British Library
8. John Cane, as quoted on the BBC News website, www.bbc.co.uk/news in February 2014
9. National Archives HW14/164

Chapter Four

1. Arthur Levenson's interview can be found in the National Security Agency online archive at www.nsa.gov/news-features/declassified-documents/oral-history-interviews/index.shtml. Levenson's interview is NSA-OH-40-80

2. As above

3. As quoted in *Alan Turing: The Enigma* by Andrew Hodges (Burnett/Hutchinson 1983)

Chapter Five

1. Aileen Clayton, writing in *The Enemy Is Listening* (Hutchinson, 1980)

2. This correspondence can be found on the National Security Agency online archive. Visit www.nsa.gov/news-features/declassified-documents/friedman-documents/assets/files/correspondence/FOLDER_365/41733539077277.pdf

3. Alan Sillitoe, *Life Without Armour* (HarperCollins, 1995)

4. As above

5. *The Woygian*, Beaumanor magazine, Winter 1946 number

6. Veterans share their memories online at http://gwulo.com/RAF-Battys-Belvedere-Hong-Kong

Chapter Six

1. Neal Ascherson, writing in the *London Review of Books*, 20 December 2012

2. *Spycatcher* by Peter Wright (Viking, 1987)

3. Meredith Gardner, as featured in the National Security Agency archives. Visit www.nsa.gov/news-features/declassified-documents/crypto-almanac-50th/assets/files/POLYGLOT.pdf

4. *Postwar: A History of Europe Since 1945* by Tony Judt (Heinemann, 2005)

5. As quoted in *The Cambridge History of the Cold War Volume 1* (Cambridge University Press, 2010)

6. As quoted in *The Cambridge History of the Cold War Volume 1*

Chapter Seven

1. Quoted from *Enigma and the Eastcote Connection* by Susan Toms. The essay can be read at www.ruislip.co.uk/eastcotemod/enigma.htm

2. Geoff Hardy, as quoted on the Cheltenham Civil Service RFC website www.pitchero.com/clubs/cheltenhamcivilservice/a/club-history-8718.html

3. Chris Barnes, writing for *The Woygian*, Beaumanor in-house magazine

4. As above

5. Kenneth Carling, writing at the website http://www.garatshay.org.uk/about_us/beaumanor.html

6. As above

7. As above

8. As above

Chapter Eight

1. For a splendid appreciation of Alexander from Stuart Milner Barry, go to: https://www.nsa.gov/news-features/declassified-documents/cryptologic-spectrum/assets/files/cono_hugh.pdf

2. As quoted in *The Secret Sentry: The Untold Story of the National Security Agency* by Matthew M Aid (Bloomsbury, 2009)

3. Stuart Milner Barry, writing in *Codebreakers – The Inside Story of Bletchley Park* (Oxford University Press, 1993)

4. William Millward, writing in *Codebreakers*, as above

5. Ralph Bennett, writing in *Codebreakers*, as above

6. Telford Taylor, writing in *Codebreakers*, as above

7. As quoted in *GCHQ – The Uncensored Story of Britain's Most Secret Intelligence Agency* by Richard J Aldrich (HarperCollins, 2010)

8. As quoted in *GCHQ – The Uncensored Story* by Richard J Aldrich

9. As quoted in *Gordon Welchman: Bletchley Park's Architect of Ultra Intelligence* by Joel Greenberg (Frontline Books, 2015)

10. For the National Security Agency's appreciation of Wilma Zimmerman Davis, go to www.nsa.gov/news-features/declassified-documents/crypto-almanac-50th/assets/files/Wilma_Z._Davis.pdf

11. Genevieve Grotjan, as featured in the National Security Agency online archives, as above

12. As quoted in *The Defence of the Realm – the Authorized History of MI5* by Christopher Andrew (Penguin, 2009)

Chapter Nine

1. George Kennan, as quoted in *Post-War: A History of Europe Since 1945* by Tony Judt

2. ES Turner, writing in the *London Review of Books*, 29 September 1988

3. *Reflections on Intelligence* by RV Jones (William Heinemann, 1989)

Chapter Ten

1. Norman Logan, writing online at 14threunion.blogspot.com/2011/05/royal-signals-hands-over-to-corps-of.html

2. Alan Stripp, writing in *Codebreakers*

3. As recalled for www.bbc.co.uk/history/ww2peopleswar

4. As above

5. As above

6. As above

7. Dennis Underwood, writing at http://www.burmastar.org.uk/stories/dennis-underwood-war-office-y-group/

Chapter Eleven

1. Walter Eytan, writing in *Codebreakers*

2. As above

3. Martin Sugarman, 'Jewish Personnel at Bletchley Park' which can be found at www.jewishvirtuallibrary.org

4. An interview with Dr Solomon Kullback – and interviews with his notable peers and contemporaries in American codebreaking – can be read at https://www.nsa.gov/news-features/declassified-documents/oral-history-interviews/

5. As above

6. Arthur Levenson interview, available at https://www.nsa.gov/news-features/declassified-documents/oral-history-interviews/

7. From the *Financial Times*, 10 July 2015

Chapter Twelve

1. National Archives HW50/50

2. As above

3. National Archives HW14/1

4. National Archives HW50/50

5. As above

6. As above

7. As above

8. As above

9. As above

Chapter Thirteen

1. *Life Without Armour* by Alan Sillitoe

2. As quoted in *The Cambridge History of the Cold War Volume 1*

3. Chris Barnes, writing for *The Woygian*, Beaumanor in-house magazine, Winter 1948

Chapter Fourteen

1. Hugh Foss, as quoted in *The Emperor's Codes: The Breaking of Japan's Secret Ciphers* by Michael Smith (Biteback, 2010)
2. As above
3. Joan Clarke, writing in *Codebreakers*
4. As above
5. As above
6. Jack Good, writing in *Codebreakers*
7. As quoted in the *Oxford Dictionary of National Biography*
8. *Chess* by C H O'D Alexander (Pitman and Sons, 1937)
9. As above
10. As above
11. *Alexander on Chess* by C H O'D Alexander (Pitman, 1974)
12. As above
13. As above
14. As above
15. As above
16. This tribute can be found on the NSA's website at www.nsa.gov/news-features/declassified-documents/cryptologic-spectrum/assets/files/in_memoriam.pdf

Chapter Fifteen

1. Melita Norwood quoted in *The Guardian*, September 1999
2. As quoted in *GCHQ – The Uncensored History* by Richard J Aldrich
3. Alexander Kendrick, writing in *New Republic*, 26 July 1948
4. As quoted in *Intercept: The Secret History of Spies and Computers* by Gordon Corera (Weidenfeld and Nicholson, 2015)

Chapter Sixteen

1. As quoted in *The Cambridge History of the Cold War*
2. As above
3. As above
4. Michael L Peterson, National Security Agency online archives, at www.nsa.gov/news-features/declassified-documents/cryptologic-quarterly/assets/files/maybe_you_had_to_be_there.pdf
5. As above
6. National Archives FO 1093/485
7. As above
8. As above
9. As above
10. As above

Chapter Seventeen

1. 'The Beginning of Intelligence Analysis in CIA', which can be found at https://www.cia.gov/library/center-for-the-study-of-intelligence/csi-publications/csi-studies/studies/vol51no2/the-beginning-of-intelligence-analysis-in-cia.html
2. *Know Your Enemy – How the Joint Intelligence Committee Saw the World* by Percy Cradock (John Murray, 2002)
3. As quoted in *The Korean War* by Max Hastings (Michael Joseph, 1987)
4. Brian Hough, quoted in *The Guardian*, 25 June 2010
5. *What's It All About?* by Michael Caine (Arrow, 1993)
6. *British Intelligence, Strategy and the Cold War 1945–41* edited by Richard J Aldrich (Routledge, 1992)
7. *Espionage, Security and Intelligence in Britain 1945–70* by Richard J Aldrich (Manchester University Press, 1998)
8. As above

Chapter Eighteen

1. From the *Oxford Dictionary of National Biography*

2. As above

3. As quoted by Andrew Hodges in *Alan Turing: The Enigma*

4. As above

5. As above

6. As above

7. As above

8. As above

Chapter Nineteen

1. Edward Said writing in the *London Review of Books*, 7 May 1998

2. Tom Nairn, quoted by Perry Anderson in the *London Review of Books*, 24 April 2008

Chapter Twenty

1. GCHQ memo in the National Archives FO 1093/485

2. *Alan Turing: The Enigma* by Andrew Hodges

Chapter Twenty-Two

1. 'The Battle of Hastings', article by Edward Crankshaw, *Observer*, 10 January 1954

2. As above

3. As above

4. *Conel Hugh O'Donel Alexander: A Personal Memoir* by Stuart Milner-Barry, which can be found online at www.nsa.gov/news-features/declassified-documents/cryptologic-spectrum/assets/files/cono_hugh.pdf

5. Alatortsev's newspaper report, picked up by Sir John Rennie's department in 1954, can now be found in the National Archives FO 371/111787

6. As above

7. Barbara Greenbaum interviewed on Turing by the BBC, 6 June 2014

8. *The Manchester Guardian*, 11 June 1954

9. *The Times*, 11 June 1954

Index

Acknowledgements

As ever, much gratitude in general to the Bletchley Park Trust, whose work in ensuring that the codebreakers are at last properly celebrated goes from strength to strength. For information on visiting the wonderfully restored Bletchley Park Museum, visit www.bletchleypark.org. Thanks also to Professor Richard J Aldrich of the University of Warwick who for some years has been leading the way with his brilliant and wide-ranging studies of GCHQ and global security. In terms of the book itself, I am particularly grateful to Jennifer Barr and Richard Green, both in terms of expert editorial judgements and also terrific enthusiasm. The same also to editor Philip Parker, who came at the manuscript with eagle-eyed flair and impressive knowledge. Many thanks are also due to Daniela Rogers for finding such striking images, Catherine Rubenstein for her laser-beam proof reading and not least to Katherine Josselyn, for sharp and clever ways of ensuring that the world is alerted to the book.